LEADERSHIP

FOR HIGHLY SUCCESSFUL MIDDLE LEVEL SCHOOLS

A National Study of Leadership in Middle Level Schools

VOLUME II

Jerry W. Valentine
Donald C. Clark
Donald G. Hackmann
Vicki N. Petzko

NATIONAL ASSOCIATION
OF SECONDARY SCHOOL
PRINCIPALS

Reston, VA

NATIONAL ASSOCIATION of SECONDARY SCHOOL PRINCIPALS

National Association of Secondary School Principals
1904 Association Drive • Reston, VA 20191-1537 USA
703-860-7200 • Fax: 703-476-5432 • www.principals.org • nassp@principals.org

ISBN 0-88210-358-X

Contents

Preface

In the winter of 1999, the Board of Directors of the National Association of Secondary School Principals (NASSP) made a commitment to continue the Association's longstanding tradition of conducting a study of middle level education every 10 years. The goal of such studies is to identify the current and evolving state of middle level education programs and leadership and to provide insight into the practices and programs in highly successful middle level schools in the United States. The documentation of typical and exemplary practices and trends has proven a valuable source of information for school leaders, policymakers, and researchers for more than two decades. Through a contract with the Middle Level Leadership Center at the University of Missouri–Columbia, a three-year study was designed that would be similar enough to previous studies to identify trends in leadership and programs and distinctive enough to address contemporary issues facing today's middle level leaders and schools.

This is NASSP's third "decade study" of middle level leaders and programs, with the initial study beginning in 1980 and subsequent studies beginning in 1990 and 2000. Each of the multiyear studies had two phases. The first phase included a detailed survey of principals from across the country to identify leadership characteristics and practices and school programs and practices common in U.S. middle level schools. The second phase of each study included the identification and study of exemplary schools and their principals to provide clearer insight about best practices in middle level schools. The schools in the second phase were characterized in the 1980 study as *highly effective middle level schools,* in the 1990 study as *successfully restructuring middle level schools,* and in the current study as *highly successful middle level schools.*

Each study has been published in two volumes, the first of which provides the latest detailed data from the national surveys about the principals and programs in middle level schools across the country. The first volume of the current decade study, *A National Study of Leadership in Middle Level Schools, Volume I: A National Study of Middle Level Leaders and School Programs* (Valentine, Clark, Hackmann, & Petzko, 2002), chronicled the leaders and programs in middle level schools in 2000 and compared current leadership and programs with the previous decade studies. Thus, trends in middle level leadership and programs were documented across the three studies.

This book, the second volume of the current multiyear study, focuses on a set of highly successful middle level schools. The first chapter reviews middle level education programs and leadership to set the backdrop for the findings presented in the remaining chapters. Data about 98 "highly successful" middle level schools and their programs and leaders are provided in chapter 2. The 98 highly successful schools are contrasted with findings from the study's national sample of schools and leaders, highlighting how the highly successful schools and their leaders are similar and distinct from typical middle level principals across the country. From the 98 schools, 6 were selected for an in-depth study. A profile of each school is presented in chapter 3, and a detailed analysis of successful programs and practices among the schools is presented in chapter 4. Chapter 5 is an analysis of the leadership of the principals of those schools. The final chapter is a synthesis of the findings from the study and recommendations for school leaders and policymakers.

Dedication

This dedication was written without the knowledge of one of the members of our research team. We did so because we want to dedicate this book to Dr. Donald Clark, professor emeritus of the University of Arizona, and his wife, Dr. Sally Clark, a professor emerita from the University of Arizona. Don is a member of this research team and, when we concluded that we would like to dedicate the book to them, we decided to ask for Don's forgiveness after the fact rather than try to get his permission beforehand. We respectfully apologize to him for not including him in this decision.

Don and Sally Clark have influenced middle level education practices for three decades. During that time they have contributed scores of manuscripts to the body of knowledge, consulted with hundreds of schools, conducted numerous major research projects that have informed our profession, helped establish state and regional middle level organizations, worked in leadership roles with NASSP and the National Middle School Association, and mentored countless teachers and principals who are now the practitioners and researchers of middle level education. Throughout this study and the 1980 and 1990 studies, Don and Sally have been trusted colleagues. They have analyzed data, written and critiqued manuscript drafts, and refined our work. I wish that all educators could experience the quality professional relationships that we have had with these two outstanding colleagues throughout our careers. Don and Sally Clark have dedicated their professional lives to the betterment of education for young adolescents. We wish to thank them for their contributions to middle level education and honor their many years of work with this dedication.

Jerry Valentine, March 2004

Acknowledgments

The concept of decade studies for middle level education at NASSP emerged under the leadership of NASSP executives Scott Thomson, Jim Keefe, John Kourmadas, and George Melton in the late 1970s. Throughout much of the 1970s and into the 1980s, educators in middle level education debated the relative merits of 7–9 junior high schools and 5–8 or 6–8 middle schools. NASSP's commitment to the 1980 study of middle level education served as a strong statement from the nation's leading secondary principals' association that the real issue should not be the name or the grade pattern of the school but the nature of the programs for the young adolescents the school served. The term *middle level* was coined for that study and has since been used extensively to describe all programs designed specifically to serve young adolescents from grades 5–9. The 7–9 junior high has all but disappeared from the educational scene, and the terms *middle*

level and *middle grades* are commonly used today to characterize schools serving young adolescents. Clearly, NASSP's 1980 commitment to the study of leadership for developmentally appropriate programs for young adolescents was significant in the evolution from junior high to middle level schools.

As noted in the introduction to volume 1 of this study (Valentine et al., 2002), the current study began under the leadership of Sue Galletti, then associate executive director for middle level education at NASSP. Current NASSP Executive Director Gerry Tirozzi and Director of School Leadership Services John Nori have continued to support the study and have secured resources to make the study available to each middle level member in the Association. Keith Taton, NASSP's past president, championed the multiyear study and has been an influential leader of middle level education throughout his long association with NASSP.

This study began with nominations from education leaders in each state who recommended several exemplary schools. From that set of recommendations, 100 schools were selected for inclusion in the study and 98 participated. From those 98 schools the research team collected a wealth of data that required time from principals, faculty members, students, and parents. Everyone who reads this book and gains insight about successful middle level schools is indebted to the respondents from the 98 schools.

Many readers will find the greatest value of this study in the chapters devoted to the six schools that were selected for in-depth analysis. Not only did the six schools complete the same extensive battery of surveys as their colleagues in the other 92 schools, they opened their schools to three days of on-site analysis by the research team. During the site visits the research team studied programs; observed classrooms; analyzed teaching strategies; and interviewed principals, teachers, parents, and students. The six schools were scrutinized in detail to understand what made them so successful.

We extend our appreciation to the faculty members of the six schools. We owe a special thanks to the six very talented principals of those schools, whose patience, cooperation, and support made much of this study possible: Cathy Andrews, Becker Middle School, Las Vegas, NV; Clara Sale-Davis, Freeport (TX) Intermediate School; Ed Vittardi, Independence (OH) Middle School; Jim Fernandez, Julius West Middle School, Rockville, MD; Sharon Neuman, Lawton Chiles Middle Academy, Lakeland, FL; and Tim Hadfield, South Shelby Middle School, Shelbina, MO. Working with each of you has been a professional pleasure.

Design of the Study

For more than a century, education leaders, policy-makers, and members of the public have been challenging the quality of education practices that have served young adolescents. In the late 1800s and early 1900s, several national committees studied U.S. education and most made recommendations for the development of programs and practices that uniquely served the needs of young adolescents. Throughout the 20th century, debate continued about the quality and appropriateness of programs intended to meet the needs of young adolescents but, more often than not, delivered in a manner more fitting for students of different age groups. The debate about high-quality education programs for young adolescents continues in the 21st century. Across the nation, states assess student progress in elementary, middle level, and high school years and raise repeated concerns about academic rigor and educational equity for all students. High-stakes testing, coupled with relative declines in revenue, have many schools on the verge of academic and financial bankruptcy. Those are but the most visible of the many challenges facing today's school leaders, and there are no easy answers to these dilemmas. The first chapter provides a detailed discussion of current knowledge about middle level programs and their leaders. It sets the context for interpreting the subsequent chapters of the study.

This book does not purport to have solutions to these complex problems. However, it can inspire insight into how highly successful middle level schools across the nation have addressed their challenges. This report can be used to contrast schools with the highly successful schools and as a guide to strategize for improvement. It shows specific organizational structures, education programs in use, and the nature of the relationships between formal school leaders and their constituents, and it can offer insight about best practices that can help to transform even the most challenging of educational settings into one of success for each student.

Overview of the Survey

The findings presented in this volume are from the second phase of the National Association of Secondary School Principals (NASSP) National Study of Leadership in Middle Level Schools. The first phase, a national sample of existing practices in U.S. middle level schools, was reported in 2002 (Valentine, Clark, Hackmann, & Petzko).

The second phase of the study focused on highly successful schools and their leaders. The purpose of this phase of the study is to provide principals, policymakers, researchers, other educators, and members of the public with insight about the programs that exist in highly successful middle level schools and the leaders who helped establish and maintain those programs.

This section explains the process used to identify and collect data from a set of 98 highly successful schools. It concludes with an explanation of how the research team identified and collected data about six middle level schools that collectively represent some of the best practices found in the composite set of 98 schools.

Highly Successful

Understanding the phrase *highly successful middle level school* is essential to the development of the study and is crucial to interpreting the findings. As the study began, a general definition was used. *Highly successful middle level school* was defined as "a school in which the principal and teachers consciously work together to effectively meet the needs of the young adolescents they serve." To select schools that fit that definition, the research team developed a set of criteria for nominators to use to recommend schools. Once nominations were made, the team asked the principals of the nominated schools to provide more detailed information about their schools.

As the research team studied the information from the nominated schools, the definition of *highly successful middle level school* changed to "a school that is effectively meeting the unique needs of its students through a variety of developmentally appropriate programs and practices befitting the students and the community." This definition was used to ensure that the schools selected for this study were (a) implementing middle level programs representative of the current research and literature about effective middle level schools, (b) making a conscientious effort to improve their programs as that knowledge expanded, and (c) studying and using student achievement data as well as other forms of student and school data to inform purposeful changes. The definition was, in essence, designed to select schools that were truly making a positive difference in the educational lives of the students they served.

Rather than attempting to identify the "best 100 middle level schools in the United States," this study attempted to identify a set of schools that fit the final definition of a *highly successful middle level school.* The analysis of highly successful schools provided high-quality information about programs and practices that schools can strive to implement. This design was congruent with the previous NASSP studies of the early 1980s and 1990s that used the terms *highly effective middle level schools* and *successfully restructuring middle level schools.*

The Nomination Process

The research team began in fall 2000 by developing criteria to enable education leaders from each state to identify highly successful schools. The criteria were developed from recommendations in *Turning Points: Preparing American Youth for the 21st Century* (Carnegie Council on Adolescent Development, 1989) and subsequent recommendations from *Turning Points 2000: Educating Adolescents in the 21st Century* (Jackson & Davis, 2000). These were selected because they represent the most current comprehensive knowledge about effective practices in middle level education. See Appendix A for the nomination criteria.

The research team then identified three or four education leaders from each state who would be most familiar with their states' middle level schools. In winter and spring 2001, the researchers contacted more than 200 leaders from state departments of education, principals' associations, and middle school associations as well as professors with expertise in middle level education. The educators were asked not only to nominate schools from their state but also to recommend others who would know the most successful middle level schools in their state. The number of submissions the nominators could make would be in proportion to the number of middle level schools in their state relative to the total number of middle level schools in the coun-

try. The nomination process was designed to obtain high-quality nominations from each state and provide a pool of 200 to 300 schools that were "highly effective" and in which the principal had been the leader of the school for at least two years.

The team sent each nominator an Internet address and asked him or her to complete a Web-based nomination form for each school he or she nominated. The form required the nominator to select the *Turning Points* recommendations from a pull-down menu and describe how the school was effectively addressing at least two or three of the recommendations.[1]

Because the forms required specific information, nominations on the basis of reputation or friendship were reduced. To complete the nomination process, each nominator had to have some in-depth insight about how the school was meeting the *Turning Points* recommendations. When the nominations were completed by spring 2001, each state was represented and 273 schools had been nominated.

The Selection Process

The research team contacted the principal of each nominated school in spring or summer 2001. The letter (Appendix B) explained the study and invited the principals to provide additional information about their schools if they wanted it to be considered for the set of 100 highly successful schools. Each letter also included a unique user ID and password to a secure Web site where the principals would complete the Nominee Response Form (Appendix C). The form explained the study and asked several open-ended questions about the school's change processes, vision and goals, challenges, evidence of meeting established outcomes for young adolescents, and leadership practices. The form also listed each of the seven *Turning Points 2000* recommendations and asked the principal to describe how his or her school was addressing each recommendation. The last section of the form included 27 demographic questions about the school, the community, and the principal.

Most principals took two to four hours to respond to the detailed questions. Of the 273 schools nominated, 141 principals completed the form. Some principals provided partially completed responses and others did not respond. Through follow-up contact with nonrespondents and those who did not complete the form, the

---

[1]Throughout the study, the research team mailed or faxed a copy of the questionnaires to respondents who had difficulty accessing the Web site. Research assistants transferred the written responses of nominators, principals, teachers, and parents to the study database.

three most common reasons for not completing the form were identified: the school was not addressing the expectations of the study adequately, so the principal chose not to respond; the response form required too much time to complete; or the principal had been relocated or had retired.

To select the set of 100 highly successful schools, the researchers established a panel of seven educators knowledgeable in middle level education and leadership. Each panel member rated a specified number of schools, and each school was rated independently by two panel members. If there was not close agreement in the ratings of a school, a third panel member rated the school.

To provide for validity and reliability in the rating process, a scoring rubric and a scoring directions booklet were developed and field-tested. Each rater was required to study the scoring rubric and the scoring directions booklet. For each question, the booklet provided the rater with a "perspective" that identified the relative level of significance of the question, a "scoring framework" that described the desired responses, and a "rater knowledge" section that provided the rater with information designed to inform the rater's understanding of the most appropriate responses for the question. Each rater was tested for reliability against an established standard. Reliability scores of 0.90 or higher were required to serve as a rater.

The research team analyzed the panel members' ratings and the 100 schools with the highest ratings were contacted in summer 2001 and invited to participate in the study (Appendix D). The responsibilities of the schools to collect additional data from teachers, students, parents, and principals were explained. Of the 100 schools, 98 agreed to participate in the study.

Data Collection From the 98 Highly Successful Schools

After each principal accepted the invitation to participate in the study, the researchers gave them instructions on how to collect additional detailed information about their school. The following sections describe the data collected from each school's principal, teachers, students, and parents.

Principal Surveys

Each principal was asked to complete the same online survey during the first phase of this multiyear study in 2000. The principals answered the first 27 questions from that national survey on the Nominee Response Form, so 163 questions remained. The online survey was divided into seven sections, each requiring 20–30 minutes to complete. The sections were: school leadership, school programs, school reform and professional development, instructional practices, curricular and cocurricular programs, school organization and programs, and leadership issues. Because the items were the same as those asked in the national sample and printed in the appendix of that book, the reader is referred to pages 155–211 of that document for a copy of the instrument (Valentine et al., 2002). The data collected from the 190 questions provided the opportunity to compare the programs and leadership of the highly successful schools with other middle level schools across the nation. Those findings are presented in chapter 2.

Teacher Surveys

The principals were asked to submit an alphabetical list of certified teachers. Specific directions were provided to ensure that the teachers were regular classroom teachers and that they had been in the school for at least one year. Using the list provided by the school, the research team created user IDs and passwords for each teacher so that he or she could go online and respond to a set of questions. Because 234 questions were identified for the teachers, the complete set was divided into three versions, with each teacher asked to complete one version. Each version contained approximately the same number of questions and required approximately 45 minutes to complete. The items were grouped by factors so that the responses could be analyzed to form a school score for each item, each factor, and each cluster of items in the surveys. The teacher survey items are in Appendix E. The findings from the survey items provided confirmation that the schools in the set were truly highly successful. The findings also provided data that were valuable in the process of identifying six schools for three-day site visits. Some findings about the six schools are discussed in chapters 3–5.

Student Surveys

The research team randomly selected 10% of the oldest group of students in each school to complete the student survey. The oldest grade, for example, grade 8 in a 7–8 school, was selected because those students would have had the longest period of time to develop an understanding of their school. The 62-item, paper-and-pencil survey (Appendix F) asked students about school activities, academic self-esteem and self-efficacy, schoolwide behavior, school adults and parents, home study conditions, and homework. The findings from the survey were helpful in identifying the six site-visit schools.

Parent Surveys

Each principal was asked to identify a parent leader who was extremely familiar with the school. The parent was sent a user ID and password and asked to log on to the study Web site and complete a few brief, open-ended questions about school improvement and change processes and the manner with which the school was addressing the recommendations from *Turning Points 2000*. The parent survey (Appendix G) provided information about the quality of the school program from the perspective of a knowledgeable parent. Like the data from teachers and students, the information collected from parents was valuable in the identification of the six site-visit schools.

Selection of Six Site-Visit Schools

After the data from the 98 schools had been collected and analyzed, the research team identified a few schools that were representative of the effective programs, practices, and leadership common to the 98 schools. By studying and profiling a small set of schools, the research team could provide all middle level principals with detailed insight about how those schools and their principals and teachers were facing the same challenges as middle schools across the country, yet they were overcoming those challenges and effectively meeting the needs of the students they served.

Six schools emerged from the analysis as representative of the demographic characteristics of the 98 highly successful schools. The six schools were more than merely demographically congruent, however. All the available data indicated that they were exemplary in the manner with which their programs, teachers, and school leaders met the needs of the unique student populations they served. Their data were among the highest on all factors of the teacher and student survey data. Their reports were among the most impressive in

the types of education programs they had developed and implemented and the manner with which they were continuing to change to better meet their students' needs. In December 2001, the research team invited six schools to participate in the site-visit portion of the study (Appendix H). Each of the schools accepted the invitation.

Data Collection from the Six Site-Visit Schools

In February, March, and April 2002, three members of the research team, or two members of the team and an additional middle level expert, spent three days at each of the six site-visit schools. Prior to the visit, each principal completed a brief survey about the school. The previsit survey was designed to provide insight about the school that would expedite the work of the team during the visit (Appendix I).

During the site visits, the team interviewed the principal and assistant principals, randomly selected teachers, student and parent leaders, and central office leaders. The team also observed instructional practices throughout the school over a two-day period (Appendix J).

Pseudonyms for the Six Site-Visits

The schools selected for the site visits were recognized alphabetically in the acknowledgment portion of the preface. For the purposes of this study, the schools have been given pseudonyms. The pseudonyms, listed alphabetically, were Einstein Middle Academy, Fourstar Middle School, Kent Middle School, Mark Twain Middle School, Pioneer Middle School, and Southside Intermediate School. A general profile of each school is presented in chapter 3. Specifics about the middle level programs and practices in the six schools are presented in chapter 4. Details about the nature of leadership in the six schools are included in chapter 5.

CHAPTER 1

Middle Level Education:
A Century of Growth and Reform

A Context for the Study
of Highly Successful Schools

Almost a century has passed since the establishment of the first junior high schools in Berkeley, CA, and Columbus, OH, in 1909. The significance of these schools cannot be overemphasized because it marked the beginning of an important reform in U.S. education: the creation and development of the middle level school. "The middle school movement," stated George and Oldaker (1985), "is one of the largest and most comprehensive efforts at educational reorganization in the history of American public schooling" (p. 1). John Lounsbury (1991) agreed and characterized the development of middle level education as the "longest-running, most extensive educational reform in the United States" (p. 68).

Although many factors have continued to contribute to the ever-evolving middle level education concept, the focus on meeting the unique developmental needs of young adolescents who are undergoing tremendous cognitive, emotional, physical, and social changes has been and remains predominant. Understanding this longstanding commitment to developmentally appropriate schools, the historical foundation of such schools, and the forces that continue to drive middle level reform provides the underpinnings for understanding the research findings reported in this book.

The Junior High School: 1900–1960

The 50 years from 1890 to the start of World War II often have been characterized as the golden age of U.S. education. During those years scholars and educators engaged in a rigorous inspection of U.S. public education and its intellectual, social, and democratic functions. This was the era of Charles Eliot, president of Harvard University, and others, who led or participated in numerous national studies of education, such as the Committee of Ten on Secondary Education and the Committee on Economy of Time in Education. It was also the era when John Dewey advocated for more

democratic and socially relevant forms such as progressive education; Edward L. Thorndike identified individual differences in students and developed educational measurement processes; G. Stanley Hall created developmental theories of adolescence, and the Commission of the Relation of School and College published its *Eight-Year Study* (Aikin, 1942; Lipka et al., 1998), which showed that innovative instructional strategies produced greater student success in college. This climate of reform nourished scholars and educators in their efforts to improve the educational experiences of young adolescents.

Recognition of the need to establish a separate school setting for young adolescents evolved slowly and was based primarily on concerns about the perceived failures of the organization of elementary (grades 1–8) and secondary schools (grades 9–12). Of particular concern was the belief that elementary schools were not dealing effectively with the needs of the students enrolled in grades 7 and 8. Early middle level reformers (Briggs, 1920; Koos, 1927) identified those needs as a more rigorous, challenging curriculum at an earlier age; teachers who were content specialists; provisions for individual differences; resources to meet the special needs of young adolescents; and a reduction in the number of dropouts and students retained at the same grade for a second or third year. Inherent in these needs were four forces that Koos (1927) characterized as responsible for "the movement of educational reorganization finding expression in the widespread establishment of junior high schools or intermediate schools" (p. 1). These forces included economy of time, concern for high student mortality and dropout rates, wide variations in learners, and needs of young adolescents (see Figure 1.1). These forces, which were important in the early formation of the junior high school, continue to influence current middle level educational programs and practices (Clark & Clark, 1994).

In their reorganization efforts to establish a separate school for young adolescents, early reformers drew strong support from the 1913 report of the Committee

Figure 1.1 **Forces that Led to the Establishment and Growth of the Junior High School 1900–1920**

Major Forces	Factors/Conditions	Responses
Economy of Time	Need for students to be exposed to natural science, algebra, geometry, and foreign languages at an earlier age; lack of academic rigor in grades 7 and 8 in elementary schools; no subject-area specialization for elementary teachers; need for preparing students for workforce	Recommendation for a 6-year secondary school; organization of 7–9 junior high schools; content-specialist teachers; subject-area departmentalization; high school coursework pushed to lower grades; vocational education
High Student-Mortality and Drop-Out Rates	A high percentage of students dropped out after grade 5, one-third reached ninth grade, and one-tenth graduated from high school; one-third of all students enrolled in school had been "left back" (repeated a grade) during the few years they spent in school	Repeating individual courses rather than an entire grade; providing for individual differences; more relevant curriculum; better instructional strategies
Wide Variation in Learners	Assumption that all students were alike led to standardized instruction and curriculum and produced a high drop-out rate; Thorndike & Cattell produced evidence of variation of learning among students; recognition of the varying needs caused by socioeconomic levels, family settings, and primary language backgrounds	Ability and achievement testing; homogeneous grouping/ability grouping/tracking; differentiated work through a partially variable curriculum; groups moving at different rates; promotion by subject; permitting "brighter" students to carry more courses; supervised study
Young Adolescents' Needs	Hall's cultural epoch theory provided the impetus needed for educators to address the special needs of adolescent youth	Organization of separate schools for young adolescents; engaging and appropriate instructional strategies; exploratory opportunities; content relevancy; guidance

Other Forces	Factors/Conditions	Responses
Overcrowding	Overcrowding in elementary or high schools	Creation of a 7–9 junior high relieved overcrowding at the elementary school (grades 7 and 8) and the high school (grade 9) levels
Momentum	High visibility and support for the junior high school (e.g., rhetoric, research, books, articles, reports)	Creation of a junior high school was deemed to offer best opportunities for learning (best on research, publications, practice, etc.)
Bandwagon	Desire by school officials to appear to be progressive or on the cutting edge of reform	Creation of junior high schools to be part of a "fad" or a trend (this process did little to change the educational processes available to young adolescents)

Note. From Koos, 1927; adapted from Clark and Clark, 1994.

on Economy of Time in Education (Baker, 1913), the first report that called for the organization of junior high schools. Educators and local school board members across the nation responded to the call for reform by establishing junior high schools in their communities. In fact, during the first 15 years (1910–25) after the establishment of the first junior high schools in Berkeley and Columbus, the number of junior high schools in the United States grew to 2,000 (Koos, 1927) and continued growing to 10,000 by 1947 (Hansen & Hern, 1971).

Throughout this period of rapid expansion, the early reformers sought to define the purposes and functions of the new junior high school. Their efforts were enhanced and supported by the report of the Commission on the Reorganization of Secondary Education of the National Education Association (1918) whose seven "cardinal principles" endorsed the junior high school concept and suggested additional organizational and programmatic components. The significance of the report, however, was in its emphasis on the larger purposes of U.S. secondary education, purposes that broadened the scope of educational aims beyond subject mastery to include citizenship, vocation, family membership, and leisure activities. These new principles, which reflected more democratic objectives for all schools, were particularly supportive of the purposes being advocated by reformers for junior high schools (Clark & Clark, 1994) and in later years by middle school reformers such as Eichhorn (1966) and Beane (1993, 1997).

On the basis of the "Seven Cardinal Principles of Secondary Education," junior high educators, scholars, and reformers continued their search for an identity and a purpose for middle level schools. A number of early junior high scholars, including Briggs (1920), Davis (1924), Koos (1927), and Pringle (1937), identified purposes and functions of junior high schools. The best known and most comprehensive model, however, was Gruhn and Douglass's "Six Functions of the Junior High School": integration, exploration, guidance, differentiation, socialization, and articulation (Gruhn & Douglass, 1947; Hansen & Hern, 1971; Van Til, Vars, & Lounsbury, 1961). Although the six functions reflected some changes in the perceived functions of early junior high schools, Gruhn and Douglass emphasized exploration and guidance, replaced the emphasis on grade-level retention with a new emphasis on socialization, placed greater importance on the function of differentiation based on individual differences, and introduced the concept of integration (Clark & Clark, 1993, 1994; Hansen & Hern, 1971; Van Til et al., 1961).

There was widespread agreement on the importance of these functions for the junior high school, and they served as a major force in guiding junior high educators in the 1940s and 1950s (Van Til et al., 1961).

By the middle of the 20th century, the junior high school had become widely accepted as the appropriate place for the education of young adolescents. In fact, the junior high school had become firmly entrenched as the school "in the middle." With four out of five high school graduates having attended school systems organized around the 6-3-3 grade-level configuration, there was a clear reversal from the 1920s, when four out of every five graduates had experienced an 8-4 grade-level organizational structure (Alexander & McEwin, 1989). It was evident that the organizational changes and programs called for by the early reformers to address the unique needs of adolescents and their variety of individual differences, as well as society's concerns about dropouts and grade retention, had been implemented and were successful (Van Til et al., 1961). The programs and practices that were evident in junior high schools across the United States included guidance programs that featured counselors and guidance periods (homerooms) and the extension of "secondary education" to include grades 7 and 8 (Hansen & Hern, 1971). Junior high schools implemented courses similar to those in high schools and organized instructors by subject matter, so subject specialists taught students. To accommodate individual differences, most students were grouped by ability, or "tracked," in the core classes of language arts, mathematics, social studies, and science (Wright & Greer, 1963).

As the 1950s progressed, however, there was a growing concern that the accepted junior high school organization and practices were falling short of fulfilling the promise of a unique place where young adolescents could be successful learners. Many believed that although accepted organizational structures were in place, the functions of the junior high school as described by Gruhn and Douglass were not being fully implemented because of the increase in tracking and ability grouping, extreme departmentalization and specialization, failure of guidance counselors to meet individual student needs (because of high pupil-to-counselor ratios), adoption of many activities that characterized senior high schools (e.g., formal dances, interscholastic competition), and widespread dissatisfaction of teachers with their assignments to junior high schools (Hansen & Hern, 1971; Lounsbury, 1954). The same organizational changes that the early promoters of junior high schools believed would meet the special needs of young adolescents—departmentalization, teacher specialization, and ability grouping—

were now being challenged as inappropriate for junior high school students (Clark & Clark, 1993).

The Emerging Middle School: 1960–1990

The 1960s brought a period of renewed interest in education reform. Although the United States was engaged in the Cold War, the federal government was embarking on a comprehensive domestic program of social and educational reform. It became a major force in shaping education with its Great Society programs such as Operation Head Start and the Elementary and Secondary Education Act of 1965 and additional funding for the National Defense Education Act and for vocational education. In addition, concern about issues such as poverty and segregation were increasing, and schools were being asked to become major players in the solution of these important social issues.

Educators were exerting considerable effort in curriculum development, making significant revisions to the major content areas. This included, for example, transformational grammar in language arts; the numerous developing science programs [e.g., ChemStudy, Biological Sciences Curriculum Study (BSCS), Physical Science Study Committee (PSSC) physics]; and the revision of mathematics content typically categorized as "new math." Many of these programs not only revised subject-area content but also promoted and incorporated innovative instructional practices such as programmed instruction, learning activity packages, inquiry learning, and individualized and personalized self-paced learning.

A major teacher shortage, particularly at the secondary level, forced educators to explore new ways of staffing their schools. Out of these efforts came flexible scheduling and innovative staff-utilization programs. The work of former NASSP Associate Executive Director J. Lloyd Trump was particularly influential. His book *Focus on Change* (Trump & Baynham, 1961) was important in establishing team teaching as a viable structure for secondary schools. As codirectors of the collaboration between the Danforth Foundation and NASSP, the Model Schools Project, Trump and William Georgiades created a comprehensive model for personalized education that legitimized many of the programs and organizational structures that have become closely linked with successful middle level schools (e.g., team teaching, teacher advisories, interdisciplinary curriculum; Trump, 1969; Trump & Georgiades, 1970).

It was in this climate of social and educational change that junior high educators and reformers were beginning to challenge the effectiveness of junior high

programs. An increasing number of educators were calling for the reorganization of junior high school grades. Grambs, Noyce, and Robertson (1961) suggested, for example, that the ninth grade should be moved to high schools in order to offer all of the college-preparation courses in one setting. Others found this suggestion appealing, believing that the provisions of the Carnegie unit as applied to the ninth grade in junior high schools were major impediments to meeting young adolescent needs (Bough, 1969). Additional support for the notion of a different grade configuration than 7–9 came from new information showing that young adolescents were maturing at an earlier age than children of previous generations (Alexander, 1984; Bough, 1969; Hansen & Hern, 1971). Bough (1969) believed that in addition to the earlier maturation of young adolescents, two other factors supported the justification for changing grade configuration: the importance, in metropolitan areas, of taking pupils out of the neighborhood ghettos and getting them into a large integrated school at a younger age; and, like Grambs et al. (1961) had advocated, the restoration of the ninth grade to the high school for college-preparation purposes.

While much of the early reform effort was aimed at reconfiguring the grade arrangement in middle level schools, a number of educators were responding to the increasing criticism that junior high schools were merely mimicking high school programs and policies. Armed with new information on young adolescent development, educators such as William Alexander and Emmett Williams (1965) and Donald Eichhorn (1966) became leading advocates of the middle school concept. In addition to supporting grade-level reorganization, Alexander and Williams (1965) also proposed changes in the basic middle level structure, including creating homerooms with 25 students and forming four-person teams of teachers with specialties in language arts, social studies, mathematics, and science. The teams would plan and implement a curriculum that integrated the subject areas with learning skills, general studies, and personal development. Eichhorn's (1966) sociopsychological model, which focused heavily on the developmental needs of young adolescents, featured two integrated curricula: analytical, which included language, mathematics, social studies, and science; and physical/cultural, which included fine arts, practical arts, physical education, and cultural studies. Instruction in Eichhorn's model was delivered in a variety of organizational arrangements including block and flexible schedules.

Defining the Middle School

As a result of the increasing pressure in the 1960s for reform in the education of young adolescents, middle level educators became embroiled in a debate about the effectiveness of junior high schools when compared with the new and emerging middle schools. Junior high schools were regarded as subject-centered, departmentalized, impersonal, miniature versions of high schools, whereas middle schools were characterized as student-centered schools that incorporated integrated curricula, teams, and advisory programs. Junior high schools were neatly categorized as schools containing grades 7–9 or 7–8, whereas middle schools typically contained grades 5–8 or 6–8. These debates continued over the next two decades, even though the "first comparative studies and surveys revealed that the new middle schools and the old junior high schools were surprising alike in actual practice" (Lounsbury, 1991, p. 68).

The rhetoric on middle level schools, fueled largely by the junior high versus middle school debates, became more focused on the organizational and programmatic structures of middle level education. Grooms (1967) promoted nongraded structures in which students could progress on a continual learning basis without recognized grade levels or grade classifications. Gatewood (1973) advocated for middle level schools with programs that focused on individualized learning and many curriculum options. Trying to move beyond simply changing schools' organizational structures, other middle level educators focused the curriculum on young adolescent learners by promoting integrated curricula, schedule and group-size flexibility, individualized and personalized instruction, a variety of learning experiences, alternative evaluation procedures, and new roles for teachers and administrators (Eichhorn, 1973; Sale, 1979; Vars, 1969).

Out of these debates and rhetoric grew a need to find a term that would describe schools that served young adolescents; a term that would be equally acceptable to junior high school and middle school educators. The terms *middle level schools* and *middle level education* were first used by the research team of the Dodge Foundation/NASSP national study of schools "in the middle" (Valentine, Clark, Nickerson, & Keefe, 1981). These terms, however, gained general acceptance among junior high school and middle school educators largely through the energetic efforts of George Melton, former deputy executive director of NASSP, who popularized the terms through his work with schools throughout the nation (Clark & Clark, 1994). By the end of the 1980s, the terms *middle level school* and *middle level education* had gained widespread accept-

ance and were the terms used by middle school and junior high school educators to describe their schools (Lounsbury, 1991).

Researchers, scholars, and educators increased their efforts in defining middle level education and identifying the attributes of good middle level schools. Building on Gruhn and Douglass's "Six Functions of the Junior High," Alexander and George (1981) listed the essential features of middle level schools as guidance, transition and articulation, block time schedules and interdisciplinary teams, appropriate teaching strategies, exploratory curriculum, and appropriate core curriculum and learning skills. In addition, on the basis of the literature and research of the 1970s, Clark and Valentine (1981, 1992) defined and organized middle level schools into three major categories: program environment, program content, and program strategies (Figure 1.2).

Joan Lipsitz (1984) was also working to define the purposes and functions of middle schools. Drawing from her comprehensive research on four successful middle level schools, she identified the following general characteristics of successful schools:

> [S]chools responsive to early adolescent development will reduce the size of the focus groups (interdisciplinary teams, schools-within-schools, house plans, teacher advisory groups), personalize the quality of adult-student relationships, give ample room for peer groups to flourish, acknowledge diverse areas of competence, involve students in participatory activities, emphasize self-exploration and physical activity, and encompass all of these in a clearly defined, structured environment. (p. 199)

Lipsitz (1984) also introduced the term *developmental responsiveness* to identify schools and programs that were aligned with the needs of their young adolescent students.

Refining the Focus

Despite the work of many scholars and researchers throughout the 1960s and 1970s, many middle level educators believed that the middle level concept still lacked a comprehensive focus that would define its purposes and practices. Although many individuals, organizations, and state departments of education contributed to build this comprehensive focus, three organizations worked during the 1980s to define middle level education: the National Middle School Association (NMSA), NASSP, and the Carnegie Task Force on Education of Young Adolescents. These organizations have had—and continue to have—a significant effect on middle level education.

Figure 1.2 Middle Level Programs

Program Environment
Schedule includes provision for both interdisciplinary blocks and single courses
Cocurricular activities are part of the regular school day
Opportunity for all students to participate in intramural and, when appropriate, interscholastic programs
Provision for community involvement in the educational program
Opportunities to learn through interdisciplinary teams, where students can interact with a variety of
teachers in a wide range of subjects

Program Content
Emphasize the acquisition of basic skills (language arts, mathematics, social studies, and science)
Available required exploratory courses (music, art, technology, etc.)
Opportunities to participate in elective classes
Provisions for both remediation and enrichment
Required reading instruction
Provisions for daily physical education
Opportunities for instruction in both health and sex education

Program Strategies
Available multimedia resources (print and nonprint)
Provision for a variety of teacher-student teaching and learning styles
Provisions for flexible learning and group size
Adaptation of curriculum to concrete/formal learning needs of students
Available teacher–adviser programs
Provisions for individualized grade reporting based on each student's ability and
including parent conferences
Opportunities for each student to explore and clarify values
Provisions for individualized/personalized programs that include diagnosis
(skills and learning style) and prescription
Organization of content into a continuous progress sequence that allows students
to progress at their individual rates

Note. Adapted from Clark and Valentine, 1981.

The National Middle School Association
The National Middle School Association (NMSA), established in 1973, is the only national education association that focuses exclusively on the education of young adolescents. In 1982 the association published *This We Believe*, which defined the characteristics of developmentally responsive middle level schools. A committee of educators and scholars developed a list of characteristics of effective middle level schools on the basis of the belief that the middle level school "is an educational response to the needs and characteristics of youngsters during early adolescence and, as such, deals with a full range of intellectual and developmental needs" (NMSA, 1982, p. 9). Effective middle level schools have:

- Educators knowledgeable about and committed to young adolescents

- A balanced curriculum based on the needs of young adolescents
- A range of organizational arrangements
- Varied instructional strategies
- A full exploratory program
- Comprehensive advising and counseling
- Continuous progress for students
- Evaluation procedures compatible with the nature of young adolescents
- Cooperative planning
- A positive school climate. (NMSA, 1982, pp. 15–22)

This list, which has undergone several revisions (NMSA, 1995, 2003), has served to successfully define and guide the work of NMSA for the past two decades. Figure 1.3 presents the current version of *This We Believe*.

Figure 1.3   **Middle Level Characteristics**

This We Believe: Successful School for Young Adolescents

The National Middle School Association believes that successful schools for young adolescents are characterized by a culture that includes:

- Educators who value working with this age group and are prepared to do so
- Courageous, collaborative leadership
- A shared vision that guides decisions
- An inviting, supportive, and safe environment
- High expectations for every member of the learning community
- Students and teachers engaged in active learning
- An adult advocate for every student
- School-initiated family and community partnerships.

Therefore, successful schools for young adolescents provide:

- Curriculum that is relevant, challenging, integrative, and exploratory
- Multiple learning and teaching approaches that respond to their diversity
- Assessment and evaluation programs that promote quality learning
- Organizational structures that support meaningful relationships and learning
- Schoolwide efforts and policies that foster health, wellness, and safety
- Multifaceted guidance and support services.

Note. From National Middle School Association, 2003.

The National Association of Secondary School Principals NASSP, established in 1916, has been a strong advocate of middle level education since its inception. NASSP has provided leadership in middle level education, starting in 1965 with its first major study of the junior high school (Rock & Hemphill, 1966). The association has supported three additional major national studies of middle level schools and leadership: *The Middle Level Principalship* (Valentine et al., 1981; Keefe, Clark, Nickerson, & Valentine, 1983), *Leadership in Middle Level Education* (Valentine et al., 1993; Keefe, Valentine, Clark, & Irvin, 1994), and the current study, *A National Study of Leadership in Middle Level Schools* (Valentine et al., 2002). NASSP also has sponsored three national shadow studies of grades 6, 8, and 9 (Lounsbury & Clark, 1990; Lounsbury & Johnston, 1985, 1988) and, in the early 1980s, formed the Council on Middle Level Education, which produced numerous publications including a monthly magazine, *Schools in the Middle*; actively participated in conferences and conventions; and provided guidance to middle level leaders across the country.

The NASSP Council on Middle Level Education publication, *An Agenda for Excellence at the Middle Level* (1985), identified 12 dimensions that must be in place to ensure that a middle level school is successful.

Incorporating many elements identified by others, a comprehensive list was developed that included an emphasis on core values, instruction, effective teaching, and transition (Figure 1.4).

The Carnegie Task Force on Education of Young Adolescents

The Carnegie Task Force on Education of Young Adolescents was established in 1987 with the mission of examining firsthand new approaches to fostering the education and healthy development of young adolescents. It also aimed to "place the compelling challenges of the adolescent years higher on the nation's agenda" (Carnegie Council on Adolescent Development [CCAD], 1989, p. 13). In *Turning Points: Preparing American Youth for the 21st Century* (CCAD, 1989), the task force suggested that a vast majority of U.S. middle level schools were failing to meet the needs of young adolescents. To remedy this situation, the authors of *Turning Points*, drawing from research and practice, developed eight essential principles for transforming middle grades education:

- Large middle grades schools are divided into smaller communities for learning.
- Middle grade schools transmit a core of common knowledge to all students.

Figure 1.4   An Agenda for Excellence at the Middle Level

> ### An Agenda for Excellence at the Middle Level
>
> *Core Values:* Everyone involved must be committed to clearly articulated core values that guide both individual behavior and institutional practices and policies.
>
> *Culture and Climate:* School improvement depends on a change in culture and climate of the institution. Specific attention must be given to altering the culture and climate of the school so it supports excellence and achievement.
>
> *Student Development:* Success in school and adjustment to adult life depend, to a large degree, on personal attributes and behaviors.
>
> *Curriculum:* The middle level curriculum must develop in young adolescents the intellectual skills and an understanding of humankind that will permit them to gather information, organize that information, evaluate the data's veracity and utility, form reasonable conclusions about the data, and plan for individual and collective action.
>
> *Learning and Instruction:*: The quality of any young adolescent's educational experience is determined by the nature of instruction provided in the classroom.
>
> *School Organization:* School organization should encourage the smooth operation of the academic program, clear communication among teachers and administrators, and maximum teacher and student control over the quality of the learning environment.
>
> *Technology:* Young adolescents should be educated to use technology competently and thoughtfully in their study of specific subjects and in their approach to complex problems.
>
> *Teachers:* Teachers require special preparation and certification which must include the study of human development, counseling, differentiated instruction, classroom management, and home–school cooperation.
>
> *Transition:* One of the main responsibilities of the middle level school is to ensure a smooth transition for students from elementary to high school.
>
> *Principals:* Successful schools enjoy strong administrative leadership, a clear sense of mission, and confidence in the capacity of administrators to handle problems that interfere with the learning program of the school.
>
> *Connections:* The success of any school is determined by the extent to which it is supported and valued by the community and by the parents of the young adolescents who attend.
>
> *Client Centeredness:* Successful schools are those that understand the uniqueness of their clients and fill their clients' needs quickly and effectively.

Note. Adapted from NASSP Council on Middle Level Education, 1985.

- Middle grade schools are organized to ensure success for all students.
- Teachers and principals have the major responsibility and power to transform middle grade schools.
- Teachers for the middle grades are specifically prepared to teach young adolescents.
- Schools promote good health; the education and health of young adolescents are inextricably linked.
- Families are allied with school staff through mutual respect, trust, and communication.
- Schools and communities are partners in educating young adolescents. (CCAD, 1989; p. 36)

At the time of the publication of *Turning Points,* Anthony Jackson, project director of the task force, reported that the response to the report was overwhelmingly positive (Jackson, 1990). He also reported:

> Nevertheless, some educators have commented that there is very little that is new in the report. "We are already doing that" is a common response to many of the recommendations in Turning Points from schools across the nation. Despite such perceptions, recent studies show that few of the recommended actions, though frequently proposed, are actually practiced in schools. (p. 1)

Jackson's comments were confirmed by numerous studies in the late 1980s. In spite of the evidence that the common elements identified by Alexander and George (1981), Clark and Valentine (1981, 1992), Lipsitz (1984), NASSP Council on Middle Level Education (1985), and NMSA (1982) were successful in creating more developmentally responsive environments (George & Oldaker, 1985; Lipsitz, 1984; MacIver, 1990), these elements were not found at that time in a majority of the country's middle level schools. In addition, numerous national studies indicated that most of the programs commonly recommended by middle level educators and the Carnegie task force were not being widely implemented (Clark & Clark, 1992). It was also evident that even when schools reported implementing programs such as interdisciplinary teaming and teacher advisories, many of the programs were not functioning in the way they were intended to function (Lounsbury & Clark, 1990; MacIver, 1990).

For middle level educators, *Turning Points* provided a wake-up call and was important in promoting middle level reform in a variety of ways (Clark & Clark, 1992):

- *Turning Points* confirmed that many of the programs that middle level educators had been trying to implement were developmentally appropriate. The report supported programs such as smaller focus groups; implementing teacher advisories, interdisciplinary teaming, and a core curriculum; and increasing parental and community involvement.
- *Turning Points* supported programs such as school–community youth service, health education integrated with life science and focused on adolescent development, teacher education programs focused on the middle grades, and extensive involvement of health and community groups in educating young adolescents.
- *Turning Points* described shortcomings of existing middle level programs and challenged educators to address them.
- *Turning Points* provided educators with guidelines for establishing a purpose for their middle level schools.
- *Turning Points* challenged middle level educators to continue their efforts in developing responsive middle level schools. Using current research and best practices, the task force developed eight principles for transforming middle level education.
- *Turning Points* gave middle level education new status as an equal partner in the education hierarchy. It provided the mission, challenges, and principles upon which middle level educators could develop strong, viable, developmentally appropriate middle level schools.

By the end of the 1980s, *middle school* had become well defined. Almost universally, middle level educators recognized the importance of schools that were developmentally appropriate to the needs of young adolescents. Although there was agreement on the general purpose of middle level schools, middle level educators, drawing from tradition, practice, rhetoric, and research, organized their schools in a variety of ways. The research of the 1980s[1] yielded the following picture of middle level schools:

- **Grade-level configuration:** By 1990, young adolescents were most likely to be enrolled in middle level schools with grades 6–8, and 7–8 was more prevalent than 7–9 (which had been the most common configuration in 1980).
- **School size:** Although enrollment size varied, a majority of middle level students received their education in schools that had enrollments of 400–800.
- **Scheduling:** The single-subject schedule (traditional high school schedule format) was still the predominate method for instructional time.

---

[1]See Alexander and McEwin, 1989; Cawelti, 1988; Clark and Clark, 1990; Epstein and MacIver, 1990; Lounsbury and Clark, 1990; Valentine et al., 1981.

- *Interdisciplinary teaming:* Approximately 40% of the schools had interdisciplinary teaming programs, but the presence of teams in a school did not necessarily mean that there was an effect on classroom instruction or young adolescents.
- *Guidance:* Schools with teacher advisory programs ranged from 29% in the Cawelti study (1988) to 66% in the CREMS study (MacIver, 1990). Schools were slow to implement teacher advisory programs.
- *Core curriculum:* In almost all cases, the required or core curriculum consisted of English and language arts, social studies, mathematics, and science. Concerns were expressed about the fact that the curriculum was influenced extensively by state mandates and requirements (Cawelti, 1988) and about its lack of relevance to young adolescent needs (Lounsbury & Clark, 1990).
- *Exploratory curriculum:* Although they were still an important part of the middle level curriculum, exploratory experiences were more narrowly defined as courses (e.g., practical arts, fine arts, technology) and were being reduced by the pressure to add more state-mandated requirements (Becker, 1990).
- *Grouping practices:* Ability/homogeneous grouping and tracking were practiced in a vast majority of middle level schools. Students were most likely to be grouped in mathematics, reading, and English and least likely to be grouped in social studies and science (Braddock, 1990).

Reforming Middle Level Schools: 1990–2003

Although reform has been ongoing, it came to the forefront of middle level education during the last decade of the 20th century, motivated primarily by the challenges presented by *Turning Points* (CCAD, 1989). The actions that came about as a result of those challenges—and the attempts to accommodate the pressures being placed on educators by the local, state, and federal government for improving student achievement, increasing accountability, and instituting high-stakes testing—contributed significantly to the efforts to reform middle level schools during the 1990s. Middle level educators were encountering the same forces identified 60 years before by Koos (1927): economy of time (more rigorous curriculum at the middle level, standards, greater emphasis on core courses, teachers with content specializations), student retention in school (engagement in learning, relevant curricular structures), variation in learners (multiple approaches to instruction, ability grouping), and needs of young adolescents (developmentally appropriate curriculum, instruction, and activities).

Implementing *Turning Points*

The release of *Turning Points* in 1989 (CCAD) gave middle level education a national presence. The book and its executive summaries were disseminated to nearly every middle school in the country, and it gave a new impetus to raise the quality of educational experiences for young adolescents. Although *Turning Points* provided a vision of a possible future and asked parents, community members, policymakers, and educators to work together to translate that vision into a better reality for all young adolescents, it did not provide a great deal of information on how to carry out that vision. The implementation of the original *Turning Points* framework of ideas and recommendations was left to innumerable individuals who added their own wisdom, knowledge, skills, and experience.

The publication of *Turning Points* was followed by major grants through the Middle Grade School State Policy Initiative of the Carnegie Corporation (Council of Chief State School Officers, 1992), and its recommendations were embraced by major education organizations such as NASSP and NMSA, which used its recommendations as a foundation for numerous national and regional conferences and publications. The appeal of *Turning Points* was that it was easy to read, its recommendations were clear and concise, it made sense, and, as a result, it energized the middle level reform efforts that had already begun.

The efforts to create small learning communities, teach a core academic program, ensure success for all young adolescents, empower teachers and administrators, staff schools with expert teachers, improve performance through better health and fitness, reengage families, and connect schools and communities led to many positive changes in middle level schools. Ongoing research about the implementation process yielded several trends that characterized the *Turning Points* implementation efforts:

- There was support for the eight principles in general, with strong preferences for some principles and weak support for others
- Most of the changes in middle level schools were structural or organizational
- There was not as much change in actual middle grade classroom practices as had been hoped
- Many middle level schools implemented pieces of the recommendations and principles—not the whole package. (Clark & Clark, 2003b; Jackson & Davis, 2000).

*Uneven Support for the Various Principles
of Turning Points*

Although there appeared to be strong support for all eight principles of *Turning Points*, in reality some were considered to be much more important than others and, as a result, received more emphasis in the implementation process. For example, principals ranked creating small learning communities, teaching a core academic program, and ensuring success for all young adolescents as the three most important principles (Valentine et al., 2002). Creating small learning communities in fact justified the efforts that many educators had made to incorporate interdisciplinary teaming, the signature program in middle level education, into their schools. Principals reported that their schools implemented this recommendation at a higher level than any of the other *Turning Points* principles. Principals also indicated that creating small learning communities would receive more emphasis in the future than any of the other recommendations (Valentine et al., 2002). That teaching a core academic program and ensuring success for all students were ranked high and identified as areas that would receive emphasis in the future is easily explained by their correlation with pressures to emphasize content standards and to ensure success for all students.

Ranked at the bottom of principals' lists (Valentine et al., 2002) were reengaging families with young adolescents and connecting schools with communities, which were recommendations that principals also had indicated were lowest in current effectiveness and were least likely to receive emphasis in the future. It is clear that principals, in spite of evidence to the contrary (Jackson & Davis, 2000), did not perceive these two areas as being important in addressing the issues of standards and student learning.

Structural Change

Evidence supported the fact that middle level educators were actively engaged in making structural changes in their schools during the 1990s (Valentine et al., 2002), and two factors appeared to be conducive to the implementation of structural change in middle level schools: many of the *Turning Points* recommendations called for organizational changes, and structural changes are generally easier and more appealing to implement than changes of attitudes and school cultures. Evidence of this was found in the increase in the number of schools with interdisciplinary teams and strong support for and implementation of exploratory programs (Valentine et al., 2002). Organizationally, these programs could be implemented by teaming teachers and scheduling the same group of students to a team or by adding or deleting courses. Altering school structures and course offerings, however, did not necessarily improve teaching and learning (Clark & Clark, 1998, 2003a; Elmore, 1995b).

Classroom Change and Learning

Although evidence from research studies in the 1990s shows many benefits of middle level school improvement efforts, these efforts had a minimal effect on changing classrooms (Clark & Clark, 1998, 2003a; Midgley & Edelin, 1998). In presenting the results from their study, Midgley and Edelin (1998) reported:

> Structural changes in middle grades education—how students and teachers are organized for learning—have been fairly widespread and have produced good results. Research indicates that the adoption of middle grade structures has improved relationships within schools and that students are experiencing a greater sense of well-being. However, our observations suggest that relatively little has changed at the core of most students' school experience: curriculum, assessment, and instruction. (p. 195)

Lipsitz, Mizell, Jackson, and Austin (1997) also believed that many middle level schools were "warmer, happier, and more peaceful places for students and adults" (p. 535). They suggested that, in spite of this positive climate, most schools "have not yet moved off this plateau and taken the critical next step to develop students who perform well academically with the intellectual wherewithal to improve their life conditions" (p. 535).

It appeared that, in spite of the many structural and organizational changes, many middle level schools continued to use traditional classroom approaches to educate young adolescents. In most cases, programs and strategies that had been recognized as successful in engaging students and fostering learning had been implemented at low levels and had been underutilized (Clark & Clark, 1998, 2003a).

*Partial, Incomplete, or Low Implementation
of the Turning Points Recommendations*

Research also indicated that high implementation of middle level school programs, including the recommendations of *Turning Points,* could have a positive effect on student learning. Felner et al. (1997), for example, in their study of 31 middle schools, examined the level of implementation of programs and its effect on student achievement and social behaviors. They found that higher levels of implementation were associated with significant increases in achievement as measured by standardized tests, self-esteem, and students' feelings of connectedness and belonging within their school. Higher levels of implementation also were associated with fewer student problem behaviors and lower fear of victimization.

High implementation of *Turning Points* recommendations also meant complete implementation of the total package. Choosing some components for implementation but rejecting others fragments the program and reduces its effectiveness. Jackson and Davis (2000) suggested:

> [E]xisting research suggests that when reforms are implemented with integrity, in a manner that leads to authentic change in curriculum, instruction, and assessment and in the organization and climate of a school, dramatic and lasting improvements in student performance can be obtained. When reforms are implemented in a limited or scattershot manner, however, as when changes in grade configuration and teacher and student grouping are not accompanied by substantial changes in teacher practices, improvement in outcomes is more limited. (p. 6)

Remaining Unsolved Issues

In addition to these trends, there were and are several *Turning Points* issues that middle level educators continue to address; issues that remain unsolved after more than 10 years of effort.

Ensuring Success for All Young Adolescents

Although most middle level educators indicated the importance of all students succeeding in their schools, it appeared that many school cultures still supported programs and structures that were developmentally inappropriate (Valentine et al., 2002). For example, ability grouping in middle level schools had increased over the past 10 years, most master schedules for middle level schools were single subject (not interdisciplinary or flexible), and the curriculum was most often delivered in a subject-centered manner using traditional, low-student-engagement instructional strategies. In addition, developmentally appropriate programs designed to offer special assistance to young adolescents, such as teacher advisories, often were undervalued and not implemented. When they *were* implemented, they were ineffective (Clark & Clark, 1998, 2003a; Valentine et al., 2002).

Staffing Schools With Expert Teachers

During the past decade, middle level education was not yet able to establish itself as a separate entity for spe-

cialized preparation of teachers and administrators. As a result, the vast majority of teachers and administrators currently in middle level schools have received preparation to be elementary or high school educators. Numerous studies support the fact that fewer than 25% of middle level teachers had specialized preparation or had certificates for teaching at the middle level (Cooney, 2000; McEwin, Dickinson, & Jenkins, 1996; Scales, 1992; Scales & McEwin, 1994). Because of this lack of preparation, most new middle level teachers must rely on on-the-job training for the basic skills necessary to survive at the middle level. This on-the-job training often lacks most of the basic ingredients recognized as being important to middle school teacher preparation (McEwin & Dickinson, 1996; McEwin, Dickinson, Erb, & Scales, 1995; National Association of State Directors of Teacher Education and Certification, 1994; NMSA, 1995).

Teach a Core Academic Program

The push by the federal government, corporate leaders, and state legislatures to mandate curriculum and content standards, raise levels of student achievement, and hold teachers and administrators accountable for student performance placed a great significance on curricular programs and instructional practices. These high-stakes demands for accountability that became part of the standards-based reform movement had and have the potential to enhance curriculum, instruction, and student learning—or greatly diminish it and narrow its scope (Clark & Clark, 1997, 2000). The question that faced all middle level educators over the past decade was: What effect will the pressure of high-stakes accountability have on developmentally responsive curriculum, instruction, and assessment? Mandated standards and the accountability that goes with them, however, do not single-handedly pose a threat to developmentally responsive middle level programs. It is how the standards are interpreted and the procedures are put in place that determine their appropriateness for educating young adolescents (Clark & Clark, 2003c).

This dilemma of developmental responsiveness and standards-based reform continues to be an issue that must be addressed by middle level educators. There is, however, a substantial amount of research that indicates that, in spite of the fears of some middle level principals (Valentine et al., 2002), standards-based reform and developmental responsiveness can be mutually supportive (Clark & Clark, 2001; Mizell, 2002; Rosenholz, 1991; Schmoker & Marzanno, 1999; Wheelock, 1998). Hayes Mizell, director of the Program for Student Achievement at the Edna McConnell Clark

Foundation, suggested that standards are not the enemy of developmentally appropriate middle school programs. Nor are they an excuse for narrowing a teacher's instruction to prepare students to pass a high-stakes test. "Standards," stated Mizell, "make clear to everyone the academic mission of the middle grades" (2002, p. 78).

Although the push for accountability and higher test scores led some critics to characterize the middle level movement as a failure, Jackson and Davis (2000) refuted this claim:

> There is, in fact, a kind of backlash against the kinds of practices recommended in Turning Points in some communities because dramatic gains in academic achievement are not yet evident in schools attempting to implement changes. If we have learned anything in the past ten years, it is that gains in student achievement and other positive outcomes for students require comprehensive implementation over an extended period of time. (p. 16)

They go on to say that "there is mounting evidence that when educators stay the course of comprehensive reform, student outcomes do improve" (Jackson & Davis, 2000, p. 16).

Middle Level Education: Expansion and Research

In summarizing middle level education during the 1990s, two major trends became apparent: (1) continued expansion and implementation of commonly accepted middle level programs and practices and (2) high research activity that enhanced the validity of middle level programs and increased knowledge about them.

Expansion and Implementation

The number of middle level schools in the United States had expanded to an all-time high of more than 14,000 schools in 2002 (Valentine et al., 2002). During the 1990s the 7–9 grade pattern nearly disappeared, with the 6–8 grade configuration becoming predominant for middle level schools. The average enrollments decreased as did teacher-to-pupil ratios. Most middle level schools, however, were staffed by teachers who often did not have middle level certification (Valentine et al., 2002).

Programmatically, almost all middle level students were provided with a comprehensive core academic program of mathematics, science, language arts, reading, social studies, and physical education. In these core courses, 85% of the schools grouped students into specific classes by academic ability, which represented a

3% increase from the results of the 1992 NASSP study (Valentine, Clark, Irvin, Keefe, & Melton, 1993). Most students had the opportunity to participate in a variety of required exploratory and elective courses and to engage in cocurricular clubs, intramural activities, and interscholastic sports. Although 79% of the schools reported the presence of interdisciplinary teams in their schools (an increase of 22% over the 1992 study), the curriculum typically was delivered in a subject-centered manner through a departmentalized or interdisciplinary teaming design. There was little evidence of theme-centered, student-centered, or integrated curriculum.

Middle Level Research: Expanding the Knowledge

The 1990s produced a significant amount of research that continued the process of confirming the effectiveness of the middle level concept, particularly as it was represented by the *Turning Points* recommendations. The research of Felner et al. (1997), George and Shewey (1995), and Jackson and Davis (2000), for example, all offered evidence of the effectiveness of accepted middle school programs. When these programs were properly implemented, they provided multiple benefits for students, including increased learning as measured by achievement tests. Other research has demonstrated the effectiveness of numerous alternative classroom instructional strategies that engage students in learning and facilitate academic success (Mayer, 1998; Newmann & Wehlage, 1995; Tomlinson, 1999; Wehlage, Newmann, & Secada, 1996; Wheelock, 1998; Wiggins & McTighe, 1998).

Establishing links between research and practice continued to be an important priority for both NASSP and NMSA. NASSP, in addition to its national study of eighth grade, *Inside Grade Eight: From Apathy to Excitement* (Lounsbury & Clark, 1990) and its two-phase, two-volume *A National Study of Leadership in Middle Level Education* (Keefe et al., 1994; Valentine et al., 1993), conducted a major middle level principal development project and evaluation study (Leadership Makes a Difference in Standards-Based Reform) funded by the Edna McConnell Clark Foundation, and in 1999 sponsored another two-phase, multiyear national study of middle level schools and leadership. NMSA published *Research in Middle Level Education,* and initiated and maintained a research page with research summaries and research articles on its Web site. NMSA's *What Current Research Says to the Middle Level Practitioner* (Irvin, 1997) provided an excellent source of research for middle level educators. Middle level research also gained legitimacy from the American Educational Research Association, with the renewed interest and expansion of middle level research with the formation of the Middle-Level Education Research special interest group.

The long-term efforts of the Program for Student Achievement of the Edna McConnell Clark Foundation also provided important information about successful middle level school practices. As a result of its sustained work and funding, the foundation identified and supported implementation of successful, developmentally appropriate standards-based reforms in large school districts throughout the nation to improve student learning. In addition, the Program for Student Achievement provided numerous publications about middle level school reform and created a middle level Web site (MiddleWeb) that features up-to-date information about middle level education. The comprehensive efforts of the foundation have demonstrated that middle grades reform is difficult and complex but also important.

Also contributing to knowledge on effective middle level practice was the National Forum to Accelerate Middle-Grades Reform Schools to Watch program. Schools to Watch has identified successful middle level schools on the basis of academic excellence, developmental responsiveness, and social equity. Through this program, the forum has found and supported middle level schools that are successfully implementing developmentally appropriate standards-based reform.

A final but important contribution to knowledge about middle level education was *Turning Points 2000: Educating Adolescents for the 21st Century* (Jackson & Davis, 2000). This publication highlights the lessons learned from the Carnegie Foundation's Middle Grades School State Policy Initiative, other national middle level improvement efforts, and the latest research in an "in-depth examination of how to improve middle grades education" (Jackson & Davis, 2000, p. xi). *Turning Points 2000*, states David Hamburg in the foreword, "combines the most up-to-date research with what has been learned from the follow-up Middle Grades School State Policy Initiative and other middle grades improvement efforts—a blend of wisdom from practice and data from systematic research." (Jackson & Davis, 2000, p. xi). Hamburg goes on to say:

> The research base on education reform has grown considerably in recent years, and this book incorporates the findings of that research. In drawing heavily on the best available research, Turning Points 2000 helps to bridge the gap between researchers and practitioners, putting practitioners in touch with research in the framework of a comprehensive and comprehensible model. (p. xi)

Anthony Jackson and Gayle Davis (2000) used *Turning Points 2000* to "describe what has happened in the 1990s in order to envision, in considerable detail, what can happen in middle grades education in the 21st century" (p. 16). They believed that the book should be "useful to advocates and decision makers working to establish policies at the local, state, and federal levels to improve the education and development of America's young adolescents" (p. 16). "[M]iddle grades education is ripe for a great leap forward," Jackson and Davis state. "Our hope is that this book will help middle grades educators maintain their courage and commitment as they continue their journey up the mountain" (p. 16).

With a central, overriding theme of *ensuring success for every student*, *Turning Points 2000* calls for middle grades schools that:

- Teach a curriculum grounded in rigorous, public academic standards for what each student should know and be able to do, relevant to the concerns of adolescents and based on how students learn best. . .
- Use instructional methods designed to prepare all students to achieve higher standards and become lifelong students. . . .
- Staff middle grades schools with teachers who are expert at teaching young adolescents, and engage teachers in ongoing, targeted professional development opportunities. . . .
- Organize relationships for learning to create a climate of intellectual development and a caring community of shared educational purpose. . . .
- Govern democratically through direct or representative participation by all school staff members—the adults who know students best. . . .
- Provide a safe and healthy school environment as part of improving academic performance and developing caring and ethical citizens. . . .
- Involve parents and communities in supporting student learning and healthy development. (Jackson & Davis, 2000, pp. 23–24)

With its focus on academic excellence, equity, and developmental responsiveness, and its emphasis on teaching and learning, *Turning Points 2000* has the potential to provide the guidance necessary for taking the next steps in improving middle level schools.

The Challenges of Leadership in Middle Level Schools

Schools are increasingly composed of a student demographic that differs significantly from that in the 1950s, when most schoolchildren were from traditional nuclear families (Reyes, Wagstaff, & Fusarelli, 1999). Growing numbers of children come from single-parent households, blended family structures, or dual-career families (Huelskamp, 1993), and the nation's schools are becoming more ethnically diverse. Minority students made up 38% of school enrollments in the fall 2000 semester, compared with 30% in 1986 (National Center for Education Statistics [NCES], 2002). During the 2000–2001 academic year, more than 13% of the total U.S. school population received special education services, and there were significant gaps in academic performance among racial and ethnic subgroups (NCES, 2002).

Middle level schools have not been universally successful in addressing concerns about student achievement, particularly in low-income communities and for students with special needs. Because of poor educational quality in many urban middle level schools, approximately half of the students in urban districts have been unable to experience success after the transition to high school (Balfanz & MacIver, 2000). A primary objective of the recent federal No Child Left Behind Act (NCLB, 2002) was to close the existing achievement gap for students who are economically disadvantaged, have disabilities, are non–native English speakers, and are from racial and ethnic minority groups (NCLB, 2002). *Turning Points 2000* advocated "equity in outcomes for all groups of students, regardless of their race, ethnicity, gender, family income, or linguistic background" (Jackson & Davis, 2000, p. 11).

These calls for excellence have significant implications for leadership in middle level schools. Successful schools must have highly skilled principals who can develop the capacity within their organizations to ensure that every student experiences success. This section provides an overview of the existing knowledge on effective leadership practices, noting the middle level principal's vital responsibility for promoting school change.

The School Reform Movement and Implications for Leadership

The publication of *A Nation at Risk* (National Commission on Excellence in Education, 1983) served as a catalyst for an educational accountability movement that has been sustained for 20 years. Schools and educators have been criticized during this era of reform for maintaining the educational status quo,

being resistant to change, and being unresponsive to student learning needs. This accountability movement initially focused at the state level, with each state implementing curriculum standards, benchmarks, and assessment measures. The enactment of NCLB, however, dramatically increased the stakes for schools from a district or state accountability framework to a national one (NCLB, 2002). The concept of local control—with each school district enjoying a high degree of autonomy—rapidly eroded as federal and state education departments increasingly focused on local school accountability.

Building-level leadership practices have undergone intense scrutiny during this reform era, with principals challenged to move beyond traditional management practices to visionary leadership activities that promote the involvement of multiple constituencies in facilitating comprehensive school change. The school leader's role, consequently, has changed dramatically and has become increasingly complex and demanding (Louis & Murphy, 1994). Principals' changing responsibilities were categorized into five areas: local management of schools, balancing management and leadership roles, increased accountability, expanded relationships with parents and community members, and school-choice dilemmas (Whitaker, 2003). Professional associations have developed new definitions of the principalship commensurate with these shifting expectations. Such groups as the National Policy Board for Educational Administration (Thomson, 1993), the National Association of Elementary School Principals (1991), the Interstate School Leaders Licensure Consortium (1996), the Institute for Educational Leadership (2000), and the National Staff Development Council (Sparks & Hirsch, 2000) influenced new conceptualizations of the principal's role while also proposing multiple—and sometimes competing—recommendations for enhancing leadership skills. A consistent theme, however, ran through the reports: The principal's leadership practices are key in forming an organizational culture dedicated to improving student performance.

The school reform movement has covered the broad spectrum of preK–12 education, but middle level schools arguably have been subject to as much intense scrutiny and condemnation as elementary or high schools, if not more. The middle school movement has been criticized for a perceived emphasis on creating a more welcoming school climate for the emerging adolescent but not concurrently attending to issues related to improving student achievement (Jackson &

Davis, 2000; Lipsitz, Mizell, Jackson, & Austin, 1997). *Turning Points 2000,* however, asserted: "The main purpose of middle grades education is to promote young adolescents' intellectual development" (Jackson & Davis, 2000, p. 10). Middle level educators should not lose sight of student achievement issues when implementing middle school programming, understanding that it is certainly possible for the curriculum to be developmentally appropriate while still retaining academic rigor (Anfara & Waks, 2001; Clark & Clark, 2003b).

The Changing Landscape of Schools and Leadership

Increasing demands for accountability, a growing emphasis on standards-based reforms, and increasingly diverse student enrollments have necessitated the reconceptualization and restructuring of schools throughout the nation. Schools in the United States have developed into loosely coupled systems (Weick, 1976) in which teachers primarily have been responsible for implementing instruction within the classrooms while principals manage the structures and processes that support instruction. Since the 1930s, middle level principals' roles have gradually shifted away from management to democratic leadership, then to humanistic leadership in the 1980s, and to instructional leadership in the 1990s (Valentine, Maher, Quinn, & Irvin, 1999). Although many have extolled the benefits of the principal's increasing responsibility as an instructional leader, Elmore (2000) noted, "Direct involvement in instruction is among the least frequent activities performed by administrators of any kind at any level" (p. 7). Standards-based reform, however, brought with it an increased emphasis on the principal's responsibility to influence the practice of teaching and the process of learning. Principals cannot ignore this important charge.

Because of the mandate for content standards and benchmarks and the increased accountability that accompany these requirements, middle level principals and teachers must be actively engaged in the development and implementation of curriculum standards. Jackson and Davis (2000) noted that, in the middle grades, standards are essential to guarantee that excellence and equity are present within the school, ensuring success for every student. Principals must take on more direct instructional leadership responsibilities, and school organizations must become more tightly coupled, to promote close alignment among the written, taught, and assessed curriculum.

Developing High-Quality Schools

The Interstate School Leaders Licensure Consortium (1996) clarified three central changes that must occur in educational institutions for high-quality schooling to exist for all students: redefining teaching and learning to challenge and engage all students, increasing community-focused and caring conceptions of schools, and increasing the involvement of external stakeholders. The following sections expand upon these themes, explaining how effective middle level leaders ensure that every student attains a high-quality educational experience.

Teaching and Learning: Promoting Success for All

In addition to demographics, other dramatic changes in the 21st century workplace are projected (Reyes et al., 1999). The U.S. Department of Labor (2002–2003) forecasts that the nation's shifting employment trends will continue to move away from the goods-producing sector to the service-producing sector. Computer and data-processing services were projected to be the fastest growing industry in the economy, with an estimated 86% job growth increase between 2000 and 2010. The seven fastest-growing education and training categories require postsecondary training, and 48 of the 50 highest paying occupations require a college degree (U.S. Department of Labor, 2002–2003). Such forecasts necessitate close examination of curricular offerings and learning activities to ensure that each child is adequately prepared for success in high school and beyond.

Curriculum

School leaders are charged with determining appropriate curricular modifications within their educational systems as they strive to prepare a dramatically changing student population for the 21st century postindustrial society. Because the nation's population is graying and fewer households contain school-age children, older adults will "exert a disproportionate influence on the political system" (Reyes et al., 1999, p. 194). Consequently, approval for proposed increases in education spending will be increasingly difficult to obtain and schools will need to reconsider the breadth of their programs and services and more directly align their efforts to providing a "fundamentally sound, basic education" (Reyes et al., 1999, p. 194). Middle level principals, who in some instances already have faced community resistance to the implementation of effective middle grades practices (Oakes, Quartz, Ryan, & Lipton, 2000), may need to more vigorously justify and defend their programs to their community.

Many loosely coupled schools and school systems suffer from disorganized, fragmented, and unconnected curricula that are not completely effective in promoting coherent learning (Beane, 1995). Jackson and Davis (2000) acknowledged that, in the middle grades, "relatively little has changed at the core of most students' school experience: curriculum, assessment, and curriculum" (p. 5). Many middle level schools have not taken the initiative to move beyond forming supportive, welcoming environments to developing schools with a challenging curriculum that fully prepares students for academic success (Lipsitz et al., 1997). Middle level leaders can ameliorate this deficiency by closely interconnecting the written, taught, and assessed components of the curriculum (English & Larson, 1996). In effective schools, educators have the essential content knowledge and skills to design and deliver an appropriate, standards-based curriculum that meets the learning needs of their students (English, 2000).

Teaching and Learning

The construction of a well-designed middle grades curriculum is only the first step in the improvement process. Teachers must then use instructional approaches that ensure that each child masters the curriculum content. Throughout most of the 20th century, instructional practices aligned with behaviorist theory, which "regards psychology as a scientific study of behavior and explains learning as a system of behavioral responses to physical stimuli" (Fosnot, 1996, p. 8). A significant amount of cognitive research related to teaching and learning has been undertaken in the past few decades, prompting educators to question their time-honored instructional practices. Whereas behaviorism tends to focus on the teacher's role in transmitting knowledge, a relatively new view of learning—constructivism—emphasizes the student's role in the learning process. Building on the work of Jean Piaget, Lev Vygotsky, and others, constructivism theorizes that individuals actively create their own knowledge from their existing beliefs and personal experiences (Fosnot, 1996). Simply stated, the instructional focus is shifting away from the act of teaching toward the process of learning. Teachers in high-quality schools create learner-centered environments in which students strive to form meaning from newly accessed content (Windschitl, 1999).

Although ideas regarding instructional methods are moving toward constructivist strategies that actively engage every student in learning, classroom practices in schools across the nation appear to be changing so slowly that it is almost imperceptible (Elmore, 1995a). Teacher-dominated instruction persists in today's classrooms, and the teaching gap between belief and practice appears to be widening (Stigler & Hiebert, 1999).

Contrary to Irvin's (1992) recommendation that middle level instruction should involve "learning how to learn, learning how to think, and learning how to cooperate" (p. 305), direct instruction methods are predominant in many middle level classrooms. Lounsbury and Clark's (1990) shadow study of eighth-grade students found that most classrooms were highly structured, with teachers relying on lectures to deliver content. Most middle level teachers infrequently used active instructional practices, instead relying on drill-and-practice and other passive activities (Jackson & Davis, 2000; MacIver & Epstein, 1993). When leaders focus their energies on instructional innovations and technologies designed to improve student learning, this trend can be reversed (Kruse, 2001). In effective schools, teachers' work in the classroom becomes "a key instrument of reform" (Kruse, 2001, p. 361). Prawat and Peterson (1999) agreed, noting that constructivist principles and practices should permeate the entire school organization.

In fulfilling the mandates of NCLB, principals must help teachers access successful research-based programs that have been proven to help most children learn. Extensive amounts of research exist that can inform middle level educators about effective instructional methods, or best practices (Zemelman, Daniels, & Hyde, 1998). Increased student learning occurs when middle level teachers implement research-based practices such as teaming and curriculum integration (Trimble, 2003).

As teachers continue to hone their craft, they should identify and implement successful instructional practices (Marzano, Pickering, & Pollock, 2001). Furthermore, as classrooms become increasingly diverse and students' learning needs become more varied, teachers must develop skills with differentiated instruction (Tomlinson, 2001b) so they can "work with students' variability instead of ignoring it" (Jackson & Davis, 2000, p. 78). In addition, teachers should become proficient with inclusion practices (Bartlett, Weisenstein, & Etscheidt, 2002) to ensure that students with special learning needs also experience success.

Assessment

Policymakers and community patrons tend to rely on standardized testing as a means of holding students accountable for individual learning and holding school systems accountable for the effectiveness of their instructional programs. NCLB requires states to test students' progress in reading, science, and mathematics. Although middle level faculties will need to comply with state and national testing mandates, changing instructional practices prompts a call for alternatives to traditional testing methods in favor of more authentic forms of assessment (Rowan, 1995). Authentic measures can be of two types: products (such as papers, newspaper articles, letters to public officials, and projects) and performances (such as skits, poetry recitations, demonstrations, and oral presentations) (Danielson, 2002). Furthermore, classroom assessments should be ongoing so teachers have opportunities to differentiate instruction and to reteach as necessary, ensuring that each child is successful (Wiggins & McTighe, 1998).

These varied assessments are necessary to discern the quantity and quality of student learning. Effective principals engage teachers in the analysis and use of assessment data to satisfy accountability mandates and identify areas in which instructional improvement should occur.

Community-Focused and Caring School Environments

In addition to developing students' academic skills, middle level schools also need to teach citizenship and promote interpersonal relationships among teachers and students (CCAD, 1989; Jackson & Davis, 2000). The terrorist attacks of September 11, 2001, reminded Americans of the importance of teaching students the basics of democracy and about their roles as citizens.

Schools traditionally have been based on the factory model of efficiency, possibly because they have displayed a tendency to focus more on the workplace needs of adults than on the individualized learning needs of students (English & Larson, 1996). As a result, many schools have gradually evolved into sterile, impersonal environments. However, the principles of the middle school movement have been successful in helping faculties form healthy and positive student-centered school cultures (Clark & Clark, 2003b). High-quality middle level schools promote a personalized learning environment (Keefe & Jenkins, 2002) that nurtures positive relationships and helps students become ethical and caring citizens (Jackson & Davis, 2000; Noddings, 1988).

Ethical and Caring Communities

School leaders should be dedicated to creating schools that serve as centers of inquiry while ensuring that each individual is treated with dignity and respect. Noting that an ethic of care should be a guiding principle, Beck and Foster (1999) believed that schools must be restructured as caring communities, calling upon administrators to "work diligently and strategically to create such conditions" (p. 353). They stated, "Schools

and systems that function as agencies of and agents for community are those most likely to support the development of human and humane persons capable of work, love, friendship, and citizenship" (p. 355).

Developing shared values is a necessary feature in the formation of caring school communities (Strike, 1999). To assist in the formation of these caring communities, many middle level schools have implemented character education programs (Lockwood, 1997). In addition, service learning has been advocated by *Turning Points* (CCAD, 1989) and *Turning Points 2000* (Jackson & Davis, 2000) as a means of instilling citizenship values and skills in young adolescents.

Moving beyond shared values into the creation of a shared vision, teachers and administrators should develop the school as a moral community that fosters unity while respecting and embracing the differences inherent in diversity (Starratt, 1996). Furthermore, "educators must become aware of the ethical implications of their work and . . . must continually strive to make and be guided by morally sound decisions" (Beck & Murphy, 1994, p. 1). In high-quality schools, educators have a moral purpose (Fullan, 2001, 2003b), and they are guided by their personal and professional ethical codes as they engage in the decision-making process.

Socially Just Schools

Successful schools establish fair, equitable, and caring environments in which each student feels accepted and valued. However, schools traditionally have been structured to educate the students who come prepared and are motivated to learn. As evidenced by the achievement gap, it is apparent that many "schools now really work for just part of the population" (English & Larson, 1996, p. 100). In a postindustrialist society that places a premium on a well-educated populace, our school systems cannot fail our students, and it is the school leader's responsibility to ensure that equitable practices and social justice exist throughout their institutions (Grogan & Andrews, 2002). Social justice should be the anchor for the educational leadership profession (Murphy, 1999). Highly successful middle level schools seek social equity, striving to educate all children (Lipsitz et al., 1997).

Forecasters predict that minority students will make up nearly half of the nation's school-age population within the next few years (Sykes, 1995). Middle level leaders must be fully committed to embracing diversity and educating all students who enter their schools. Beyond diversity, high-quality schools must be responsive to every student, and they must honor differences in class, race and ethnicity, gender, sexual orientation, and academic ability. Although the current financial crisis in most states may hinder efforts to address social justice issues (Marshall & McCarthy, 2002), successful leaders will keep this issue as a central element of their schools.

Stakeholder Involvement

Effective leaders seek to create schools as centers of inquiry that involve and empower individuals within the organization as well as stakeholders in the greater school community. A primary leadership focus should be to develop strong social ties within the school by fostering trust, establishing channels for new information, and communicating and enforcing norms and expectations (Smylie & Hart, 1999). Teachers, in particular, must have frequent opportunities to interact and collaborate with their colleagues to plan, assess, and improve their practice. Interdisciplinary teaming structures are particularly effective in developing "cultures of collaboration" (Clark & Clark, 1994, p. 192), which provide an effective avenue for school restructuring. Such collaborative efforts help build a cohesive faculty that focuses on teacher learning, engages in reflection on practice, and promotes continuous improvement (Kruse, 2001).

Involvement of Internal Stakeholders in School Governance

Implicit in the development of stronger connections within a school is the expectation for greater faculty member involvement in school governance. School-based decision making provides an opportunity for principals to cultivate leadership skills within faculty members, in the process stimulating teachers to become "leaders of leaders." Teacher empowerment and participatory management build organizational learning capacity (Marks & Louis, 1999), promote trust among teachers and administrators, and support a structure for teacher collaboration and reflection (Youngs & King, 2002). However, as relationships become more complex and individuals are required to relate to one another in new ways, role conflicts often can occur. Successful leaders learn the skills to manage conflict and build consensus as they negotiate and define the boundaries created by changing role structures (Short & Greer, 1997).

Middle level schools have a unique opportunity to facilitate democratic governance through an interdisciplinary teaming approach. Although principals should be continually informed about and involved in the work of the teams (Arnold & Stevenson, 1998), the teaching teams "must have substantial

autonomy in decisions about student instruction" (Jackson & Davis, 2000, p. 137). Teams also provide an opportunity to develop leadership capacity within faculty members by giving them assignments such as team leader, parent liaison, and curriculum coach (Shapiro & Klemp, 1996).

The heart of middle level school governance and communication is the building leadership team, often referred to as the program improvement council (George & Alexander, 1993) or the school improvement team (Painter, Lucas, Wooderson, & Valentine, 2000), which includes, at a minimum, the principal and teacher representatives from throughout the school faculty. This team is responsible for the development of the school's annual comprehensive school improvement plan and oversees its implementation (Jackson & Davis, 2000). However, in spite of the fact that collaborative decision-making models are in place in most middle level schools, researchers caution that most principals continue to make a high percentage of school decisions (Clark & Clark, 2002a; Valentine et al., 2002). Leaders must ensure that teacher-leaders operate in a truly democratic fashion and are granted sufficient authority to make decisions.

Working collaboratively with the leadership team, the principal is a key agent in mobilizing support for change while ensuring that the focus is on improved student learning. Because change is "resource-hungry," leaders also provide sufficient time for faculty members to meet, reflect, and make decisions as well as contribute the necessary funding to ensure that reforms are adequately implemented and sustained.

Successful leaders also ensure that their democratic governance models include parents (Goldring & Sullivan, 1996) by working to establish effective two-way communication and actively soliciting parental input in decision making (Blase & Blase, 2000). An additional positive outcome of empowerment is improved relationships among teachers and students, which promote greater student participation in decision making. Empowered teachers, in turn, give students "increased choice and responsibility for their own learning" (Short & Greer, 1997, p. 157).

Improved student achievement does not simply emerge as a by-product of site-based management and teacher empowerment (Miller, 1995). School-based reforms must focus on student achievement goals to ensure improved student learning, and faculty members must reach data-informed decisions (Quinn, Gruenert, & Valentine, 1999). As educators strive to reach a more complex and profound understanding of teaching and learning, their reflection and practice must be informed through accessing the growing research related to best instructional practices, particularly as it relates to the effects of teacher behaviors on student cognition.

Facilitating Connections With Families and External Stakeholders

Effective leaders develop associations with key stakeholders and resources outside the school, because "[t]hese external ties perform a crucial function of bringing new information, perspectives, and challenges to teachers inside the school" (Smylie & Hart, 1999, p. 433). One approach is the establishment of school–family–community partnerships (Epstein, Coates, Salinas, Sanders, & Simon, 1997; Kettler & Valentine, 2000), which recognize the shared responsibilities of the home, school, and community in promoting students' learning and development. Another approach is to facilitate links through coordination and collaboration among human service agencies (Smrekar & Mawhinney, 1999). Integrated services for children and their families, such as the full-services school model (Dryfoos & Maguire, 2002), bring a variety of services into the school setting, including drug and alcohol counseling, mental health services, violence prevention education, child care, nutrition education, dental and medical services, parenting classes, and GED programs for parents. These integrated services assist in "bridging the worlds of families and schools" (Smrekar & Mawhinney, 1999, p. 452), firmly establishing the school as an essential element within the community.

Leadership for Change

There is growing evidence that high-quality principal leadership is essential for school reform to occur (Valentine et al., 1999), particularly if improved student achievement is the goal. Conducting a meta-analysis of 30 years of quantitative educational leadership research, Waters, Marzano, and McNulty (2003) found a substantial positive relationship between leadership and student achievement, with an average effect size of .25. Cotton's (2003) meta-analysis of qualitative research confirmed the significant role of the principal in effecting change and thus influencing student success. Effective middle level principals practice visionary leadership, willingly accepting "their role as a catalyst and as vision keeper" (Brown & Anfara, 2003, p. 21). The following sections discuss the importance of reflective practice, instructional leadership, and transformational leadership in promoting school change.

A review of the extensive literature related to accountability, school reform, and effective leadership

practices discloses the presence of a constant theme: Effective principals use reflective practice (Schön, 1987) and they have the ability to help teachers reflect on their practice (Mullen, Gordon, Greenlee, & Anderson, 2002). McCarthy and Kuh (1997) discussed the importance of "reflective practitioners who are informed by leadership theory, education research, and craft knowledge" (p. 262), and Blase and Blase (1998) depicted a process of "reflective supervision" as the principal works with the professional staff members. Murphy (2002) brought the elements of instructional leadership, transformational leadership, and reflective practice together, asserting that leaders should be moral stewards who invest themselves in defining purpose and reflective analysis, educators who keep curricular and instructional leadership at the core of their practice, and community builders who "learn to lead by empowering rather than by controlling others" (p. 188).

The principal's changing role related to school accountability reveals that middle level leaders must possess the ability to transform their organizations and to be the "principal change agent" (Hipp, 1997, p. 45) for the school. However, to build a school's capacity to engage in critical reflection and to promote improved learning for all students, principals must first have in-depth knowledge of curricular standards and effective teaching practices. Marks and Printy (2003) described the significance of instructional leadership that is "shared" between formal leaders and teacher leaders and concluded that schools that lack transformational leaders also lack effective instructional leaders. Transformational leadership, however, does not imply instructional leadership. Both are essential and complementary, supporting the importance of what they call "integrated" leadership (p. 392). Shared instructional leadership and transformational leadership form the core of effective principal practices.

Collaborative Instructional Leadership

The standards movement has placed "student learning at the center of the administrator's role" (McCarthy, 2002, p. 213). Principals must have "a common understanding of good classrooms and good schools" (Grogan & Andrews, 2002, p. 241), adopting collaborative instructional leadership approaches in which they partner with internal and external stakeholders to promote the formation of a shared vision and common goals. This schoolwide vision should be "built solidly on a compassionate understanding of the characteristics and needs of young adolescents" (George & Alexander, 1993, p. 504). Curriculum and instructional leadership should focus "on teacher growth rather than compliance, teacher collaboration for instructional improvement, and facilitation of teachers' reflective inquiry" (Mullen et al., 2002, p. 181).

Middle level principals should make successful learning for every student their "number one leadership priority" (Clark & Clark, 2002b, p. 51). Although instructional leadership is only one element of organizational behavior, even routine principal responsibilities should be given a curricular interpretation so they are grounded in the teaching-learning dimensions of the school organization (Glatthorn, 1997). Schools should shift from an emphasis on teaching to an emphasis on learning, and principals should function as learning leaders (DuFour, 2002). Lambert, Walker, Zimmerman, and Cooper (2002) used the term "constructivist leadership" to describe how standards-based reform and authentic assessments can be implemented. Equity, diversity, and multiculturalism can be addressed through constructivist-based accountability (Lambert et al., 2002).

Middle level principals and their faculty members must have a solid understanding of effective curriculum, instruction, and assessment practices. They must possess knowledge about emerging adolescents' physical, cognitive, emotional, and social characteristics so that their learning organizations address the developmental needs of children. However, this knowledge is not always present in many middle level schools:

> A continuing difficulty in providing developmentally responsive schools for young adolescents is widespread ignorance about the characteristics, needs, and interests of the age group. Many people, both inside and outside the profession, are not only unenlightened about the age group, but hold negative stereotypes about them. (McEwin et al., 1996, p. 157)

Consequently, as middle level principals strive to be effective change agents within their school, they must ensure that these changes are grounded in a thorough understanding of the needs of middle level learners. Principals must promote curriculum reforms and instructional methods that are responsive to young adolescents' developmental needs (McEwin et al., 1996).

Leaders must be knowledgeable consumers of educational research and be proficient with the uses of various technologies to access and analyze classroom and school data (Trimble, 2003). Principals must be committed to data-informed decision making—collecting, analyzing, and using data to determine their effectiveness in meeting their school improvement plans (Lipsitz et al., 1997; Quinn et al., 1999). To reduce achievement gaps that exist within their schools, educators must "explicitly monitor the gap reduction (not just overall achievement trends) and take appropriate action" (Fullan, 2003a, p. 14). Furthermore, principals cannot effectively supervise their staff members and lead them, as individuals and a group, to higher levels of performance if they do not have a conceptual understanding of "how schools succeed, how great teaching is accomplished, and how students learn well" (Glickman, 2002, p. 6). Blase and Blase (1998) acknowledged a growing acceptance of more democratic and collegial approaches to supervision and encouraged leaders to build professional dialogue among educators.

The term *collaborative instructional leadership* was coined to highlight the collegial nature of this significant responsibility because principals cannot engage in instructional leadership activities in isolation. Inherent within this approach are principal behaviors that foster reflective practice. Blase and Blase (1999) noted, "[P]rincipals who are effective instructional leaders use a broad-based approach; they integrate reflection and growth to build a school culture of individual and shared critical examination for improvement" (p. 370). These practices facilitate the formation of professional communities in schools.

At the middle level, the interdisciplinary teaming structure provides an effective mechanism for supporting teachers' development of their craft. The provisions for common planning time, flexible scheduling, common adjacent classrooms, and team autonomy are a few of the features that facilitate teacher collaboration and continual professional growth (Flowers, Mertens, & Mulhall, 2000b), which is indispensable in promoting school change.

Effective staff development activities directed toward changes in teacher behaviors can result in improved student performance (Clark & Clark, 1994; Gilles, Cramer, & Hwang, 2001). They should be "intensive, of high quality, and ongoing" (Lipsitz et al., 1997, p. 536). Because the majority of middle level teachers did not receive specialized training in middle level practices for young adolescents in their preservice programs, staff development activities should include these components and remain connected to the school improvement plan (Flowers, Mertens, & Mulhall, 2002).

Transformational Leadership

In reviewing the educational leadership literature of the past few decades, Leithwood, Jantzi, and Steinbach (1999) categorized approaches to school leadership into six models: instructional, transformational, moral, participative, managerial, and contingent. Although much of the school leadership literature focuses on instructional leadership, Leithwood et al. argued that this approach focuses only on first-order changes within the school culture—changes in core technology. They believe that a comprehensive approach to contemporary leadership must "help those in, and served by, current and future schools respond productively to the significant challenges facing them" (Leithwood et al., 1999, p. 21). Fullan (2002) agreed, noting that the principal's singular role as an instructional leader is too limited to transform a school's teaching and learning culture. Marks and Printy (2003) noted the importance of "integrated" leadership, in which leaders demonstrate transformation and shared instructional skills. Leaders can extend the focus on learning and instruction through the creation of leadership teams, a concept Elmore (1999) called "distributed leadership."

Transformational leadership first drew attention in 1978 through the work of James McGregor Burns. More recently, Bass (1998) has defined transformational leadership as including the components of idealized influence (being ethical and moral role models), inspirational motivation (motivating or inspiring by providing meaning and challenge to followers' work), intellectual stimulation (encouraging innovation and creativity), and individualized consideration (accepting individual differences, while acting as a coach or mentor). Most transformational leadership models underrepresent the significance of managerial practices that are inherent in administrative positions. Transformational leadership should encompass leadership and management roles (Leithwood & Jantzi, 2000). As schools become more decentralized, leaders must become more skilled with responsibilities that may be considered managerial in nature, such as generating and targeting resources for school improvement (Monk & Plecki, 1999), addressing legal issues (including employment and termination decisions), administering special education programs, and maintaining internal and external communication channels.

Although modifying the instructional practices employed within a school is indeed important, such changes will not become sustainable without school restructuring, which Leithwood et al. (1999) described as a second-order change. In their view, transformational leadership is the most effective approach because it is comprehensive, fits the school context in which it is exercised, and ensures that the school culture is transformed as changes become institutionalized. Schlechty (1997) agreed, adding that transformational leadership creates the capacity within organizations to support reforms, an approach Fullan (1993) described as "reculturing." Finally, Smyth (1996) argued that transformational leaders should create socially just schools that are committed to whole-school change. This type of learning community, Smyth emphasizes, includes parents and teachers in the decision-making process, establishes a process of consultation with the local community, and strengthens students' connections with their own cultures. Brown and Anfara (2003) agreed, explaining that "[e]xemplary middle schools and their visionary leaders find it essential to involve all stakeholders in the change process" (p. 23).

Summary

The purpose of this portion of NASSP's national study of middle level schools is to provide principals, teachers, policymakers, and other educators and noneducators with insight about the programs, practices, and leadership in highly successful middle level schools. As a unique level of education devoted specifically to young adolescents, the middle school "concept" has been under close scrutiny for three decades. In any environment, close examination is important; in today's environment of high-stakes testing and declining fiscal resources, such examination is imperative, and middle level education has welcomed the scrutiny.

The literature about middle level programs, practices, and leadership reported in this chapter provided the foundation for the analyses of 98 highly successful schools. Understanding this basic literature about middle level programs and leadership is essential for interpreting the findings reported in the following chapters.

In the quest for understanding highly successful middle level schools and their leaders, programmatic and leadership success stories in urban, suburban, and rural settings, in small, medium, and large enrollment schools, and in low-, middle-, and high-income communities were discovered. The composite data about the 98 highly successful schools that participated in the study and the detailed analyses of the six site-visit schools will be a valuable source of insight and, hopefully, inspiration for those who serve young adolescents. This book is not a recipe for success. It is a compilation of information about important components found in successful schools from which thoughtful, reflective educators can glean important knowledge and then apply that knowledge in their ongoing quest for success.

CHAPTER 2

98 Highly Successful Middle Level Schools

Programs, Practices, and Leadership

The 98 highly successful schools from across the nation are meeting the developmental needs of their students, aggressively addressing the challenges in their local school setting, and looking inwardly and asking how they can improve. This chapter provides details about the 98 schools and contrasts their characteristics, programs, and leaders with what is typical across the nation. Middle level educators can compare their programs and practices with both sets of data and generate goals and strategies for improvement.

Basic demographic characteristics are presented in the first section of this chapter. Details about the middle level programs in the 98 schools, including curriculum, instructional design, assessment methods, transition strategies, and cocurricular programs are presented in the next section, and characteristics of the principals and their leadership practices are addressed in the subsequent section. The chapter includes tables detailing the 98 schools and contrasting their characteristics with the findings from the NASSP national study of middle level schools across the country (Valentine, Clark, Hackmann, & Petzko, 2002). The final section is a synthesis of selected findings from the chapter.

Demographic Characteristics

The 98 highly successful schools were selected because they stand out from other schools in what they do and how they do it, and the positive effects for students. The 98 schools are implementing programs and practices that are making a difference in the lives of their students, much more so than typical U.S. middle level schools. The study was designed to identify a set of highly successful schools, regardless of the demographic variables associated with the schools. There was no attempt to match the demographic conditions of the highly successful schools with typical conditions from the national sample of schools. The following paragraphs provide brief discussions of the demographic variables (Table 2.1).

School Grade Patterns

Among the approximately 14,100 middle level schools in the United States, the most common middle level grade pattern is 6–7–8, followed distantly by grades 7–8 (Valentine et al., 2002, p. 1). The highly successful schools were not significantly different from the national sample for any of the grade level categories.

Student Enrollment

Approximately half of the middle level schools across the country had fewer than 600 students enrolled. In contrast, nearly half of the highly successful schools enrolled between 800 and 1,400 students. The highly successful schools tended to be larger than typical schools across the country. Although there were some excellent examples of small schools in the set of 98, and two superb small schools in the six site-visit schools, the percentage of smaller middle level schools in the study was not proportionate to the number of small schools across the nation.

Per-Pupil Expenditure

The highly successful schools in this study spend more money per pupil than typical schools across the nation. Compared with the national sample, a smaller percentage of schools from the highly successful group spent less than $4,000 per student, and a higher percentage of highly successful schools spent more than $7,000 per pupil. The percentage of schools from both groups spending between $4,000 and $7,000 were similar (about 66% of each group).

Classroom Teacher-to-Pupil Ratio

The highly successful schools were larger and tended to spend more money, but they had higher pupil-teacher ratios than is typical across the nation. This translates into larger class sizes, which is not uncommon in larger schools that are able to use staff members somewhat more efficiently than smaller schools. The most notable differences between the highly successful schools and the national sample were in the percentage of schools with an average class size of fewer than 20 students and the percentage of schools with an average class size between 26 and 30 students. There were fewer highly successful schools with average class sizes below 20 students and more with average class sizes above 25 students.

Student Ethnicity

The student demographics of the highly successful schools were slightly different from the national sample. In the 98 schools, the average percentage of Caucasian and African American students were each 2% less than the average percentage for the national sample. The average percentage of Asian American students in the highly successful schools was 3% higher than in the national sample.

Free and Reduced-Price Lunch Programs

The percentage of students eligible for free or reduced-price lunches in the highly successful schools was 7% lower than the average for the national sample schools. The number of schools with more than half of their students eligible for free or reduced-price lunches was 6% lower in the highly successful schools.

Demographic Summary

The demographic conditions in both sets of schools provide insight for comparing the conditions and environments of the 98 highly successful schools relative to the nation's middle level schools. Among the demographic characteristics, grade pattern and student ethnicity were most similar, and student enrollment, per-pupil expenditure, teacher-pupil ratio, and free and reduced-price lunch programs were less similar. However, no demographic characteristic was classified as extremely different.

Programs and Practices in Highly Successful Middle Level Schools

This section reports on the educational programs and instructional practices of the 98 highly successful

Table 2.1 Demographic Characteristics of Highly Successful and National Sample Schools

School grade patterns	Highly successful	National sample
5–6–7–8	8	10
6–7–8	54	59
7–8	22	17
7–8–9	8	6
Other	8	8
Student enrollment	**Highly successful**	**National sample**
Less than 400	15	27
400–599	15	24
600–799	21	22
800–999	25	14
1,000–1,399	24	11
1,400 or more	0	2
Per-pupil expenditure	**Highly successful**	**National sample**
Less than $4,000	11	24
$4,000–$4,999	29	29
$5,000–$5,999	25	22
$6,000–$6,999	13	13
$7,000–$7,999	11	6
$8,000 or more	11	6
Class teacher/pupil ratio	**Highly successful**	**National sample**
Less than 1:11	0	1
1:11–15	3	7
1:16–20	17	20
1:21–25	40	40
1:26–30	35	28
1:31–35	4	4
1:36 or higher	<1	<1

(continued next page)

schools, contrasting the data with that of the national sample that was reported in Volume I of this study (Valentine et al., 2002). For ease of comparison, the findings are reported in the same categories as the national sample volume: Curriculum, Organizational Designs for Instruction, Assessing and Reporting Student Progress, Articulation and Transition, and Cocurricular Activities and Interscholastic Sports.

Table 2.1 *(continued)*

Student ethnicity	Highly successful	National sample
Caucasian	77	79
African American	8	10
Chicano/Hispanic	8	8
American Indian	1	1
Asian American	5	2
Other	1	<1
Free and reduced-price lunch programs	**Highly successful**	**National sample**
Average percentage of students receiving free or reduced-price lunch	25	32
Percentage of schools with 50% or more students receiving free or reduced-price lunch	11	17

Curriculum

Required and Elective Courses

In *Turning Points 2000,* Jackson and Davis (2000) advocated for middle level schools to deliver "a curriculum grounded in rigorous, public academic standards for what students should know and be able to do, relevant to the concerns of adolescents and based on how students learn best" (p. 23). At the middle level, this curriculum is commonly delivered through mandatory core-academic subjects, required exploratory courses, and elective offerings.

Principals of the highly successful schools reported that their commonly required core subjects were English/language arts, mathematics, science, social studies, reading, physical education, and health education. Consistent with the national sample, the inclusion of reading, physical education, and health education as required core subjects diminished with each successive grade.

In addition to the core subjects, other required or elective subjects commonly offered throughout the middle grades were typing/keyboarding, computer education, art, foreign language, home/family living, industrial education, vocal music, chorus, instrumental music, orchestra, general music, dramatics, career education, and study skills (Table 2.2).

Curriculum Design

The curriculum becomes more coherent and relevant to students when connections are made among the disciplines (Beane, 1993; National Middle School Association [NMSA], 1995). Curriculum design and delivery approaches range on a continuum from highly structured by content area (discipline-centered) to highly integrated (student-centered). The discipline-centered approach, in which instruction is delivered in departmentalized settings, was used in 25% of the highly successful schools. Topic-centered designs, which link content among disciplines but primarily through departmentalized class settings, were employed by 33% of schools. Twenty-seven percent used theme-centered approaches, focused on interdisciplinary themes, and relied on interdisciplinary instructional settings. Student-centered approaches were used in 15% of schools. In this model, teachers and students identify themes and units, and instruction is delivered almost entirely in an interdisciplinary team format (Table 2.3).

Although the highly successful schools were more likely to employ methods that facilitated a more integrated approach to teaching and learning, one-fourth of the highly successful schools used the discipline-based method.

Core Curriculum Delivery

Principals identified the organizational formats in which students received instruction across the core curricular areas of English/language arts, math, science, social studies, and reading. The formats were self-contained classrooms, interdisciplinary teaming, departmentalized instruction, and disciplinary teaming. Approximately three-fourths of the highly successful school respondents reported that interdisciplinary teaming was the instructional approach used across the content areas in grades 6, 7, and 8 (Table 2.4). Percentages were slightly lower in reading because the subject is not included in the curriculum core for some schools. The percentages also were lower in grade 5 (in which approximately one-fourth of schools employed self-contained classrooms) and grade 9 (in which two out of five schools used a departmentalized approach).

Interdisciplinary teaming was used in approximately one-half of the national sample schools. Consequently, it is clear that the highly successful schools were more committed to implementing interdisciplinary teaming.

Table 2.2 Required and Elective Core Curriculum Content Areas in Highly Successful Schools

Course	Grade 5		Grade 6		Grade 7		Grade 8		Grade 9	
	Req.	Elec.	Req.	Elec.	Req.	Elec.	Req.	Elec.	Req.	Elec.
English/Language arts	100	0	100	2	100	1	100	3	100	25
Mathematics	100	0	100	2	100	1	100	1	100	13
Science	100	0	100	0	100	1	100	0	100	0
Social studies	100	0	100	0	100	0	100	1	100	13
Reading	91	0	88	11	74	23	68	25	38	50
Physical education	100	0	92	9	91	13	85	21	88	38
Health education	82	0	77	8	71	9	64	12	25	0
Sex education	36	27	45	8	52	9	52	8	25	0
Spelling	91	0	72	3	49	3	45	3	0	0
Typing/Keyboarding	64	27	45	23	26	29	17	36	13	38
Computer education	73	18	56	27	47	34	43	48	38	38
Art	100	9	70	28	54	49	32	69	13	88
Crafts	0	9	2	16	3	15	1	21	0	25
Foreign language	18	18	39	25	21	49	17	63	13	88
Home/Family living	27	0	33	9	35	27	30	36	0	100
Industrial education	18	9	33	13	34	32	25	48	13	88
Vocal music	36	18	20	44	5	52	3	54	0	50
Chorus	0	45	9	72	5	84	2	87	0	88
Instrumental music	1	55	6	91	4	92	3	93	0	100
Orchestra	0	45	3	53	2	60	1	63	0	100
General music	73	9	33	27	20	26	13	20	0	25
Speech	0	0	6	6	4	21	3	21	13	50
Drama	0	27	14	27	4	35	2	43	0	63
Career education	36	0	23	2	25	8	30	12	25	13
Study skills	18	9	27	11	17	17	16	16	0	13
Agriculture	0	0	0	3	1	5	1	8	0	25
Journalism	0	9	3	9	1	17	1	29	13	38
Creative education	0	0	2	2	1	1	1	2	0	13
Photography	0	0	0	5	0	4	0	9	0	38
Other	0	0	5	8	4	11	8	17	0	25

Note. Req.= required; Elec. = elective.

Exploratory/Elective Curriculum Delivery

Middle level educators endorse an interdisciplinary approach for delivering core and encore (i.e., exploratory and elective) courses, although it can be challenging to deliver encore courses through interdisciplinary avenues. Practices in the highly successful schools were evenly distributed between interdisciplinary teaming and departmentalized instruction, with roughly one-third of schools employing each approach for required and elective exploratory subjects (Table 2.5). In contrast, approximately three-fifths of the national sample used a departmentalized approach.

Table 2.3 Curriculum Design Practices, by Grade Organization

Design	Total		5–6–7–8		6–7–8		7–8		7–8–9		Other	
	HS	NS	HS	NS	HS	NS	HS	NS	HS	NS	HS	NS
Discipline centered	25	38	26	41	27	36	18	40	31	45	48	40
Topic centered	33	27	33	27	31	28	35	24	33	29	25	27
Theme centered	27	21	29	20	26	21	32	22	20	17	18	18
Student centered	15	14	12	12	16	15	15	14	16	9	9	15

Note. HS = highly successful schools; NS = national sample schools.

Service Learning

Ninety-three percent of the responding principals reported implementing service learning in their schools. Service learning was designed to engage students in activities to improve the school and community and promote responsible citizenship and student personal growth. In contrast, 80% of schools in the national sample incorporated some form of service learning. Service learning is required for all students in 16% of schools, is completed only in cocurricular settings in 32% of schools, and is conducted as an elective class in 9% of schools. Although the National Center for Education Statistics (NCES, 1999) noted that only 38% of middle level schools were involved in service learning as recently as 1999, it appears to have proliferated rapidly and is now common practice in some form throughout the nation's middle level schools.

Character Education

Character education programs, which aim to raise students' awareness of issues such as social equity, citizenship, respect, and responsibility (Deitte, 2002), are becoming more common at the middle level. Often, these programs focus on areas such as citizenship education, drug education, health education, and self-esteem (Murphy, 1998). Eighty percent of the principals in the highly successful schools reported that their schools provided character education; 30% integrated this curriculum into core classes; 27% incorporated this content in noncore classes, 19% delivered the curriculum in a stand-alone format during the regular school day, and 4% used a cocurricular format. Seventy-three percent of the national sample schools reported having a character education curriculum in place.

Table 2.4 Organizational Format for Core Curriculum, by Grade, for Highly Successful Schools

Format	English/Language arts					Mathematics					Science					Social studies					Reading				
	5	6	7	8	9	5	6	7	8	9	5	6	7	8	9	5	6	7	8	9	5	6	7	8	9
Self-contained classroom	26	11	7	8	2	26	12	7	8	2	25	8	7	8	2	25	11	6	6	2	26	13	8	8	0
Interdisciplinary teaming	62	75	78	77	59	62	73	77	76	60	63	75	78	76	59	63	76	78	79	59	64	70	70	69	50
Departmentalized instruction	7	7	11	12	39	7	8	12	13	37	7	9	11	13	39	7	6	12	12	32	7	10	16	14	50
Disciplinary teaming	5	7	4	3	0	5	7	4	3	1	5	7	4	3	0	5	7	4	3	7	3	7	6	9	0

Table 2.5 Organizational Format for Exploratory Subject Areas, by Grade, for Highly Successful Schools

Format	Grade 5		Grade 6		Grade 7		Grade 8		Grade 9	
	Req.	Elec.	Req.	Elec.	Req.	Elec.	Req.	Elec.	Req.	Elec.
Self-contained classroom	18	20	10	8	6	9	6	10	15	7
Interdisciplinary teaming	32	10	34	23	35	22	32	23	34	24
Departmentalized instruction	35	30	33	33	33	46	31	46	18	69
Disciplinary teaming	5	0	3	1	2	1	2	0	0	0

Note. Req. = required; Elec. = elective.

Table 2.6 Instructionally Responsive Programmatic Practices

Practice	Little/No importance		Somewhat important		Very important	
	HS	NS	HS	NS	HS	NS
Interdisciplinary teams of 2–5 teachers sharing common students, common planning time, housed in close proximity	1	9	3	14	96	77
Exploratory course offerings that provide required (not elective) curricular opportunities for all students	8	8	14	20	78	72
Adviser–advisee program regularly scheduled for 15 minutes or more during each classroom day	5	21	34	31	61	48
Cocurricular program separate from regular graded courses, but occurring during the school day, designed to provide students with the opportunity to pursue leadership roles, special interests, and socialization	12	17	32	41	56	42
Intramural activities offered for all students during or immediately after the regular classroom day	8	18	32	34	60	48

Note. HS = highly successful schools; NS = national sample schools.

Organizational Designs for Instruction

Instructionally Responsive Programmatic Practices

Middle level experts generally agree on five programmatic practices that are responsive to the developmental and instructional needs of young adolescents: interdisciplinary teaming, exploratory courses, adviser–advisee programs, cocurricular programs, and intramural activities. When compared with the national sample, principals of the highly successful schools were much more supportive of all five practices; interdisciplinary teams were rated as "very important" by 96% of the principals, required exploratory courses by 78%, adviser–advisee programs by 61%, cocurricular programs by 56%, and intramural activities by 60% (Table 2.6). It is worth noting that the highly successful school principals showed almost unanimous support for interdisciplinary teaming.

Implementation of Practices

Principals were asked to note current implementation levels and future plans for the five programmatic practices. The highly successful schools were more effective in attaining full implementation than the national sample. In the highly successful schools, interdisciplinary teaming was reported as fully implemented by 81% of the schools, required exploratory courses were fully implemented in 75% of schools, adviser–advisee programs were fully implemented in 47% of schools, cocurricular programs were fully implemented in 43% of schools, and intramural activities were fully implemented in 47% of schools (Table 2.7).

When comparing their personal beliefs about the importance of each characteristic to their schools' levels of implementation, however, it becomes apparent that several principals were not completely satisfied with their schools' current status. Depending on the characteristic, 10%–26% reported that they were either considering or had committed to full implementation within the next two years. Clearly those principals were striving to move their schools toward higher levels of implementation in the near future.

Instructional Schedules

A school's schedule has a substantial influence on instructional design and delivery. An effective scheduling approach provides sufficient flexibility to accommodate students' learning needs and facilitate curriculum integration (Hackmann & Valentine, 1998). Models that provide blocks of time for teaming and interdisciplinary instruction are recommended throughout middle level literature.

Table 2.7 Importance, Current Implementation, and Plans for Future Implementation of Instructionally Responsive Programmatic Practices for Highly Successful Schools

Practice	Importance of characteristic[a]			Current implementation[b]			Plans for implementation[c]				
	1	2	3	1	2	3	1	2	3	4	5
Interdisciplinary teams	1	3	96	5	14	81	4	4	7	3	82
Required exploratory course offerings	8	14	78	13	13	75	13	6	4	3	75
Regularly scheduled adviser-advisee program	5	34	61	16	37	47	20	15	11	5	49
Cocurricular program	12	32	56	26	31	43	32	14	8	3	43
Intramural activities	8	32	60	16	37	47	15	21	7	6	52

[a]*Importance of characteristic:*

1 = little or no importance;
2 = somewhat important;
3 = very important.

[b]*Current level of implementation:*

1 = no implementation;
2 = partial implementation;
3 = full implementation.

[c]*Plans for future implementation:*

1 = Do not implement characteristic fully and plan to continue as we are;
2 = Do not implement fully but are considering full implementation in two years;
3 = Do not implement fully but plan to do so in next two years;
4 = Implement characteristic fully but plan to discontinue in next two years;
5 = Implement characteristic fully and plan to continue to do so.

Table 2.8 School Schedule Serving Most Students

Schedule	Total		5–6–7–8		6–7–8		7–8		7–8–9		Other	
	HS	NS	HS	NS	HS	NS	HS	NS	HS	NS	HS	NS
Daily disciplinary	23	46	25	48	20	41	20	55	33	58	29	42
Daily interdisciplinary	55	38	75	37	63	41	53	32	0	27	43	40
Alternating-day disciplinary	14	11	0	10	11	12	20	11	50	12	0	9
Alternating-day interdisciplinary	7	4	0	3	3	5	7	2	17	3	29	5
Self-contained classroom	1	1	0	2	3	1	0	0	0	0	0	4

Note. HS= highly successful schools; NS = national sample schools.

Principals of the highly successful schools identified the primary schedule used to serve most of the students in their school. The most common model, used in 55% of schools, was a daily interdisciplinary schedule, which typically has 6–8 periods, with most of the instructional time scheduled in flexible blocks for the interdisciplinary teams. Twenty-three percent of schools used a daily disciplinary schedule, a departmentalized approach that usually has 6–8 periods. The alternating-day disciplinary schedule was used by another 14%; this model commonly consists of four blocked classes meeting on rotating days. Seven percent employed an alternating-day interdisciplinary schedule, which usually employs four blocks on rotating days, with flexible interdisciplinary blocks of time. Finally, 1% used self-contained classroom schedules, with one teacher teaching most or all of the core subjects. Sixty-two percent of highly successful schools had schedules that permitted the use of interdisciplinary teaming (either daily period or alternating day), compared with 42% of schools in the national sample (Table 2.8).

Interdisciplinary Teaming

Interdisciplinary teaming, a practice often described as the heart of the middle school philosophy, consists of a group of two or more teachers who share a group of students and a common schedule and who are responsible for designing and delivering their core curriculum (George & Alexander,

1993). In the national sample, 79% of responding principals reported having one or more interdisciplinary teams operating in their buildings. Reinforcing the significance of this practice, 95% of highly successful school principals reported either full or partial implementation of teaming in their schools; all principals of 5–8 and 6–8 grade level structures, and 83% of the 7–8 and 7–9 schools reported full implementation (Table 2.9).

Core Subject Content on Teams

The number of subjects included in the teaching core for teams can vary from two to six, but the most common arrangements include four or five subjects. Forty-three percent of these schools' teams included English/language arts, social studies, math, science, and reading; 41% included those subjects minus reading (Table 2.10).

Ideally, teachers of the same team should teach all of the team's students the core subjects. However, in the highly successful schools, that was slightly less likely

Table 2.9 Schools With Interdisciplinary Teams by Grade

Type	Total	5	6	7	8	9
Highly successful schools	95	90	96	95	94	100
National sample schools	79	59	79	76	69	22

Table 2.10 Team Subject Content by Grade Organization

Subject	Total		5–6–7–8		6–7–8		7–8		7–8–9		Other	
	HS	NS	HS	NS	HS	NS	HS	NS	HS	NS	HS	NS
Math, science, social studies, English/language arts, reading	43	47	88	63	45	52	14	28	63	29	38	42
Math, science, social studies, English/language arts	41	43	38	21	30	44	48	48	50	57	88	50
Social studies, English/language arts	3	8	13	11	2	5	5	10	0	29	0	8
English/language arts, reading	4	5	25	16	4	3	0	3	0	0	0	8
Math, science	2	4	13	11	2	3	0	3	0	0	0	0
Other subject content included	18	22	38	26	17	19	24	28	13	29	0	17

Note. HS = highly successful schools; NS = national sample schools.

than in the national sample. Seventy-nine percent of the respondents adhered to this practice, compared with 83% in the national sample.

Teacher Assignment to Teams

The number of subjects included in the core curriculum influences the number of teachers who make up the team. The most frequent staffing pattern was four-person teams (35%), but five-person teams (25%) and teams of six or more (21%) also were common (Table 2.11). In 84% of the schools, administrators appointed the teachers to teams either with teacher input (65% of those responses) or without input (19%). In 11% of schools, teachers selected their own teams. Replacements for team members were appointed by the administration with teacher input (69%), appointed administratively without teacher input (15%), or selected by the team (16%).

Team Leadership

Effective team leaders are vital for high performance. Within the highly successful schools, 50% of the teams selected their own leader, 33% of the teams rotated this responsibility among the members, 24% of team leaders were appointed by the administration, and 14% of the teams had no formally identified leader. When provided, compensation for team leaders took two forms: financial compensation (34%) or released time from teaching responsibilities (6%).

Teaming Issues Related to Students

Eighty-six percent of the respondents noted that three-fourths or more of their student body (excluding special education students) received their core curriculum through interdisciplinary team instruction. Students were assigned to heterogeneous teams in 100% of the

Table 2.11 Number of Team Teachers by Grade-Level Organization

Teachers	Total		5–6–7–8		6–7–8		7–8		7–8–9		Other	
	HS	NS	HS	NS	HS	NS	HS	NS	HS	NS	HS	NS
Two	5	3	13	0	4	4	0	0	13	0	0	8
Three	15	15	0	32	24	13	0	14	0	14	25	8
Four	35	35	50	21	28	34	47	34	25	43	38	59
Five	25	23	38	15	22	25	29	28	38	14	13	8
Six or more	21	24	0	32	22	24	24	24	25	29	25	17

Note. HS = highly successful schools; NS = national sample schools.

highly successful schools; in contrast, 93% of responding schools used heterogeneous placements in the national sample.

Location of Team Classrooms

Grouping all the classrooms of the interdisciplinary teachers in close proximity facilitates a sense of shared identity and belonging among teachers and students and a flexible time schedule designed to meet individual, small-group, and large-group student needs. In the highly successful schools, 45% of principals reported that all classrooms were adjacent, 47% stated that "most" classrooms were adjacent, and 8% could not maintain adjacent classrooms for their teams. In the national sample, only 26% of the respondents reported that all classrooms were adjacent.

Team Planning Time

The development of highly functioning teams requires a provision for common planning time in addition to time for individual planning. Research consistently discloses that teams with high levels of common planning time are more likely to demonstrate gains in student achievement, develop an integrated curriculum, and view team activities in a positive fashion (Flowers, Mertens, & Mulhall, 1999, 2000a, 2000b). Sixty-six percent of the highly successful schools provided common and individual planning periods for team teachers, 27% provided only common planning time for the team, and 7% provided one planning period that was not necessarily at the same time for the entire team.

To promote close working relationships among the core and encore teachers, some schools strove to create common planning time with both groups. In the highly successful schools, 15% scheduled a common planning time for core and exploratory teachers, 57% provided common planning time for exploratory teachers, 27% provided one planning time for exploratory teachers that was not scheduled with other core or exploratory teaching colleagues, and 1% provided no planning time for exploratory teachers (Table 2.12). Principals in 36% of the highly successful schools reported that their teachers spent more than four hours weekly working as a team, a figure

that is much higher than the 22% in the national sample. Forty-nine percent of highly successful schools reported that their teams spend two to four hours working together weekly, and 15% indicated that their teams collaborated for fewer than two hours each week.

Team Effectiveness

To achieve high performance levels as a team, team teachers need sufficient time to mature as a group. Teams also should be restructured occasionally to promote the infusion of new ideas. Nearly half the principals (48%) believed that the ideal length of time for teams to remain together was five or more years; 23%, four years; 23%, three years; and 6%, only two years.

Grouping Students for Instruction

Ability Grouping

For the purposes of instruction, students can be assigned to classrooms either in homogeneous or heterogeneous groups. The practice of tracking, which groups students by ability into "higher" groups and "lower" groups, each with a limited, focused curriculum, is fervently opposed by most middle level advocates (Jackson & Davis, 2000; NMSA, 1995). The use of flexible grouping, however, which allows teachers to

Table 2.12 Planning Time for Interdisciplinary Teams and Exploratory Teachers

Type	Highly successful	National sample
Interdisciplinary teams		
One common planning time for all team members, plus an individual planning time	66	59
One planning time at the same time for all team members	27	37
One planning time not necessarily at the same time for all team members	7	11
Exploratory teachers		
Common planning time with core teachers	15	14
Common planning time with exploratory teachers	57	37
Planning time, not common with core or exploratory teachers	27	47
No planning time provided	1	2

assign students to short-term groups on the basis of specific learning needs and activities, is recommended as an effective process to differentiate instruction. Sixty-one percent of highly successful schools grouped students into specific classes, such as reading or math, by ability; 23% permitted flexible grouping within the classroom; and 17% reported no form of ability grouping. Forty percent reported no ability grouping or the use of flexible groups, compared with 28% in the national sample. In addition, 14% of principals of the highly successful schools in which ability grouping was present reported that they were considering eliminating this practice.

Gifted and Talented Programs

Providing an engaging curriculum for G/T students is an important task so high-ability students will be wholly challenged and engaged in school (Rosselli & Irvin, 2001). When compared with the national sample, highly successful schools were more likely to offer G/T programming and reported more frequent use of all delivery options. Providing G/T students with released time

for special classes was offered in 49% of the highly successful schools; 46% provided individualized assignments in heterogeneous classes, 36% clustered G/T students in special classes with individualized assignments, 14% offered summer programs, 8% developed cooperative programs with other institutions, and 20% listed additional alternatives (Table 2.13).

Inclusion Practices

Students with special needs and disabilities are entitled to a curriculum that is both challenging and appropriate to their developmental needs. In fact, the *Turning Points 2000* recommendations (Jackson & Davis, 2000) call for "ensuring success for every student" (p. 30). Educational researchers advocate that students with disabilities and special needs should be integrated into the regular classroom setting for both the core and exploratory curricula, a practice commonly known as inclusion. As a group, the highly successful schools are embracing this philosophy. Seventy-eight percent reported that special education students spent the majority of their core-curricular time in regular educa-

Table 2.13 Organizational Format of Gifted/Talented Programs by Grade-Level Organization

Format	Total HS	Total NS	5–6–7–8 HS	5–6–7–8 NS	6–7–8 HS	6–7–8 NS	7–8 HS	7–8 NS	7–8–9 HS	7–8–9 NS	Other HS	Other NS
No gifted/talented program	9	16	25	9	6	17	10	8	13	20	13	22
Released time for special classes	49	45	50	68	53	43	38	33	50	47	50	50
Heterogeneous classes with individualized assignments	46	35	75	32	45	35	43	25	38	53	38	39
Clusters of gifted/talented students in heterogeneous classes with individualized assignments	36	26	25	18	34	31	38	31	50	7	38	6
After school, evening, or weekend programs	24	22	50	23	28	22	19	28	0	20	0	11
Summer programs	14	6	38	14	15	5	10	3	13	7	0	11
Cooperative program with another school/organization	8	8	13	0	11	10	5	8	0	13	0	0
Other	20	9	25	9	19	5	19	17	13	7	38	0

Note. HS = highly successful schools; NS = national sample schools.

tion classes, and the remaining 22% reported that students with special needs divided their time equally between regular education and special education settings. In the exploratory area, 99% reported that students with special needs spent their time in regular classrooms (Table 2.14). Only 57% of principals in the national sample reported that special education students spent the majority of their core-curricular time in regular

Table 2.14 Inclusion Practices (Core and Encore Classes) by Grade-Level Organization for Highly Successful Schools

Practice	Total		5–6–7–8		6–7–8		7–8		7–8–9		Other	
	C	E	C	E	C	E	C	E	C	E	C	E
Special education students spend most of their time in regular education classes	78	99	75	100	81	98	81	100	71	100	57	100
Special education students spend about equal time in regular education and special education classes	22	1	25	0	19	2	19	0	29	0	43	0
Special education students spend most of their time in special education classes	0	0	0	0	0	0	0	0	0	0	0	0

Note. C = core subjects; E = encore subjects.

Table 2.15 Education Technology Usage in Middle Level Schools

Type of Educational Technology	Used by Teachers		Used by Students	
	HS	NS	HS	NS
No educational technology used in our school	0	<1	0	1
Internet support of instruction (Internet used to obtain information for reports and projects)	90	91	88	90
Computer-assisted instruction	83	89	84	91
Electronic mail	83	81	64	64
Media-enhanced project demonstrations	79	74	87	81
Educational television channels/programs	74	68	71	69
Computer-managed instruction	59	56	58	61
Web pages for courses	64	47	N/A	N/A
Internet-based instruction (Web-based coursework)	45	37	44	38
Interactive video (within school)	31	26	28	26
Media-enhanced exit performances	24	18	35	24
Distance education (remote access combining several technologies)	17	17	14	16
Interactive video (remote access)	10	9	13	8
Other	4	0	3	2

Note. HS = highly successful schools; NS = national sample schools.

classrooms, and 9% said their special education students spent most of their time in special education classrooms.

Multigrade Grouping

Middle level educators group students across grade levels for varied purposes. This practice, often called multigrade or multiage grouping (McLaughlin & Doda, 1997), may occur in core classes, in elective courses, or through multigrade advisory programs. Highly successful school principals reported more frequent use of multigrade grouping practices than those in the national sample. Twenty-four percent reported using multigrade grouping for instructional purposes, 6% used this approach for scheduling purposes, 3% employed this grouping for social purposes, and 20% reported other multigrade grouping practices; 47% said they did not use multigrade grouping.

Multiyear Instruction

To facilitate close relationships among students and teachers, some student teams progress through the middle grades as an intact group—a multiyear instructional practice commonly called "looping." Looping practices were recommended in both *Turning Points* reports (Carnegie Council on Adolescent Development, 1989; Jackson & Davis, 2000). Eight percent of principals in the highly successful schools reported that looping was practiced at all grade levels with all students in their schools, 10% employed looping at all grade levels but with only a portion of their students, and 2% provided looping for all students but only at some grade levels. Eighty percent did not engage in any form of looping.

Instructional Uses of Technology

NMSA (1995) recommended the use of technology by teachers and students to enhance the learning environment. Comparing the types of educational technology used by teachers and students in the highly successful schools and those in the national sample displayed consistent patterns between both groups. However, teachers in highly successful schools were more likely to use Web sites for their courses (64% vs. 47%), and students in highly successful schools were more likely to access media in exit performances (35% vs. 24%; Table 2.15).

Table 2.16 **Principal Estimates of Assessment Practices Used by Teachers**

Assessment	Total HS	Total NS	5–6–7–8 HS	5–6–7–8 NS	6–7–8 HS	6–7–8 NS	7–8 HS	7–8 NS	7–8–9 HS	7–8–9 NS	Other HS	Other NS
Multiple-choice tests	16	22	14	21	15	23	19	22	18	19	16	21
Short-answer tests	14	13	14	14	12	13	15	10	21	14	14	13
Essay tests	13	12	14	12	13	13	14	11	12	11	13	12
Student projects	19	11	19	11	18	10	23	15	24	11	18	13
Fill-in-the-blank tests	9	10	9	10	8	10	10	8	19	11	7	8
Matching tests	7	9	7	8	7	9	7	7	15	11	6	10
Demonstrations to peers	11	8	11	9	10	8	14	8	11	8	8	8
Portfolios	10	7	11	7	9	7	11	7	10	6	11	8
Demonstrations to adults	6	4	6	3	6	4	9	4	3	4	6	5
Mastery checklists	7	4	5	5	7	4	5	6	11	4	6	3

Note. HS = highly successful schools; NS = national sample schools. Rounding accounts for totals not equaling 100%.

Table 2.17 Methods of Reporting Student Progress in Core Subjects for Highly Successful Schools

Reporting Procedure	Grade 5	Grade 6	Grade 7	Grade 8	Grade 9
Letter scale (A, B, C)	82	87	86	83	100
Word scale (excellent, good)	73	34	30	30	38
Number scale (1–5)	27	18	15	14	0
Satisfactory/Unsatisfactory; Pass/Fail	36	35	33	32	38
Informal written notes	91	75	71	71	63
Percentage marks (e.g., 86)	64	56	54	53	50
Progress in relation to potential	36	28	29	27	38
Performance demonstrations	82	56	47	46	50
Student portfolios	73	52	50	51	63
Rubrics	91	79	74	72	63
Teacher-led parent conferences	73	75	75	74	75
Teacher-led parent/student conferences	73	60	58	56	38
Student-led parent/teacher conferences	36	38	38	35	25
Product/Project development	82	62	58	56	50
Formative assessment	46	56	47	46	13
Summative assessment	64	57	55	56	25
Exit performance (when leaving grade)	18	9	10	17	25

Assessing and Reporting Student Progress

Assessment Practices

Curriculum content, instructional practices, and assessment strategies should be in close alignment (Jackson & Davis, 2000) to ensure student academic success. Increasingly, experts are advocating for authentic assessment practices that mirror real-life experiences and require students to actively demonstrate their mastery of curriculum concepts (Wiggins & McTighe, 1998). When estimating the percentage of time in which teachers used varying assessment practices, the responses of highly successful school principals did not vary dramatically from the national sample respondents (Table 2.16). To a small degree, however, principals of the highly successful schools estimated slightly lower percentages for traditional student tests (multiple-choice, fill-in-the-blank, matching) and slightly higher percentages for more authentic measures (projects, essays, demonstrations to peers and adults, portfolios, mastery checklists).

Student Retention Issues

Educators frequently struggle with decisions related to pupil promotion and retention when students do not demonstrate sufficient academic progress. The retention issue is fraught with concerns for educators, students, and parents because students who repeat a grade are more likely to drop out of school (Jenkins & Weldon, 1999). However, social promotion can be viewed as an equally unattractive alternative for at-risk students. When compared with the national sample, highly successful school principals were more likely to report that their schools promoted all students in the past year. Seventy-three percent of the highly successful schools retained no students in grade 5, 61% reported no retentions in grade 6, 51% reported no retentions in grade 7, 63% reported none in grade 8, and 75% reported no retentions in grade 9. In contrast, the corresponding percentages in the national sample were as follows: 64% in grade 5, 44% in grade 6, 39% in grade 7, 43% in grade 8, and 38% in grade 9.

Reporting Student Progress to Parents

Educators encourage a wide variety of methods to report student progress to parents (NMSA, 1995; Tomlinson, 2001a; Wiggins, 1996). When compared with the national sample, the principals of the highly successful schools reported similarly high usage of tra-

Table 2.18 Impact of Standardized Testing, by Grade Organization

Effect	Total		5–6–7–8		6–7–8		7–8		7–8–9		Other	
	HS	NS	HS	NS	HS	NS	HS	NS	HS	NS	HS	NS
Student achievement	59	54	50	58	65	54	62	60	43	45	43	48
Best middle level curricular and instructional practices	56	57	50	58	52	52	62	69	57	55	71	60
Student motivation toward achievement	67	57	50	57	73	54	72	60	43	45	57	65
Teacher autonomy and motivation	51	48	38	63	48	43	67	61	43	55	43	46
Administrative ability to assess student achievement	86	80	75	74	92	81	81	86	72	82	86	76

Note. HS = highly successful schools; NS = national sample schools. Ratings reflect "very positive impact" or "somewhat positive impact" responses.

Table 2.19 Reporting and Using Student Progress Data Internally and Externally

Method	Used internally for school improvement		Reported to school district		Reported to external agencies (e.g., state)	
	HS	NS	HS	NS	HS	NS
Distribution of letter grades	78	75	40	42	19	0
Standardized test scores	98	97	97	95	84	83
Proportion of students demonstrating content skill or mastery	96	82	72	68	59	52
Samples of student work (individual pieces)	90	79	26	18	10	9
Portfolios of student work (representative samples from entire year)	78	70	11	14	6	4
Performance demonstrations (live or recorded)	70	63	10	11	3	2
Teacher-generated narratives or descriptions of student progress	73	60	18	14	2	3

Note. HS = highly successful schools; NS = national sample schools.

ditional methods such as letter and number scales, pass/fail, and teacher-led parent conferences. However, the highly successful schools also reported much higher usages of a variety of alternative reporting methods, such as rubrics, informal written notes, product/project development, formative and summative assessments, portfolios, and conferences that included students (Table 2.17).

Standardized Testing for School Improvement

Legislation at both the state and national levels is holding schools accountable for documenting gains in student achievement; standardized tests are increasingly being used to demonstrate improvements in learning, although many educators view those tests to be inappropriate as the sole indicator of student progress (Clark & Clark, 1994; Stake, 1999). Principals were asked whether the increased emphasis on standardized testing had a positive or negative influence in five areas. When the responses of "very positive" or "somewhat positive" effects were combined, principals of the highly successful schools and in the national sample generally viewed the results with some favor (Table 2.18). The principals of the highly successful schools had, to a small degree, a more favorable opinion. In particular, highly successful school principals stated that standardized testing positively affected their ability to assess student achievement (86%) and motivate students to achieve (67%).

Internal and External Progress Data

Educators can use varied student performance measures to assist them in program evaluation, school improvement, and reporting to internal and external constituents. These data sources can include the following: grades, standardized-test scores, the proportion of students who achieve mastery, student work samples, student portfolios, student performance demonstrations, and teacher-generated descriptions of student progress. The majority of principals in the highly successful schools and in the national sample reported using these data for internal school improvement purposes, although the highly successful schools were more likely to use this information (Table 2.19). These data were not likely to be reported outside the building to the school district or external agencies such as the state; however, more concrete assessment forms, such as standardized-test scores and the proportion of students demonstrating content mastery, were used internally, reported to the district, and shared with external agencies.

Articulation and Transition

Grade-Level Articulation

Elementary students can experience a variety of fears and concerns as they prepare to move to the middle

level, and these concerns can resurface when middle level students prepare to become integrated into their high school settings. These fears can create additional stress that affects students' self-esteem, motivation, and academic performance (Mullins & Irvin, 2000; Thomason & Thompson, 1992). Therefore, middle level educators must strive to make this articulation process as comfortable as possible, both as students enter the building and as they exit for their next educational experiences.

Generally, principals of the highly successful schools provided favorable reports about articulation problems related to student entry into the middle level (Table 2.20). Issues that were rated as minor or major problems were student orientation, student grading practices, instructional delivery systems, teaching methodology, subject content/sequence, and pupil promotion policies. Concerns were more apparent, however, when noting middle level–to–high school articulation problems. The same topics were noted as concerns, with student orientation, student grading practices, instructional delivery systems, and teaching methodology being rated as particularly problematic.

Principals of the highly successful schools noted fewer articulation problems at the elementary-to-middle level transition than the national sample. However, responses were mixed when they reported middle level–to–high school transition problems; 4 of the 11 topics rated lower marks than in the national sample. This might imply that as schools are more effective at implementing best practices at the

Table 2.20 Articulation Problems Identified by Middle Level Principals for Highly Successful Schools

Type	Elementary level			High School level		
	None	Minor	Major	None	Minor	Major
Orientation of students	78	22	0	43	50	7
Student grading practices	52	45	3	51	40	9
Instructional delivery systems	66	32	2	35	50	15
Teaching methodology	69	25	6	32	52	17
Subject content and sequence	63	28	9	63	28	9
Pupil promotion policies	74	20	6	71	25	5
Student records	84	14	2	81	18	1
Granting subject credit	98	1	1	87	10	3
Counseling services	84	11	5	75	19	6
Cocurricular activities	90	9	1	84	15	1
Interscholastic sports	92	7	1	82	15	3

middle grades, the dissonance between those practices and typical high school practices are more pronounced and thus create more transition issues for the students leaving the more-effective middle level schools. Schools with more-effective middle level programs and practices may have to work more closely with their high schools than typical middle level schools to ease the transition for their students into the high school setting.

Transition Practices

To resolve students' entry and exit concerns, middle level educators typically provide an array of programs and services to help students transition to their new school. The majority of the principals of highly successful schools reported employing most of these transition practices when students moved from elementary to middle level

and from middle level to high school. These percentages typically ranged 10%–20% higher than the responses in the national sample. The practices most frequently reported involved counselors and administrators actively seeking information on incoming at-risk students, parent orientation activities, spring student orientation activities, and counselors working with incoming students at the sending school (Table 2.21).

Cocurricular Activities and Interscholastic Sports

Cocurricular Activities

Middle level educators strive to provide a balanced array of cocurricular programs, intramural activities, and interscholastic sports that are appropriate for young adolescents (George & Alexander, 1993). Principals of

Table 2.21 Transition Practices for Highly Successful Schools

Practice	Elementary to middle	Middle to high school
Receiving school's counselors/administrators actively solicit information about incoming students who may be at risk academically or socially	98	74
Activities or events are carried out that are specifically designed for parents of incoming students	89	77
Incoming students go to receiving school in spring of prior year for orientation activities	89	70
Receiving school's counselors go to sending school to meet/work with incoming students	86	89
When incoming students come to receiving school for orientation, current students play significant roles in the process	77	48
Receiving school students to go sending school to meet/orient incoming students	64	54
Incoming students come to middle level school in the fall without older students present for orientation activities	44	39
When incoming students come to receiving school for orientation, counselors conduct orientation process without significant assistance from teachers or students	19	46
When middle level students to go receiving school for orientation, receiving school's teachers play significant roles in the process	N/A	34
Other	30	10

the highly successful schools, when compared with respondents in the national sample, were much more likely to support cocurricular programs and intramural activities, and their schools were more likely to fully implement these practices (Table 2.22).

Principals of the highly successful schools identified the cocurricular activities offered for their students at each grade level. The highly successful schools provided many more opportunities than the national sample at grades 5, 6, 7, and 8. Grade 9 was the exception, with the national sample schools reporting more activities. Activities offered across the grades in a high percentage of the highly successful schools included drama, intramural sports, music groups, publications, service clubs, student clubs, and student government (Table 2.23).

Interscholastic Sports

The topic of interscholastic sports raises more controversy than any other practice at the middle level (George & Alexander, 1993). Supporters of athletic programs point to the need to develop skills and talents of budding athletes, whereas critics point to both the physical and emotional harm that can be imposed on students who are subjected to intense competition at this important developmental stage. Aware of the prevailing local support for competitive athletics programs,

middle level educators recognize that proposals to cut or reduce interscholastic programs would likely be met with significant resistance in many communities.

Although many middle level educators would argue against interscholastic sports in at least grades 5, 6, and 7, a high percentage of the highly successful schools offered sports in these grades. In grade 5, 54% offered sports for boys and 64% offered girls' sports; in grade 6, 64% offered boys' sports and 66% offered girls' sports. In the national sample, only 14% offered interscholastic sports for boys and girls in grade 5 and 36% in grade 6. Percentages were more comparable in grades 7, 8, and 9, where the percentages ranged in the mid- to upper-80% mark (Table 2.24). The most common sports for boys included basketball, football, soccer, track, and wrestling. Typical offerings for girls included basketball, soccer, softball, track, and volleyball.

When principals were asked whether sports should be offered at each grade level, the responses tended to mirror the practices within their school. Consequently, because interscholastic sports were offered in more of the highly successful schools than in the national sample schools, these principals as a group expressed greater levels of support for athletics than did the national sample (Table 2.25).

Table 2.22 Importance, Current Implementation, and Plans for Future Implementation of Cocurricular Programs and Intramural Activities

Type		Importance[a]			Current level of implementation[b]			Plans for future implementation[c]				
		1	2	3	1	2	3	1	2	3	4	5
Cocurricular programs	**Highly successful**	12	32	56	26	31	43	43	3	8	14	32
	National sample	17	41	42	35	39	26	30	17	14	4	35
Intramural activities	**Highly successful**	8	32	60	16	37	47	52	6	7	21	15
	National sample	18	34	48	34	29	37	29	13	12	4	42

[a]*Importance of characteristic:*

1 = little or no importance;
2 = somewhat important;
3 = very important.

[b]*Current level of implementation:*

1 = no implementation;
2 = partial implementation;
3 = full implementation.

[c]*Plans for future implementation*

1 = Do not implement characteristic fully and plan to continue as we are;
2 = Do not implement fully but are considering full implementation in two years;
3 = Do not implement fully but plan to do so in next two years;
4 = Implement characteristic fully but plan to discontinue in next two years;
5 = Implement characteristic fully and plan to continue to do so.

Table 2.23 Cocurricular Activities Offered, by Grade

Activity	Grade 5		Grade 6		Grade 7		Grade 8		Grade 9	
	HS	NS	HS	NS	HS	NS	HS	NS	HS	NS
Dance	1	4	20	13	26	18	27	20	13	56
Debate	0	0	9	6	12	9	16	12	38	56
Drama	46	21	70	41	74	54	72	61	88	94
Honor society	0	0	19	15	33	33	43	39	38	69
Intramural sports	55	43	66	58	70	54	67	53	50	44
Mini-courses	18	18	36	22	33	20	32	19	13	13
Music groups	46	46	73	58	77	68	78	71	63	100
Publications	46	14	63	37	71	55	81	64	75	88
Service clubs	55	14	75	52	76	58	79	59	75	75
Student clubs	46	36	81	65	84	71	84	71	88	94
Student government	91	68	92	80	91	86	91	87	88	100
Other	9	11	13	9	24	10	23	10	50	0

Note. HS = highly successful schools; NS = national sample schools.

Table 2.24 Interscholastic Sports Offered, by Grade, for 98 Highly Successful Schools

Type	Grade 5		Grade 6		Grade 7		Grade 8		Grade 9	
	Boys	Girls	Boys	Girls	Boys	Girls	Boys	Girls	Boys	Girls
No interscholastic sports	46	36	36	34	15	14	11	11	13	13
Have interscholastic sports	54	64	64	66	85	86	89	89	87	87
Baseball	0	0	2	0	15	2	18	2	50	13
Basketball	18	18	16	16	73	73	76	76	88	88
Cheerleading	9	18	6	16	19	39	20	43	38	50
Football	9	9	5	2	45	14	52	18	75	25
Golf	0	0	3	3	17	19	20	19	50	63
Gymnastics	0	0	0	2	0	7	0	7	0	25
Hockey	0	0	2	0	3	3	5	5	13	25
Soccer	0	0	9	9	21	21	24	25	75	75
Softball	9	9	3	6	8	28	8	34	13	63
Swimming	0	0	5	5	14	15	16	18	75	63
Tennis	0	0	3	3	21	21	23	24	75	75
Track	18	18	20	22	65	67	70	71	75	75
Volleyball	0	9	2	9	11	60	12	65	25	88
Wrestling	0	0	11	5	50	23	54	24	63	25
Other	0	0	9	11	20	24	20	25	25	25

Table 2.25 Principal Opinions Favoring Offering Interscholastic Sports

Type	Grade 5		Grade 6		Grade 7		Grade 8		Grade 9	
	Boys	Girls	Boys	Girls	Boys	Girls	Boys	Girls	Boys	Girls
Highly successful	54	54	72	72	84	84	89	89	87	87
National sample	21	21	48	47	79	79	83	83	100	100

Note. Number indicates the percentage of respondents who support sports at that grade.

Table 2.26 Opinions About Grade at Which Greater Emphasis Should be Placed on Intramural Rather Than Interscholastic Activities

Level	Total HS	Total NS	5–6–7–8 HS	5–6–7–8 NS	6–7–8 HS	6–7–8 NS	7–8 HS	7–8 NS	7–8–9 HS	7–8–9 NS	Other HS	Other NS
All middle level grades	37	39	38	25	35	41	59	42	25	43	14	27
Grades 8 and below	11	6	0	5	4	3	6	10	50	21	43	6
Grades 7 and below	12	15	13	5	10	13	12	17	0	29	43	27
Grades 6 and below	39	36	50	55	51	37	24	31	25	7	0	40
Grade 5	0	4	0	10	0	6	0	0	0	0	0	0

Note. HS = highly successful schools; NS = national sample schools.

Table 2.27 Age Appointed to First Assistant Principalship

Years	Highly successful Total	Highly successful Male	Highly successful Female	National sample Total	National sample Male	National sample Female
24 or younger	1	2	0	<1	<1	0
25 – 29	22	32	12	14	16	8
30 – 34	19	21	17	21	24	14
35 – 39	26	17	33	20	20	19
40 – 44	8	2	14	15	12	24
45 – 49	4	2	6	8	6	10
50 – 54	2	0	4	1	<1	3
55 or older	0	0	0	<1	<1	<1
Not applicable	18	24	14	21	21	21

Table 2.28 Age Appointed to First Principalship

Years	Highly successful Total	Highly successful Male	Highly successful Female	National Sample Total	National Sample Male	National Sample Female
24 or younger	0	0	0	<1	<1	0
25–29	9	15	4	7	9	3
30–34	20	27	14	18	21	11
35–39	28	30	25	24	26	18
40–44	24	13	33	22	21	26
45–49	12	13	12	19	16	27
50–54	3	0	6	8	6	12
55 or older	4	2	6	1	<1	3

Intramurals vs. Interscholastics

Principals gave their opinions regarding the grade level at which greater emphasis should be placed on intramural activities over interscholastic sports. Responses from the highly successful school principals and the national sample indicated that 39–40% believe that the threshold is at grades 6 and below (Table 2.26). When reviewed by grade configuration, approximately half of the principals of 5–6–7–8 and 6–7–8 schools responded with grades 6 and below. Principals of 7–8 schools raised this emphasis to grades 7 and below, and principals of 7–8–9 schools moved the level to grades 8 and below.

Leadership in Highly Successful Middle Level Schools

Several decades of research have confirmed that effective leadership is essential to school success and student achievement. Recent meta-analyses, both quantitative and qualitative, affirm the significance of effective leadership and identify leadership dimensions most essential for student achievement (Cotton, 2003; Marzano, 2000; Waters, Marzano, & McNulty, 2003). Jackson and Davis (2000) have been extensively quoted regarding this conviction with respect to middle level schools, stating that the research consistently identifies a relationship between high-achieving schools and strong, competent leaders. The purpose of this section is to describe the characteristics of the principals of the highly successful schools and to compare them, where appropriate, with the principals of the national sample schools. This section examines four general areas about principals: their personal characteristics, their professional background and experience, their collaborative leadership practices, and their perceptions regarding the challenges and satisfaction of their position.

Personal Characteristics

Principals of the highly successful schools began their careers as principals and assistant principals at an earlier age than was typical of principals from the national sample. Younger appointments to both the assistant principalship and the principalship were more common for male than female principals in both sets of schools (Tables 2.27 and 2.28).

Principals in the highly successful schools have served more years as middle level principals, more years as principals, and more years as principals in their current schools than is the case for principals of the national sample schools (Tables 2.29, 2.30, and 2.31). For example, 29% of the principals of the highly successful schools have been principals for fewer than seven years compared with 52% of the principals of the national sample schools. Male principals of the highly successful schools and the national sample schools have been middle level principals longer, have more total years of experience as principals, and have been in their current schools longer than their female counterparts.

Professional Background and Experiences

Other than the age of administrative appointment, elements of the professional backgrounds of the two groups of principals are far more similar than they are different (Table 2.32). Because principals of highly successful schools were appointed to administrative positions earlier than were principals in the national sample, they have less nonadministrative (teaching) experience. With that exception, their backgrounds are generally comparable. Approximately half of the principals of both groups had taught, been a counselor, or held another nonadministrative position for 1–9 years at the middle level prior to assuming the position of principal. Almost all of the principals in both groups had some nonadministrative K–12 position before assuming the principalship. In addition, in both sets of schools, females tended to have considerably more nonadministrative experience than males.

Table 2.29 Total Years as Middle Level Principal

Years	Highly successful			National sample		
	Total	Male	Female	Total	Male	Female
1	6	4	8	12	11	13
2–3	8	2	14	26	25	32
4–6	19	17	21	23	22	27
7–9	22	26	18	15	15	16
10–14	30	28	31	14	16	9
15–19	10	15	6	6	7	2
20–24	3	6	0	3	4	<1
25 or more	2	2	2	1	<1	<1

Table 2.30 Total Years as a Principal

Years	Highly successful			National sample		
	Total	Male	Female	Total	Male	Female
1	5	2	8	10	9	12
2–3	9	4	14	20	18	26
4–6	15	15	16	22	21	26
7–9	21	24	17	14	13	16
10–14	30	28	31	16	17	15
15–19	12	17	8	9	11	3
20–24	5	6	4	5	6	1
25 or more	3	4	2	4	5	<1

Table 2.31 Years as Principal of Current School

Years	Highly successful			National sample		
	Total	Male	Female	Total	Male	Female
1	11	11	12	15	15	16
2–3	16	6	23	32	30	38
4–14	68	79	59	46	46	44
15 or more	5	4	6	7	9	2

Table 2.32 Professional Backgrounds

Experience	Highly successful	National sample
Nonadministrative experience at all levels		
4 or more years	95	96
Nonadministrative experience at middle level		
None	19	20
1–9 years	53	52
10 or more years nonadministrative experience at any level	Females: 71 Males: 38	Females: 72 Males: 55
Assistant principal at all levels		
No such experience	18	23
1–3 years	33	32
4–6 years	33	26
7 or more years	16	19
Assistant principal at middle level		
No middle level AP experience	39	45
1–3 years	33	29
4–6 years	16	17
7 or more years	12	10
Non-principal leadership experience		
Athletic coach	37	57
Athletic director	17	27
Counselor/Guidance position	8	9
Dean or registrar	11	8
Department chairperson	33	37
Team leader	27	30
Activity sponsor/adviser	56	60
Highest degree earned		
Master's degree	18	18
Master's degree +	33	40
Educational specialist	16	17
Master's degree + all course work toward doctorate	9	10
Doctor of education	13	8
Doctor of philosophy	8	3
Principal certification		
K–12	48	46
Secondary	39	39
Middle	6	4
Elementary	3	7
Other	4	3

Experience as an assistant principal was generally similar for the two groups. The majority of principals in both groups had served as an assistant principal, and those from both groups typically served in that role for less than six years. Principals of the highly successful schools were more likely than the national sample principals to have been assistants at the middle level.

Principals from both sets of schools had served in many leadership capacities other than those of an assistant principal or principal. More than half of principals of the highly successful schools had held positions as activity sponsors or advisers, 37% had been the coach of one or more athletic teams, 33% had been department chairpersons, 27% had been team leaders, and 17% had been athletic directors. These experiences were similar to those of the national sample. However, fewer of the principals of the highly successful schools had been athletic coaches or athletic directors than the national sample principals. Principals in the highly successful group had higher levels of formal educational study, with considerably more principals of the highly successful schools holding doctorates.

Background Specific to the Middle Level
Most principals of the highly successful schools and the national sample did not have comprehensive backgrounds specific to the middle level prior to appointment as a middle level principal. Only 20% of both groups had teaching experience at the middle level, and many did not have middle level assistant principal experience. Seldom were principals of the highly successful middle level schools or their national sample counterparts certified specifically as middle level principals, and the principals in both groups did not tend to hold graduate or undergraduate majors in middle level education. Although only 8% of the principals of the highly successful schools held a master's degree or an educational specialist degree with a major in middle level education, this was almost twice as many as the national sample respondents. The most striking difference between the two sets of principals was the number of courses taken that were specific to middle level education (Table 2.33). More than half (54%) of the principals of the highly successful schools had taken three or more courses specific to middle level education, compared with only 29% of their national sample counterparts.

Reasons for Entering Administration
When asked for their reasons for pursuing a career as a middle level principal, the top three reasons for principals in both groups were the opportunity to help students, the desire to be helpful to others, and the opportunity to exercise leadership (Table 2.34). Females in highly successful schools were the most likely to indicate that the opportunity to improve curriculum and instruction was an important motivator. Male principals in the national sample were more likely than other principals to identify salary as a reason for entering the profession. The lowest-rated reasons for both groups were recognition by others, social status and prestige, and excellent hours and vacations.

When asked who had been the most influential to them during their first year as a principal, both groups identified another principal or a central office administrator (Table 2.35). Females in highly successful schools were far more likely to be influenced by a central office person than were their male counterparts. A notable difference between the principals of the highly successful schools and national sample principals was the influence of someone from higher education. Although the relative percentages were small (5% vs. 1%), principals in the highly successful schools were more likely than their national sample colleagues to identify a university professor as influential during their first year as a principal. Perhaps most disconcerting, however, is the fact that 8–10% of both groups reported that no one had been influential. That even one-tenth of new middle level principals have no mentor, coach, or professional support system is potentially an enormous obstacle in the continuous improvement of middle level schools.

Value Placed on Developmental Experiences
The principals at highly successful schools and the national sample of principals had more in common for the value they placed on experiences in their careers. A majority of the principals from both groups reported that their experiences as assistant principals and teachers were of the greatest value in their leadership development. More than 50% of the principals reported that their participation on leadership teams was also of great value. In contrast, the majority of both groups of principals rated their university coursework and university field experiences as having only moderate or less value. The largest discrepancy between the two groups was the value of participation in professional development activities, with 66% of the principals from the highly successful schools and 49% of the national sample principals characterizing these experiences as having great value.

Principals were asked what components should be included in preparation programs for middle level principals. Both groups identified skills in interpersonal relationships, collaborative decision making, staff supervision and evaluation, and instructional leadership as four of the top five recommendations (Table 2.36). Noteworthy was the significant difference in the importance of middle level best practices. Ninety-eight percent of the principals in the highly successful schools believed the study of middle level best practices was very useful or essential, compared with 83% of the national sample principals. Principals of highly successful schools also ranked community and parent issues considerably higher than did the national sample. In general, a higher percentage of principals in highly successful schools categorized more of the concepts as essential than did their national sample counterparts. Principals of highly successful schools rated managerial concepts, such as scheduling, less highly than principals from the national sample rated them.

Professional Development Activities

Similar to the principals in the national sample, most principals of highly successful schools had participated in one or more professional development activities in the past two years, including local activities, national conferences, and private consultations. The same was true for membership in national professional organizations, with most principals in both groups belonging to one or more national professional organizations, such as NASSP, NMSA, and the National Association of Elementary School Principals. The principals of the highly successful schools held more leadership positions in professional organizations than did their national sample colleagues. Principals of highly successful schools also valued their professional development experiences to a greater extent than did the national sample principals, with 66% of the highly successful school principals rating their involvement in professional development as having great value in their development, compared with 49% of the national sample principals.

Table 2.33 Number of Middle Level Education Graduate Courses Taken

Courses	Highly successful			National sample		
	Total	Male	Female	Total	Male	Female
None	14	14	14	37	37	40
1–2	32	34	31	34	34	35
3–5	34	37	31	20	21	15
6 or more	20	15	24	9	8	10

Table 2.34 Reasons for Entering Education Administration

Reason	Highly successful			National sample		
	Total	Male	Female	Total	Male	Female
Opportunity to help students	2.9	2.9	3.0	2.9	2.9	2.9
Be helpful to others	2.9	2.9	2.9	2.7	2.7	2.8
Opportunity to exercise leadership	2.9	2.8	2.9	2.7	2.6	2.8
Use my abilities	2.8	2.8	2.9	2.7	2.7	2.7
Opportunity to improve curriculum and instruction	2.8	2.6	2.9	2.6	2.6	2.7
Opportunity to work with people	2.7	2.7	2.8	2.6	2.5	2.6
Opportunity to be creative and original	2.7	2.6	2.8	2.5	2.4	2.6
Stable and secure future	2.0	2.1	2.0	2.1	1.5	2.0
Good salary	1.9	1.9	1.9	2.1	2.2	1.8
Recognition by others	1.5	1.5	1.5	1.4	1.4	1.3
Social status and prestige	1.4	1.4	1.4	1.4	1.5	1.3
Excellent hours and vacations	1.2	1.2	1.2	1.2	1.2	1.1

Note. Average of responses: 1 = little/no importance; 2 = somewhat important; 3 = very important.

Table 2.35 Position of Person Most Influential During First Year as a Principal

Influence	Highly successful			National sample		
	Total	Male	Female	Total	Male	Female
Another principal	38	43	35	44	44	45
A central office administrator	27	18	35	22	22	23
Friend or family member	1	0	2	8	6	14
Another administrator in my building	3	3	4	5	6	5
A teacher(s)	7	10	4	5	6	3
Support staff	3	5	2	2	2	0
A professor	5	5	4	1	1	0
No one	8	10	6	10	10	7
Other	8	8	8	3	3	5

Implementation of Collaborative Leadership Practices

In *Turning Points 2000*, Jackson and Davis stated that middle level schools should be organized and should function through a democratic governance system with structures and processes that are systematically inclusive, collaborative, and focused on the improvement of student learning. "The system should give all 'stakeholders' in the school—teachers, administrators, support staff, parents, students and community members—a primary voice in planning and implementing school improvement efforts" (2000, p. 146). The principals of highly successful schools concur with this recommendation and implement it to a significant degree.

Most of the highly successful school principals embraced the concept of collaborative leadership and had implemented leadership teams (94%), as did most of the national sample schools (88%). In both groups, the team was most often described as formal and the most common size was more than seven members. A larger percentage of principals of highly successful schools characterized their teams as not required by any sort of state or district mandate than did principals in the national sample. The composition of the teams showed differences worthy of further examination. Highly successful schools were more likely than the national sample to include team leaders on the school leadership team and less likely to include parents and community members. Fifty-two percent (52%) of the highly successful schools included team leaders, compared with 44% of the national sample; 33% of the highly successful schools included parents, compared with 44% of the national sample; and 13% of the highly successful schools included community mem-

bers, compared with 22% of the national sample.

The specific decision-making authority of the leadership teams was investigated. In the highly successful schools and the national sample schools, leadership teams participated in the formulation of the school's mission, vision, and goals as well as implementing reform initiatives, developing grading practices, and establishing student-conduct rules. In most situations, including those involving curriculum, budget, and the addition of a course or program, decisions were made through discussions or recommendations.

When the roles of parents, students, and other stakeholders were analyzed apart from their participation on leadership teams, noteworthy tendencies were apparent (Table 2.37). Principals of highly successful schools were very likely to involve parents and citizens in establishing objectives and priorities for the school, considering program changes, and planning finance and fundraising. When compared with the national sample, principals of the highly successful schools were also more likely to involve parents and citizens in program evaluation and the determination of student rights and responsibilities, as resource persons, and as tutors. They also were less likely to use parents in the selling of concessions or as teachers' aides.

Also significant were the perceptions of respondents regarding the desire of parents, citizens, and students to participate as stakeholders. More than 90% of the principals of highly successful schools indicated that such desire was increasing or remained the same as it had been on the part of parents and students, compared with 74% of the national sample. Eighty-nine percent said the same for citizens groups, compared

Table 2.36 Principal Recommendations for the Preparation of Middle Level Principals

Experience	Highly successful	National sample	Very useful		Essential	
			HS	NS	HS	NS
Interpersonal skills/relationships	3.64	3.5	24	32	71	58
Middle level best practices	3.62	3.2	34	46	64	37
Collaborative decision making	3.60	3.3	34	42	63	44
Staff supervision/evaluation	3.59	3.5	35	31	62	60
Instructional leadership	3.58	3.4	36	40	62	49
Organizational development/change process	3.51	3.2	35	39	58	41
Oral/Written communication skills	3.47	3.4	33	40	57	48
Program evaluation, assessment, and accountability	3.42	3.3	44	46	49	37
Curriculum development	3.40	3.3	44	35	48	42
Internship/Field experiences	3.36	3.0	38	36	49	35
Special education/IDEA	3.34	3.2	46	44	44	40
Technology	3.31	3.3	57	43	37	41
Legal issues	3.29	3.3	46	40	42	45
Site-based management	3.23	2.9	45	48	39	22
Community/Parent issues	3.17	2.6	52	53	33	24
Standards-based reform	3.16	2.8	48	42	34	20
Scheduling	3.06	3.2	44	44	32	37
Mentorships	3.02	2.8	57	45	23	17
Budget/Finance/Fiscal management	3.00	2.9	46	36	27	30
School board relations/politics	2.66	2.6	51	44	9	12
Research methods	2.54	2.3	43	33	9	6
Foundations/Theory	2.21	2.1	25	18	6	6

Note. HS = highly successful schools; NS = national sample schools. Average of responses: 1 = not useful; 2 = somewhat useful; 3 = very useful; 4 = essential.

with 79% of the national sample; 99% indicated that student interest was increasing or the same, compared with 84% for the national sample. In all cases, principals of the highly successful schools reported far less of a decline in interest than did the national sample counterparts. It is evident that the principals of the highly successful schools are upholding Jackson and Davis's (2000) recommendations regarding stakeholder involvement. Parents are involved in a variety of meaningful ways in highly successful schools, and their desire to participate is continuous, if not escalating. Parent, student, and citizen involvement are both beneficial and viable components of highly successful middle level schools.

Challenges and Satisfaction for Principals

Despite the challenges of the job, persistent media attacks, and increasing federal and state mandates and accountability, it is important to note that an overwhelming percentage of respondents in both groups would choose the job of middle school principal again. Principals who indicated that they would definitely or probably do so composed 91% of the highly successful school group and 82% of the national sample (Table 2.38). Females in highly successful schools were the most likely to definitely or probably choose the position again (94%). When the respondents who would definitely choose the job again were isolated, principals

Table 2.37 Parent/Citizen Involvement

Type	Highly Successful	National Sample
Objectives and priorities for the school	81	73
Program changes and new programs being considered	79	70
Student activities	75	77
Finance and fundraising	76	65
Volunteer tutor	75	70
Volunteer aide	71	80
Resource person for programs and activities, including instruction	69	61
Student behavior, rights, and responsibilities	62	51
Evaluation of programs	58	45
Operates concessions, etc., for benefit of the school	57	70
Sponsors/moderates student groups	47	43

Table 2.38 Principals' Likelihood to Choose Administration Again

Choice	Highly successful			National sample		
	Total	Male	Female	Total	Male	Female
Definitely yes	69	74	65	50	52	43
Probably yes	22	13	29	32	30	38
Uncertain	7	8	6	11	12	9
Probably not	1	3	0	6	5	7
Definitely not	1	2	0	1	1	3

of the highly successful schools emerged with a higher response rate. Sixty-nine percent of the principals of the highly successful schools indicated that they would definitely choose the job again, compared with 50% of the national sample principals. Male principals of highly successful schools were the most likely to definitely choose the job again (74%), followed by their female colleagues (65%). Females in the national sample were least likely to definitely choose the job again (43%).

Principals of highly successful schools assessed the quality of work of other school personnel as exceedingly high. Ninety percent ranked the quality of general classroom teachers as excellent. Assistant principals, special education teachers, office and support staff members, counselors, and team leaders were also rated as excellent by a majority of the principals. There was no single area where school personnel were rated as less than good by principals of the highly successful schools.

When comparing highly successful schools with the national sample, an interesting trend emerged. In both cases no areas were rated as less than good, and the same categories of personnel received a majority of excellent ratings. However, in all cases, principals of the highly successful schools rated each category higher than the national sample. For example, 90% of the principals in the highly successful schools rated their teachers as excellent, compared with 67% of the national sample; 83% of the principals in the highly successful schools rated their special education teachers as excellent, compared with 62% of the national sample. The importance of quality faculty and staff members cannot be disregarded in light of these data.

When respondents were asked to acknowledge their level of satisfaction with other specific elements of the principalship, both groups identified that the rapport they had with students, administrative colleagues, teachers, and community members produced their highest levels of job satisfaction. Principals of highly successful schools also identified the results they achieve as highly important. Minimal differences were noted between the groups in satisfaction with other elements of the job, including rapport with the supervisor, general working conditions, and salary. Lowest on the list for both groups of principals was the amount of time spent on the job, which was the only issue that received a less-than-satisfactory rating from both sets of respondents.

The data indicating the actual amount of time middle level principals spend on the job yielded noteworthy results (Table 2.39). More than 90% of both groups spent more than 50 hours per week on the job. However, 33% of the highly successful school principals and 39% of the national sample reported an average workweek of 60–69 hours, and 18% of the highly successful school principals and 9% of the national sample described that average to be more than 70 hours per week.

When asked how they actually spent their time, as opposed to how they *felt* they should spend their time, the results were indicative of some of the challenges of the position as well as some of the differences between the principals of the highly successful schools and the national sample principals (Table 2.40). Both groups reported that they spent the greatest amount of time on school management and personnel issues. Notable differences were evident, however, in other areas. Principals of highly successful schools spent the next greatest amount of time on planning and program development, whereas national sample principals spent it on student activities and behavior. The greatest of the differences was with reference to student behavior. The national sample principals ranked issues related to student behavior as their fourth-highest time allocation, whereas the principals of the highly successful schools ranked it seventh. Both groups reported that they spent the least amount of time working with the community and on professional development.

There was considerable agreement as to how principals felt they should spend their time. Principals of the highly successful schools and the national sample of principals agreed that the top three areas for time expenditure should be program development, planning, and personnel. Both groups agreed that community, student behavior, and district office activities should consume the least amount of their time. The two groups agreed that professional development should be in the middle of their time allocation, not the lowest priority. When the discrepancies between time allocation and preferred time allocation were scrutinized, it was evident that, with the exception of the amount of time allocated to professional development, principals of the highly successful schools were able to appropriate their time more consistently with what they believed to be their priorities than were the national sample principals.

The amount and type of authority granted to middle level principals also revealed some interesting patterns. More than 60% of both groups of principals reported a high or moderate level of authority in the determination of the school's budget; however, principals of the highly successful schools indicated a much higher level of unrestricted authority in the allocation of discretionary funds than did their national sample colleagues (51% vs. 35%). When hiring teachers, the majority (65–69%) of both groups reported that they made the selection and the central office endorsed it; however, principals in highly successful schools indicated that they held more authority in decisions regarding alternative staffing than did the national sample principals (83% vs. 70%). The results suggest that principals in highly successful schools

Table 2.39 Principals' Self-Reported Hours for Average Work Week

Hours	Highly successful	National sample
Less than 40	3	1
40–49	0	5
50–59	46	46
60–69	33	39
70 or more	18	9

Table 2.40 Principals' Rank of Time Allocation for a Typical Workweek

Task	Highly successful		National sample	
	Do spend	Should spend	Do spend	Should spend
School Management	1	5	1	4
Personnel	2	2	2	2
Program Development	3	1	5	1
Planning	4	3	6	3
Student Activities	5	6	3	6
District Office	6	9	7	9
Student Behavior	7	8	4	8
Professional Development	8	4	9	5
Community	9	7	8	7

Table 2.41 Perceptions of Principals About Roadblocks That Prevent Them From Doing the Kind of Job They Would Like to Do

Obstacle	Highly successful (avg.)	National sample (avg.)	Highly successful			National sample		
			Not a factor	Moderate factor	Serious factor	Not a factor	Moderate factor	Serious factor
Time required by administrative detail at the expense of more important matters	2.2	2.2	9	64	27	11	61	28
Lack of time for myself	2.2	2.2	15	48	37	18	47	35
Regulations/mandates from state/district governing boards	2.1	2.1	15	61	25	18	54	28
Inability to obtain funding	2.0	2.1	25	48	27	20	49	31
Inability to provide teacher time for planning and professional development	1.8	2.1	38	43	19	25	45	30
Parents apathetic or irresponsible about their children	1.6	2.0	43	51	7	20	55	25
Problem students (apathetic, hostile, etc.)	1.6	2.0	43	53	5	23	59	18
Insufficient space and physical facilities	1.9	2.0	37	40	23	31	45	32
Resistance to change	1.6	1.9	46	52	2	22	62	16
Variations in the ability and dedication of staff	1.6	1.9	43	51	6	27	61	12
Time required to administer/supervise cocurricular activities	1.6	1.8	45	48	7	33	53	14
Long-standing tradition in the school/district	1.5	1.8	58	33	9	39	47	14
Lack of knowledge among staff regarding programs for middle level students	1.3	1.7	69	28	2	40	50	10
Deficient communication among administrative levels	1.4	1.7	61	36	3	42	48	10
Pressure from the community	1.5	1.6	58	38	3	48	48	4
Teacher tenure	1.4	1.6	63	37	7	51	35	14
Lack of districtwide flexibility (all schools conform to the same policy)	1.5	1.6	57	36	7	51	38	11
Collective bargaining agreement	1.4	1.6	62	34	5	55	32	13
Lack of data on program successes/failures	1.3	1.5	69	30	1	57	38	5
Teacher turnover	1.4	1.5	65	28	7	61	33	6
Too large a student body	1.5	1.5	57	33	10	66	23	11
Lack of data about student skills and styles	1.3	1.4	68	30	2	60	36	4
Lack of competent administrative assistance	1.2	1.3	84	14	2	73	21	6
Lack of competent office help	1.2	1.2	85	12	2	79	18	3
Too small a student body	1.1	1.1	91	8	1	86	13	<1

Note. Average of responses: 1 = not a factor; 2 = moderate factor; 3 = serious factor.

Table 2.42 Middle Level Principals' Career Plans for the Next Three to Five Years

Plan	Highly successful	National sample
Remain in current position	39	38
Retire	10	18
Retire–continue in educational leadership in another retirement system	7	4
Retire–seek a position in higher education	8	2
Seek a different principalship at the middle level	7	6
Seek a principalship at the high school level	3	5
Seek a principalship at the elementary school level	0	<1
Seek a position as a superintendent	9	10
Seek a central office position other than superintendent	14	15
Seek a position at a junior college or university	1	1
Seek a position in a state department of other education service agency	3	<1
Seek a position as a teacher, counselor, or assistant principal	0	<1
Leave the field of education	0	<1

28% percent of the principals of the highly successful schools assessed this factor as a moderate problem, compared with 50% of the national sample. These data, when combined with the previously discussed knowledge of highly successful school principals regarding middle level issues, strongly suggest that the faculty members and the leaders in highly successful middle level schools have more knowledge about middle level concepts and best practices than do their national sample counterparts.

Principals in the national sample also identified several roadblocks that were not perceived as significant roadblocks by the highly successful school principals. The national sample principals identified the inability to provide teacher time for planning and professional development, resistance to change, and variations in ability and dedication of teachers as moderate or serious factors hindering success. The principals of the highly successful schools were less inclined to rate those factors as serious. National sample school principals also noted apathetic or irresponsible parents and problem students as far more serious factors than did the principals of the highly successful schools.

When asked to speculate on their plans for the next five years, both groups of principals gave very similar responses (Table 2.42). Almost 40% intended to stay in their current position. A similarly sized group planned to stay in K–12 administration, although perhaps at another school or the central office. Approximately 25% intended to retire, some to work in another system and others to seek a position in higher education. Three times as many of the principals from the highly successful schools intended to seek a position in higher education than did national sample

may have more authority to use their judgment in making decisions that could affect specific middle level best practices, such as cocurricular programs, exploratory courses, and service-learning projects.

When principals of highly successful schools were asked about possible roadblocks to success in their schools, their answers were strikingly similar to the answers of the national sample (Table 2.41). Both groups identified the time required for administrative detail at the expense of more important matters, lack of time for themselves, regulations and mandates from state and district governing boards, and the inability to obtain funding as the most consequential factors that created roadblocks to success. The exceptions were particularly interesting. For example, when asked about lack of knowledge among staff members regarding programs for middle level students, 69% of the principals of the highly successful schools assessed this factor as not a problem, compared with 40% of the national sample of principals;

principals (9% vs. 3%). Virtually none of the principals of either highly successful schools or the national sample intended to leave the profession of education other than through retirement.

Despite the strenuous workweeks, the lack of time and opportunity for personal growth and professional development, increasing governmental mandates, and decreasing funding, the principals in the national sample and the highly successful schools described satisfaction with their job and a continued commitment to education. Most would choose the principalship again—many without any doubts. Most garner their greatest job satisfaction from the rapport that they have with students, parents, and teachers, and care little about prestige or salary. As a whole, there are more similarities than differences in the challenges they face and the satisfaction they derive from the job.

However, important differences between the two groups of principals were evident. Principals of the highly successful schools seem to spend their time in closer alignment with their priorities than the national sample principals. They had more discretionary authority and noted fewer roadblocks to success. They were less concerned about the ability and dedication of their faculty members and were more confident in the faculty members' knowledge of middle level concepts and best practices. When synthesized, results from this section of the study suggest that principals of highly successful schools are more able to focus on a vision for their school and to mobilize resources to achieve that vision.

Summary

When compared with the national population of 14,100 middle level schools across the country, as represented by the national sample of schools from the first phase of NASSP's multiyear National Study of Leadership in Middle Level Schools, the 98 highly successful schools selected for study were generally similar in basic demographic characteristics. In essence, the environments within which the schools operated were typical of the settings for thousands of schools across the country.

The programs and practices present in the highly successful schools more closely reflected the existing literature about effective middle level schools than the practices of the national sample schools. This was to be expected because the criteria for the selection of the schools were based upon the most recent literature about effective programs and continuous school improvement. However, some specific differences are worthy of note. For example, the highly successful schools were more likely to design instruction for integrated learning. Interdisciplinary teaming was more common among the highly successful schools as were the recommended components of teaming, such as heterogeneously grouped students, a common set of students, common planning times, and adjacent classrooms. Service learning, character education, G/T programs, inclusion of special education students, multigrade grouping, multiyear instruction, cocurricular programs, and intramural activities were also more common in the highly successful schools.

The leaders of the highly successful schools were tapped for administrative positions earlier in their careers than were the counterparts in the national sample of schools. They had served more years as middle level principals, more years as principals, and more years as principals in their current schools. The principals of the highly successful schools had taken more middle level education coursework and had experienced more-effective professional development focused on middle level education. They also had attained significantly higher levels of formal education than had the national sample of principals. The principals of the highly successful schools spent more hours per week at their job, but they were more likely to invest their time in activities that they felt were most appropriate for their role, and they were more satisfied with their jobs than their counterparts. Many challenges of the job that were labeled as roadblocks by the principals in the national sample were not perceived as roadblocks by the principals of the highly successful schools.

Although there were many similarities between the highly successful schools and the national sample of schools, as well as between the principals of the schools, it is evident that the highly successful schools and their leaders are distinctive on numerous key programmatic and leadership issues. Perhaps most important, the leaders of the highly successful schools have worked more effectively with their faculties and communities and collaboratively developed, maintained, and refined their exemplary schools. Without question, the 98 highly successful schools and their leaders are outstanding examples of quality middle level education.

CHAPTER 3

Six Highly Successful
Middle Level Schools

Six of the 98 highly successful schools were identified in December 2001 for in-depth study. The goal of this portion of the study was to provide detailed information for principals across the nation about the programs, practices, and leadership present in schools that effectively address the needs of the students they serve. The schools were selected because they represent the many effective practices that are characteristic of the larger set of 98 schools. However, the six schools were more than just representative; they were exemplary. They excelled on most of the traits analyzed in the study of the 98 schools. Their ability to design, implement, maintain, and continually improve educational settings that met the specific needs of the students they serve is exceptional. Each of the schools accepted the invitation to participate in this portion of the study (Appendix H).

Data Collection and Analysis

A three-person team composed of at least two members of the national study research team and one additional middle level leader conducted three-day visits to each school during February, March, and April 2002. Prior to the site visit, each principal was asked to complete a previsit survey to provide information about the school that would expedite the work of the site-visit team (Appendix I). During the visit the teams followed specific procedures (Appendix J) to ensure consistency of data collection. The teams conducted audiotaped interviews with principals, assistant principals, teachers, students, and parent leaders from each school. The interviews were transcribed for analysis, and researchers took notes during the interviews (Appendix K).

The interview notes and transcripts, as well as the written responses from the nominators and principals from the information required for inclusion in the set of 98 schools, provided a substantial volume of qualitative data about each of the 6 schools (which are identified by pseudonyms throughout the study). Each

research team member was assigned the responsibility of analyzing the data from at least one of the six schools. Prior to the analysis the research team members identified major threads of anticipated findings on the basis of prior literature, their experiences during the site visits, and the quantitative data collected from the set of 98 schools and the 6 site-visit schools. The research team members studied the interviews and all written materials, and all data were coded according to the anticipated, preassigned content threads. The profiles presented in this chapter were developed by summarizing the information for each school. The findings about programs and practices for chapter 4 and about leadership for chapter 5 were developed by sorting the details of the major threads and synthesizing that information collectively for the six schools.

Highly Successful Schools

This study did not attempt to identify the "best" 100 middle level schools in the nation. The intent was to study 100 "highly successful" schools and learn from their successes. *Highly successful middle level schools* were defined in the introduction as schools that effectively met the unique needs of their students through a variety of programs and practices appropriate to the young adolescents and communities they serve. The definition was used to ensure that the chosen schools were implementing programs and practices that represented the best knowledge of middle level educational practices, making a conscientious effort to continuously improve their programs, and studying and using data to inform their efforts. The goal was to identify a set of exemplary middle level schools, and the analysis of the data from the study affirms the accomplishment of that goal.

Likewise, the selection of 6 highly successful schools from the 98 schools was not intended to identify the 6 "best" middle level schools in the nation. The goal was to identify and study 6 schools that were so exemplary that they were clearly at the fore of middle level practices among the 98 schools. Throughout the process of visiting and studying the six schools, there was no question whether each school deserved its selection. The schools have implemented programmatic practices designed for the needs of the students they serve. School administrators and teachers work collaboratively to establish effective learning environments. Processes are in place to foster continuous improvement to maintain programs at high levels. The schools arrived at their levels of excellence through comprehensive designs and years of intense effort to provide exemplary services.

The following section of this chapter provides a contextual overview of the six schools and their principals. The schools are then profiled individually, with details about the school's demographics, development, facilities, programs, curriculum standards, and leadership. chapter 4 includes details about the programs and practices in the six schools and chapter 5 analyzes the leadership of the six schools. From these predominately qualitative findings most educators and noneducators can reflect on the challenges of middle level education and the manner with which the six schools addressed similar challenges.

A Collective View of the Six Schools

This collective look at the six schools has three subsections. The first includes basic demographic information

about the six schools. Information about the six principals and selected leadership characteristics provide general insight about the principals of the schools. The final section includes information about school program design and delivery.

School Characteristics

Einstein Middle Academy, Kent Middle School, Mark Twain Middle School, and Pioneer Middle School have grades 6–7–8, while Fourstar Middle School has grades 5–6–7–8 and Southside Intermediate School has grades 7–8. Enrollment ranged from 180 at Twain to 1,485 at Pioneer. Pioneer and Kent are located in the suburbs of major metropolitan areas and are primarily bedroom communities. Fourstar is in an outlying suburb of another major metropolitan area but is more of a small town that the suburbs enveloped. Einstein and Southside serve small cities and would be characterized by most as urban schools. Most of the students who attend Southside (66%) are eligible for free and reduced-price lunch programs, as are 40% of the students who attend Twain. Ethnic diversity is most evident at Kent, and the percentage of ethnic minorities throughout the school is greatest at Southside (Table 3.1).

Table 3.1 Site-Visit School Demographics

Characteristic	Einstein Middle Academy	Fourstar Middle School	Kent Middle School	Mark Twain Middle School	Pioneer Middle School	Southside Intermediate School
Grade levels	6–7–8	5–6–7–8	6–7–8	6–7–8	6–7–8	7–8
Enrollment	550	309	1,046	180	1,485	589
Community type	Small city	Suburb small town	Metro suburb	Rural small town	Metro suburb	Small city
Student ethnicity[a]	69% Caucasian 29% African American	94% Caucasian 3% Asian American	48% Caucasian 17% African American 18% Chicano/Hispanic 16% Asian American	96% Caucasian 2% African American	72% Caucasian 9% African American 10% Chicano/Hispanic 8% Asian American	37% Caucasian 13% African American 50% Chicano/Hispanic
Students receiving free or reduced-price lunch	20%	4%	29%	40%	12%	66%

[a] Student ethnicity >1% reported

Leader Characteristics

Three of the six principals were male, three female. They averaged nearly eight years of total principal experience and six years in their current school. Five of the six had experience as an assistant principal. The principals had between five and eight years of experience as teachers and/or counselors before entering administration. The majority of the teaching and principalship experience was at the middle level, but that was not true for the years of experience as assistant principals, with two principals having experience at the elementary level and two at the high school level (Table 3.2).

Program Design and Delivery

Einstein was redesigned as a math, science, and technology magnet school in the mid-1990s, and Kent was in the process of redesigning itself as an International Baccalaureate Middle Years Programme (MYP) school at the time of the site visit. In contrast, Pioneer was designed to be a "true" middle school before it opened its doors in the early 1990s. Twain was a small school rejuvenated in the late 1990s by the arrival of a new principal and participation in a comprehensive school reform initiative. Fourstar was a middle school poised for change when the current principal arrived there in the late 1990s. Southside was a school deep in failure, serving students of color and in poverty until the current principal arrived in the mid-1990s.

Each of the six schools has interdisciplinary teaming as the foundation for instructional delivery, and students are assigned heterogeneously. Each schedule is daily, except for Southside's alternating-day block schedule. Each school has a required exploratory curriculum that is supplemented by electives. Three of the schools have adviser-advisee programs. Overall, the programmatic characteristics of the six schools are reflective of the recommendations about middle level schools found in such basic middle level documents as *Turning Points 2000* (Jackson & Davis, 2000) and *This We Believe* (National Middle School Association, 1995).

Profiles of the Six Schools

The following profiles describe the development of each school, the design of the schools' facilities, the schools' programs and curriculum, and the leadership and relationships among the adults who make each school a positive environment for students. The schools are presented in alphabetic order by pseudonym.

Einstein Middle Academy

Einstein Middle Academy is a math, science, and technology magnet middle school of grades 6–7–8. It is located in the center of downtown in a city of approximately 80,000 people within a greater metropolitan-area population of 225,000. Einstein is one of 137 schools in a county school district that serves nearly 500,000 residents. The community is in the geographic heart of a southeastern state, and the area is one of the nation's premier citrus production regions. Einstein is within an hour's drive of two of the nation's major metropolitan areas, one with a

Table 3.2 Site-Visit School Principal Background (Years of Experience)

Characteristic	Einstein Middle Academy	Fourstar Middle School	Kent Middle School	Mark Twain Middle School	Pioneer Middle School	Southside Intermediate School
Gender	Female	Male	Male	Male	Female	Female
Teacher	8 ES	6 ML	5 ML 1 HS	5 ML	7 ML	6 ES
Assistant principal	1 ML 3 ES	2 ML	9 HS 11 ML	0	3 HS	4 ES
Principal (total)	8 ML	10 ML	6 ML	1 ES 3 ML	11 ML	2 ES 6 ML
Principal at site-visit school	8	3	6	3	9	7

Note. ES = elementary school; ML = middle level school; HS = high school.

population of approximately 3.5 million and the other with a population of approximately 1.5 million residents. The population of the community Einstein serves increased 11% in the 1990s and similar growth is projected for the current decade.

The median age of residents of the county is 39.7 years, with population categories rather evenly distributed across all age groups. The ethnicity of the community is primarily Caucasian (69.5%). Other ethnic populations include African American (21%), Hispanic American (6.4%), and Asian American (1%). Of the 550 students enrolled at Einstein, 69% are Caucasian, 29% African American, and 1% each are Hispanic American and American Indian. Twenty percent of the students at Einstein receive free or reduced-price lunch.

School Development

Einstein is the product of a court-ordered desegregation plan issued in 1992. Of the 19 middle schools in the district, Einstein is one of two middle schools designed to serve as a magnet school for math, science, and technology. The student population is primarily from 20 local elementary schools, including one main feeder magnet school from which comes approximately half of the incoming sixth-grade population. To maintain a multicultural balance, active recruitment is conducted each year to attract minority students from local elementary schools.

Einstein opened as a middle school and has operated for 11 years with interdisciplinary teams, common planning times for team members, advisory periods, and a commitment to effectively meet the developmental needs of young adolescents while maintaining high academic expectations. The evolution of the school toward a "true" middle school has been a gradual and purposeful journey, with faculty study groups considering the most appropriate programs and strategies for their students.

School Facility

Since its inception in 1992, Einstein has had three names and has operated in two locations. Under the leadership of the current principal, the school moved to its present location—a former high school facility—in summer 1995. In addition to having been the city's three-story high school, Einstein's new location had been the city's junior high school and an alternative school. The facility, located downtown, was vacant for several years before it was renovated prior to becoming Einstein's current location.

The facility is reminiscent of most multistory high schools constructed in the first half of the 20th century. It has a traditional design, with classrooms along both sides of the hallways throughout the building. Stairwells are so narrow that the direction of student traffic flow within the stairwells is designated for efficiency and safety and is followed by students and staff members.

The remodeling process did not structurally change the facility to address contemporary middle school organizational concepts. Classrooms are typical in size and do not accommodate multiple class groups. Science classrooms are not located in proximity to other core classes for interdisciplinary teaming. Einstein's faculty members work within that limitation, functioning as teams even though all team classrooms are not adjacent.

After nearly a decade of use, Einstein looks as if it were only just remodeled. It is an impeccably clean, pleasant, and inviting environment for students and staff members. Pictures and memorabilia in the main entry provide a tour through the history and heritage of the school. The corridors are laden with pictures of people and events reflecting the magnet themes of the school. The principal, staff members, and students have created a culture of respect and pride.

School Programs

The core curriculum for grades 6, 7, and 8 includes classes in language arts, math, science, social studies, and an integrated lab. The students and faculty members are organized as interdisciplinary teams across those five subject areas. Integrated lab classes were designed to engage students in hands-on learning experiences across the content areas. The primary emphasis of the sixth-grade integrated lab is to share an environmental experience both in the classroom and outdoors. Students use math, computer, and science process skills to learn about the state's water systems, including springs, rivers, lakes, estuaries, and marine habitats.

The seventh-grade integrated lab takes students out of their books and into the world with various media technologies. They study Earth-science topics such as meteorology, geology, astronomy, and natural resources. The highlight of the school year is a field trip to a state forest where students explore a natural cave system.

An emphasis is placed on problem solving, engineering, technology, and communication skills in the eighth-grade integrated lab. Students build their own working machines and construct and fly hot-air balloons. They learn to use a variety of software programs and create spreadsheets, databases, and slide show presentations. They also learn to use scientific calculators, digital cameras, and video cameras.

Throughout the series of integrated lab classes, students develop the skills to create electronic portfolios that represent their interests and learning achievements. They present the portfolios to parents during school "portfolio fairs."

The sixth-grade exploratory program at Einstein includes a 12-week rotation of computers, physical education, and the study of concepts from Stephen Covey's *The 7 Habits of Highly Effective People* and *The 7 Habits of Highly Effective Teens*. The seventh-grade exploratory curriculum is physical education, computers, and Spanish.

Electives are available to students at each grade, and the number of options increase with each grade. Sixth- and seventh-grade electives are band, strings, chorus, art, and TV productions. The eighth-grade electives are band, strings, show choir, guitar, honors Spanish, honors Latin, art, computers, aerodynamics, economics, public speaking, yearbook, and TV production. Students in the school's lowest quartile on the state assessment program are required to take reading during one of their two elective periods.

An adviser–advisee class provides each student with an adult advocate who develops a positive, supportive relationship with the student. The class period also provides time for intramural sports, clubs, and other supportive student activities. School clubs and after-school activities at Einstein include the National Junior Honor Society, a world language club, math counts, a history club, a science Olympiad club, a scrapbook club, student council, a video/news club, Future Business Leaders of America, an environmental club, Fellowship of Christian Athletes, an economics team, and a chess club.

Curriculum Standards

Einstein has a rigorous academic curriculum based on state and county standards. All classes are designed to be challenging. Parents and students are informed that the classes are advanced and that standards are high. Faculty members "firmly believe that if we set high standards, students will rise to the occasion." Since the school's inception, eighth-grade students have performed at the top of the county's testing program. Nearly all students regularly perform at the top two levels of the state assessment exams. For example, in 2000, 100% of eighth-grade students scored at those levels on the state writing and mathematics assessments and 97% scored at those levels on the reading assessment.

In addition to state assessments, student work is assessed in a variety of ways. Students complete individual and group projects, make visual and oral presentations, display projects and products, and complete a comprehensive electronic portfolio. Portfolios include students' personal academic goals and document class work and accomplishments, such as analyses of books read and various lab activities. Students conduct student-led conferences three times a year with their parents and present their portfolios. Parents are encouraged to engage with the electronic portfolios and are provided time during conferences to add their own reflections to the portfolio for the student to read the following morning at school.

Leadership and Relationships

Without a doubt, the principal at Einstein is the driving force behind the success of the school. She is dedicated to the accomplishments of the school's mission and goals. The principal sets the tone and standards for the entire faculty, challenging all staff members to meet individual student needs without compromising high expectations. Her self-perception, as well as the teachers' perceptions of her, is of a participative leader who engages teachers in the decision-making process. The principal said, "If the teachers help make the decision then they are more likely to go ahead and support it and actually do it." The principal's self-described and well-documented process for change is to establish a pilot program if a new idea warrants consideration. If the pilot program is successful, it should be adopted by the whole school. If it is not, then it does not merit the necessary time and energy to be maintained. The principal works with faculty members and community members to generate new ideas through faculty meetings, the school advisory council, and a very high use of e-mail communication with faculty members and parents. The principal's parent e-mail lists are extensive, and she conscientiously replies to groups and to individual parents, teachers, and community members.

Teachers describe their principal as a collaborative leader who fosters positive administrator–teacher relationships. They respect her ideas, judgment, and overall leadership. They view her as exceptional in the development, nurturance, and implementation of a vision for the school and in promoting cooperation among the faculty members to work toward that vision. They also view her as a leader who empowers them by respecting their ideas and needs and by supporting their efforts to accomplish their work. One parent-leader described the principal's interpersonal skills as "amazing."

Einstein is an excellent example of a school that is accomplishing its defined mission as a magnet middle school in an exceptional manner. The staff members and school leaders are committed to that mission and to the establishment of a school environment that supports that mission. The decisions they make and the programs they implement consistently enhance their mission. As soon as you walk through the front door at Einstein you can sense the academic integrity of the school. As you spend time visiting with students, teachers, and leaders, you know you are in a school that is dedicated to high standards and academic success for all students.

Fourstar Middle School

Fourstar Middle School is a 5–6–7–8 middle school of 309 students. It could be described as a prototypic middle school using a daily interdisciplinary block schedule, interdisciplinary teaming for all teachers, common planning times for all teachers, exploratory courses, an adviser–advisee program, cocurricular programs, intramural activities for younger students, and interscholastic opportunities for older students.

The Fourstar community is on the northern edge of a midwestern state, 20 miles from a major metropolitan city. This small community, surrounded by relatively new suburban communities, is described as "a neighborhood of character and charm" serving 7,100 residents. Compared with state averages, the Fourstar community has a high median family income and a low unemployment rate. The average resident age is 43. Eighty-nine percent of the adults have a high school degree and 29% have a college degree. The community's population is 97% Caucasian.

The Fourstar public school district serves the community with a 9–12 high school, a 5–8 middle school (Fourstar), and a K–4 elementary school. The high school has 370 students and the elementary school has 392 students. The community also has a K–8 parochial school of approximately 400 students.

Fourstar's ethnic population is only slightly different than the community's population. Fourstar has a population that is 1% African American, 1% Hispanic American, and 3% Asian American. Four percent of Fourstar students receive free or reduced-price lunch.

School Development

When Fourstar's current principal arrived at the school in the late 1990s, he found a school poised to move to a higher level of effectiveness. The principal met with existing teaching teams and began to develop faculty-wide commitment to a true middle school philosophy. Staff development focused on "middle school 101," including the study of *Turning Points* and *This We Believe*. Parents were involved in detailed discussions about educational best practices for young adolescents. Through the leadership of the new principal, the "teaching team" became the locus of operations at Fourstar. Teachers were provided with both the opportunity and the responsibility to meet the needs of their students. In two years Fourstar evolved to a highly effective student-centered middle school. Today, the principal, teachers, and parents continue to study and refine educational programs based upon knowledge of middle school best practices.

School Facilities

Fourstar is a traditional two-story brick facility originally built in 1922 and remodeled several times. The school is scheduled to move to the existing high school facility in fall 2004 following the opening of a new high school. The current middle school facility includes a cafeteria in the basement, a gym on the main floor, a media center on the second floor, and a single-room loft that houses a computer lab that, many years ago, was the projection room for community movies projected into the gymnasium so local youth would have a theater. The community's K–8 parochial school is located across the street from the middle school facility. Indicative of the level of cooperation in the community, the schedules of the two schools coincide so students can participate in common activities before, during, and after school. Also indicative of the school–community relationship was the purchase of the current middle school property so the city can establish a senior housing facility when Fourstar moves to its new location.

School Programs

Fourstar personifies many of the characteristics often touted in developmentally appropriate middle schools. At the heart of the school programs is interdisciplinary teaming. With a school enrollment of slightly more than 300 students, each grade (5–6–7–8) has a three-person or four-person team. In grade 5, one teacher teaches math, another science, another social studies, and another language arts. Each member of the team also teaches reading. The grade 6 team includes a math teacher, a science teacher, and a language arts teacher; each teacher also teaches social studies and reading. In grades 7 and 8, students are grouped by math/science and language arts/social studies with four teachers. Teachers can mix the students by the pairs of subjects as well as by the four individual subjects. Each teacher for grades 7 and 8 also teaches reading, focusing on nonfiction because that is an area specifically tested on the state assessment.

In addition to the core curriculum, all students have one period of "enrichment, remediation, or intervention," including band, choir, and study hall. The study hall provides teachers with the opportunity to work directly with students on their team who need academic support. Each student has two periods of exploration, designed to expose students to a variety of content areas. Students begin the school day in a 7-minute homeroom to establish the educational tone for the day. They conclude the day with a developmentally appropriate 18-minute homeroom. In grades 5 and 6, the afternoon homeroom is designed to help students learn to organize their work for home and for the following day. In grades 7 and 8, teachers use the time to meet individual student needs, including support for projects and other forms of academic assistance. Each grade eats lunch separately in a 20-minute time slot, and each grade has a 20-minute recess period immediately before or after their lunch period.

In 2000 Fourstar received a state grant that provided 40 laptop computers for classroom learning. Wireless technology was installed in the school to provide maximum flexibility. Staff development was provided to help teachers design learning experiences that incorporated the capacity of the laptops. In recent years the school has developed other unique programs, including a staff-designed process for recognizing students "doing things right" and an eighth-grade interdisciplinary unit that engages students with senior citizens.

Curriculum Standards
The curriculum at Fourstar is designed to meet state standards in writing, reading, math, social studies, and science. Students at Fourstar have consistently performed at a very high level on state assessments. In 2001, 100% of the sixth-grade students met the state's proficiency standard in writing; 78% met the standards in reading, 90% in math, 90% in citizenship, and 90% in science. All of these scores were well above the state averages.

Leadership and Relationships
The successes of the Fourstar programs correlate with the arrival of the current principal. During his first year, he invested significant time listening to staff members, parents, community members, and students. The dialogue fostered a broad understanding of existing practices and defined desired outcomes. It also established a trusting and collaborative atmosphere that enabled significant program change and development in subsequent years. Within two years after the principal's arrival, Fourstar was receiving recognition as one of the top middle schools in the state. Faculty members and school leaders worked together to study the knowledge of middle school best practices and use that

knowledge to change or refine their practices. They realize that they have made significant progress and that Fourstar must continue to evolve to effectively meet the changing needs of future students. Each year faculty members and school leaders design and work toward a defined set of goals. Unlike most schools that design a vision and goals as a whole school, the principal at Fourstar describes visioning as "unique to the interdisciplinary teams more than schoolwide." The evolution of Fourstar underscores the importance of collaborative relationships, the study of best practices, and the commitment of school leaders and staff members to meet the needs of the students in their community.

Kent Middle School
Kent Middle School is a 6–7–8 school of 1,046 students, located approximately 20 miles outside of a major metropolitan area on the Atlantic seaboard. Some described its location as a bedroom community of a larger urban area; others categorized it as an independent and major employment center; and still others have called it an "older, established community that is the antithesis of the larger urban community in its proximity." The range of descriptors is indicative of the defining characteristics of the Kent community, given that *diverse* was the adjective most often used to portray the unique qualities of the school and the population it serves.

Kent draws from four feeder schools that represent the full range of the community's diversity. Some students live in multimillion-dollar homes, whereas others live in subsidized housing. A substantial number of the students come from families where the wage earners are employed in professional, technical, managerial, or sales positions, whereas 29% of the students qualify for free or reduced-price lunch. Thirty-five percent of the families in the community have children under age 18. The student population is even more ethnically diverse than the city: 48% of the students at Kent are Caucasian, compared with 60% of the city population; African Americans represent 18% of the student population and 10% of the larger community. The Hispanic student population is 18% compared with 12%, and the Asian student population is 16% compared with 15%. Twenty-five percent of the students are considered "international," and 13% speak English as a second language. Fourteen percent of Kent students qualify for special education services, and there are extensive opportunities for gifted and talented students as well. The faculty's belief that "all children can learn, just in different ways and at difference paces," and the school goal of closing the achievement gap exist in a context that not only accepts but also embraces the challenges presented by such a diverse student population.

School Development

Kent is one of three middle schools in the community and is part of a large county system that serves 137,000 students. In 1977 a district advisory committee on the middle and junior high school recognized that the students would benefit from a philosophy and environment designed specifically for early adolescents. The committee recommended that a comprehensive plan be established to systematically convert the existing junior high schools to middle schools with the necessary financial and human resources. Kent and two other junior high schools were the first, chosen to be converted during the 1978–1979 school year. The conversion to a middle school was an integral part of the response to declining enrollment in the secondary schools, as well as a commitment to offer all sixth-, seventh-, and eighth-grade students a middle school education.

School Facility

Kent is situated within a residential area in the center of its city. The school was built in the 1960s as a junior high school and was extensively renovated during 1992–1994; however, by 2002 the school population had already exceeded its intended capacity by approximately 100 students. Despite crowded conditions, extensive efforts have been made to ensure that teaching teams and elective departments are generally housed in close proximity and that each of the 14 teams or departments has its own office. There are 53 standard classrooms; a complete gym and locker-room facility; specialized rooms for instructional music, chorus, and family and consumer sciences; as well as two art facilities and a TV studio. The media center contains a book collection of 15,000 titles and a 10-unit computer hub. In addition, there are two separate computer labs and at least two computers in each classroom.

The safety and security of students at Kent is part of the school's overall mission statement. Despite the fact that the school is adjacent to a 12-lane commuter highway, intruders or "stranger danger" have not been a problem. A police resource officer is assigned to Kent, which also houses the main office of the district's police resource program. The building is used extensively for community activities; it is described as in use every evening (6–11 p.m.), seven days a week, 12 months a year.

School Programs

Interdisciplinary teaming is used in all grade levels, and the exploratory curriculum offers an arts rotation as well as other elective courses. The school expects students to perform community service, which is consistent with middle school best practices. There also are a variety of after-school activities, including clubs and interscholastic sports. Core-subject teachers have common planning times during which daily team meetings, student progress reviews, and parent meetings are held. Communication with parents is considered the key to addressing how to best meet the needs of each student. Ability grouping is used in English and mathematics courses, and honors classes are also available. Other classes are heterogeneously grouped, with gifted students clustered into mixed-ability classes and students with disabilities primarily served through inclusion.

Kent's schedule is best described as a daily disciplinary schedule, where students have seven class periods and move to a different teacher every 47 minutes. Grade-level teams serve approximately 150 students each, and students receive more than 90% of their instruction within those multidisciplinary teams. Interdisciplinary instruction is increasingly evident at Kent owing, at least in part, to the expectation of the International Baccalaureate MYP that instruction and curriculum are integrated "whenever possible." The five interactive themes of MYP—approaches to learning, community service, health and social education, environment, and man the maker—connect subjects to each other and the outside world. The sixth-grade outdoor education program, a voluntary after-school enrichment program for gifted students, and the service-learning requirement at Kent each are examples of integration of content and application of knowledge and skills.

In support of the school goals of improving reading scores, reading is taught across the curriculum at all grade levels. Teachers have engaged in extensive professional development in teaching reading, and a reading specialist is one of three staff members who work closely with teachers to enhance instructional effectiveness. In the two years prior to the site visit, reading scores doubled and the number of books that were checked out from the media center was twice that of the previous year.

The recent development of a program to reduce bullying demonstrates the school's responsiveness to safety and security concerns. The schoolwide program includes lessons for students, a faculty inservice, and a parent component. The program has been evaluated as having a positive outcome; faculty members are more proactive, and more bullying situations are being reported and resolved. In general, teachers, parents, and students report that students get along well and that the ethnic and racial diversity of the school enriches the environment rather than causing problems.

Curriculum Standards

In recent years curriculum design and instructional practices have been driven by Kent's application to become an

MYP school. MYP was selected as the reform initiative that would best support the school's goals of challenging all students, improving reading scores, and closing the achievement gap. The MYP emphasis on subject integration, health and social education, and critical-thinking and problem-solving skills, as well as the required community service component, were perceived by the school community as consistent with its mission of success for every student. Kent was accepted as an MYP school the year following the site visit, and the program is currently moving into the ongoing evaluation phase.

Kent has participated in a districtwide effort to back-map and align the curriculum with state standards. Currently, it is participating in a countywide venture to develop K–12 curricular standards, essential questions, and suggested assessments. At Kent, each team establishes curricular goals for each nine-week period. Teachers post those goals in their classrooms, and evidence of goal accomplishments is expected to be observed during classroom visitations. The standards are high and, although the standards may be difficult for some students to achieve, most students are successful because of the support of teachers who recognize that students learn in a variety of ways and through different means.

Teachers at Kent engage in a high percentage of instructional strategies that actively engage students in learning. The percentage of instruction at Kent considered to be "student active engaged learning" leading to higher order thinking was substantially higher than the national study composite and the second-highest of the six site-visit schools. In addition, Kent was considerably lower than the national study composite in student seatwork and disengagement. Teachers are continually analyzing student progress and outcomes through a variety of assessments, beginning to bring increasingly authentic assessments into the learning process, and adapting instruction to improve student achievement.

Leadership and Relationships

The principal of Kent cares deeply about students, and models that value in his style, decisions, and expectations. He sets an ethical standard of "treating each child as if he/she were your own." The faculty members demonstrate a commensurate student focus with frequent statements that reiterate their beliefs that all students can be successful at Kent, that faculty members will not give up on a student, and that faculty work is characterized by dedication and commitment. As one teacher said, "This is not a school for everybody [faculty]. You have to want to work here, and be committed to work with each student because that child is someone's child."

The principal's style is described as direct, honest, and upfront. As one teacher said, "What you see is what you

get." The principal has a highly visible presence in the school and is well respected by students, teachers, and parents. The principal's self-described leadership style—and the teachers' descriptions of his leadership style—is more directive than collaborative. Yet there is widespread agreement that he is a good listener and ideas and changes come from the bottom-up as well as the top-down. Teachers make suggestions or initiate proposals either directly to the principal or through the school's instructional leadership team (ILT). Even with a perceived directive style, the practices in the school are indicative of collaborative and participative decision making on major school issues.

The ILT, which meets weekly, includes the principal, assistant principals, three teacher specialists (the staff development coordinator, a literacy and reading specialist, and the MYP facilitator), team leaders, and department heads. The team provides leadership for instructional improvement initiatives and curriculum development. There is widespread agreement that the ILT is effective as a vehicle to communicate ideas and concerns and, in most cases, to bring the faculty members to a point where they can either support a change event or, at a minimum, understand why one needs to occur. The ILT also determines professional development topics for the entire faculty. The topics are addressed in half-day released days that occur six times throughout the year, with follow-up sessions as well as other specific topics that are addressed in team meetings or after-school sessions.

The faculty members at Kent are highly collaborative and student-focused. Teachers cited the cohesiveness of grade-level teams, coordinated planning, the benefits of mentors, and the feeling of "family" as indicators of a highly collaborative school culture. Additional comments about the culture referred to people "taking care of each other," planning together, sharing ideas, and seeking and offering help. The culture was a reason teachers wanted to teach at Kent. One teacher said, "I love this faculty because we really are [collaborative]. Face it, we live with each other. That permeates everything we do."

Mark Twain Middle School

Mark Twain Middle School, which is situated in the northeastern portion of a Midwestern state, serves approximately 180 students in grades 6–7–8. Twain is one of four schools in a district that encompasses the southern half of a county of fewer than 5,000 inhabitants and whose primary source of economic revenue is derived from farming and agribusiness-related industries. Enrollment in the 800-student district has decreased approximately 10% in the past four years, so the community has not been immune from the same population declines experienced by many farming regions across the nation. Neighboring communities also consist primarily of small towns and farms, and Twain is a three-hour drive from the nearest major metropolitan area.

The median age of county residents is 40.5 years, with 27.6% residents under age 20, 28.6% in the 20–44 age bracket, 22.8% aged 45–64, and 20.8% aged 65 and over. The community is ethnically homogeneous, with 98.6% of the population of Caucasian descent; other ethnicities include African American (0.6%), American Indian (0.4%), Asian American (0.2%), and Hispanic American (0.1%). The composition of Twain's student body parallels the county: 96% of students are Caucasian, 2% are African American, 1% are American Indian, and 1% are Asian American. Forty percent of the students receive free or reduced-price lunch.

School Development

Twain was formed when the district's two junior high schools were consolidated into one school at the beginning of the 1995–1996 school year. Twain draws from two feeder elementary schools that are located in the school system's two largest towns of 1,000 and 2,000 inhabitants—communities that previously housed the two junior high school facilities. The school opened as a middle school with a faculty dedicated to serving the developmental needs of young adolescents and committed to high expectations for academic success. However, because of the school's small enrollment, teachers were assigned to teach across the 6–8 grade levels, so interdisciplinary teaming was not implemented.

School Facilities

When the decision was made to consolidate the two junior high schools, school officials determined that the most efficient use of district resources was to erect a new middle school on the high school campus. Twain is physically connected to the existing high school, which also houses the superintendent's office. This addition was designed to complement the single-story high school building that is reminiscent of many of the nation's schools built in the 1960s. The new middle school was constructed in a similar traditional fashion with classrooms lining each side of a long corridor, but the classrooms, office space, and gymnasium are distinct from the high school, so each organizational structure can establish its own identity.

Although the two schools operate as separate entities and are led by two different principals, middle and high school students cross paths frequently throughout the school day. The library and cafeteria are shared spaces, and the counselor serves both sets of students. Because many faculty members have teaching assignments shared between the two schools, middle school students attend music and art classes in the high school, and some high school classes are taught in middle school classrooms.

After seven years, Twain is exceptionally well maintained, and it is obvious that the administrators, faculty members, staff members, and students take tremendous pride in their building. Student work is displayed above the lockers along each side of the hallway, reflecting the teachers' desire to recognize their students' successes and encourage a commitment to excellence. Hallways, classrooms, and the principal's office suite are virtually spotless. Because of the school's relatively small enrollment, traffic flow is very manageable during transitions.

School Programs

Twain uses an eight-period disciplinary schedule, with the fourth period dedicated to advisory and study hall. The core curriculum in sixth, seventh, and eighth grades includes English, social studies, mathematics, and science; reading is an additional core class in seventh grade. All students enroll in physical education/health classes each year. The sixth-grade exploratory wheel includes quarter courses in keyboarding, library skills, study skills, and reading. The seventh-grade exploratory curriculum offers computers, career exploration, industrial technology, and geography.

Because of the small enrollment, elective offerings in the sixth grade are restricted to either vocal music or band. Seventh- and eighth-grade students who do not enroll in band complete an exploratory wheel of study skills, computers, introduction to agriculture, and current events.

In addition to band and choir, students have an opportunity to participate in several cocurricular offerings, including student government, science club, newspaper, dramatics, and peer tutoring. Intramural sports are provided for all three grades. Seventh- and eighth-grade students also have opportunities to participate in dance team, cheerleading, softball, basketball, track, and football.

Curriculum Standards

Twain has implemented a curriculum based upon state standards. The school district created vertical curriculum teams for each discipline that include teachers in grades 6–12, with the stated purpose of improving student achievement at all grades. Each team has developed measurable learner objectives for its respective curricular area that serve to guide instruction in the middle level and high school grades.

Twain and the school district use student achievement data to inform curriculum and instructional decisions. For the past several years, Twain faculty members have collectively studied ways to incorporate active-learning approaches into their daily lessons. They regularly collect schoolwide observational data on their instructional practices, analyze the data, and discuss methods to provide more-authentic experiences, incorporate cooperative learning, and provide differentiated instruction for their students.

The past year's building goals related to increasing use of authentic assessments and increasing students' reading comprehension. Students complete monthly assessments that parallel the state content-area exams. The monthly assessments are used as formative data to guide instruction and to identify improvement areas for students. To ensure that students are successful on state examinations, Twain has implemented a structured study hall one period each day. This study period enables the teachers to provide individualized assistance to students who need more time for instruction. Those students who demonstrate mastery of concepts are permitted to report to the gymnasium for supervised play or they may work on class projects or reports. In addition, mandatory after-school tutoring sessions are held each week for students who are at academic risk, with the school providing bus transportation for students whose parents are unable to pick them up after tutoring. Parent-teacher conferences are held each quarter so regular communication channels between home and school are maintained.

The school's intense focus on student achievement has begun to pay dividends. The school attained state "accreditation with distinction," and the percentage of students attaining proficiency (scores above grade level) on state achievement tests has improved steadily. For example, in 2002, 52% of students scored at the proficient level in communication arts, up from 25% in 2000.

Leadership and Relationships

After spending only a small amount time at Twain, visitors agree that the school truly has established a sense of community. The close relationships can be attributed partly to the school's small enrollment and the nature of the small rural communities where teachers have lived and worked together for many years. Also important is the principal's effectiveness as a collaborative instructional leader. As a former teacher at Twain, he had earned the respect of students, parents, and teaching colleagues before assuming the principalship. He displays a genuine concern for students and faculty members and continually strives to be a role model for the staff by maintaining a focus on the school's vision and mission. Disciplinary problems are virtually nonexistent in the school, due in part to the positive relationships that exist among the principal, faculty members, staff members, students, and parents.

Stating that "data drive our goals," the principal has provided focus to the faculty members' collective efforts to increase student achievement. An identified systemic change process has been used for several years, and teachers are empowered to implement reforms through numerous avenues. A three-person school improvement team guides the development of building goals, and these faculty members chair the three "focus" teams that are charged with developing action plans related to the goals. Summer professional development days that are part of the district's differentiated contract agreement provide an opportunity for the middle school faculty members to examine data, identify areas for celebration and concern, and reach a consensus on goals for the upcoming school year.

Teachers view their principal as a resource, and they appreciate his supportive leadership style. Describing him as a "strong leader, who knows what he wants and what the school needs," they acknowledge his exceptional skills in promoting their collaborative efforts toward school improvement. Teachers often provide the principal with positive feedback on students so he can compliment individual students on their successes. Their one concern, however, is losing him to another system; one teacher said, "Our principal is special and super; it will be hard to keep him."

Pioneer Middle School

Pioneer Middle School, a Blue Ribbon 6–7–8 school, is located in the suburbs of a major southwestern city. The school, which opened in August 1993, is part of a mixed-use, master-planned, multigenerational, and fully integrated community of 65,000 residents. Development of the community began in 1990 with a projected population of 160,000 once it is fully developed in 2015. It has been ranked as the best-selling master-planned community in the United States in eight of the past nine years. The suburb is home to eight golf courses, numerous houses of worship, cultural facilities, nearly 100 village and neighborhood parks, a 93-mile trail system, employment centers, medical centers, and more than 40 active neighborhoods offering more than 100 model homes by 18 homebuilders. Also included in the community are provisions for sub-communities that exclusively serve retirees and apartment complexes for low-income families.

The median age of community members is 41.5 years, with the largest age groups in the 0–20 (24%) and 65+ (21%) brackets. The ethnic distribution in the community is primarily Caucasian (82.2%). Also represented in the community are Asian Americans (6.2%), Hispanic Americans (5.4%), and African Americans (3.5%). Of the 1,485 students enrolled at Pioneer, 28% are ethnic minorities, a figure that has increased during the nine years the school has been in operation and that makes the school more ethnically diverse than the community itself. Twelve percent of the students enrolled in the school receive free or reduced-price lunch.

Pioneer is one of 275 schools of a large county school district that changed its K–12 grade level configuration in 1989 to K–5, 6–8, and 9–12, primarily because of overcrowding in existing elementary and middle level schools. In 1991 the school board voted to change the names of all junior high schools to middle schools and to adopt the middle school philosophy. Initially the change was not widely embraced, and many of the district middle level schools held on to their junior high philosophies and organizational and teaching practices. Changes in central office leadership, particularly a new superintendent knowledgeable about middle school research and practices, led to directives to principals to implement middle level programs in their schools. Although resistance still exists, currently there is strong support for middle level education in the district and among many principals and teachers.

School Development

From the very beginning of its planning, Pioneer was designed to be a "true" middle school. Playing a major role in the school's physical and programmatic design was the principal-designee, who was still the principal at the time of the site visit. With a strong, clear vision and extensive knowledge of middle level education and an outgoing, collaborative approach, the principal educated the school board's community representative and other members of the community about the research and proven benefits of the middle level concept. With the support of the area superintendent, the principal was able to involve parents, teachers, administrators, counselors, and support staff members in designing a middle level school that included the accepted components of the middle school philosophy and that incorporated the research, recommendations, and practices supported by the Carnegie Council on Adolescent Development's *Turning Points*.

School Facilities

As part of the community master plan, Pioneer was built adjacent to a beautifully landscaped park with an amphitheater that is frequently used for school and community activities. The school facility, which also serves as a hub for community activities, is a single-story structure. With the exception of the playing fields, the building structure completely surrounds the school, offering a secure and open environment with spacious courtyards. The courtyards are decorated with banners, brightly painted windows, hand-painted

murals, and numerous posters and other graphics focused on school pride and goals. The interior walls are filled with rich displays of student work and projects.

The instructional wings of the school are organized by grade level with the classrooms of interdisciplinary teams adjacent or nearby. The school also has four computer labs, each with 38–40 computers. In addition, all classrooms are wired for access to the Internet and for closed-circuit television. Pioneer also has a dance studio, a large orchestra room, and a guitar room. The school's library contains audiovisual materials, a wide selection of magazines and journals, and 15,000 book titles. A large gymnasium that is used for physical education classes is also used for intramural programs, athletic contests, and schoolwide assemblies. Athletic fields are also available and are used by physical education classes every day.

School Programs

Six months prior to the opening of Pioneer (under the direction of the principal-designee) teachers attended a number of after-hours workshops on middle level practices and identified those practices that would be implemented and the type of instruction that would best meet the needs of the young adolescents attending Pioneer. As a result of these workshops, middle level programs and practices based on research were implemented. The school was organized and continues to be structured around a teaming approach that includes, in addition to basic core-subject teachers, related arts and special-learning teachers who work together to plan for a common group of students. The school schedule provides for teams of teachers at each grade level to have flexibility to block instructional time and plan together daily.

All students are involved in encore classes that include the fine and performing arts and physical education. In 1998 the school added a dance program that has become very popular. Professional dancers volunteer by providing assistance with choreography and by interacting directly with students. In addition to the traditional music programs of choir, band, and orchestra, students may choose to take guitar and learn to play acoustic and electric instruments. Every year art students enter and win school, community, and national competitions.

Students and teachers have access to many support services. Student services include crisis intervention, counseling, and preventive/evaluative diagnostic services. The daily homeroom helps all students develop satisfying and supportive peer and adult relationships. A full-time "learning strategist" helps teachers become comfortable with interdisciplinary curriculum and its development, teaming, and other commonly accepted components of the middle level concept. The position, created by the principal when the school opened in 1993, also helps teachers develop new and appropriate instructional strategies. In addition, the learning strategist plays a major leadership role in the school-based professional development program.

Faculty members sponsor 36 after-school activities in which students can develop new skills and explore areas of personal interest. All students participate in school-wide intramural programs during homeroom. Teachers and students also participate in school-sponsored and community-sponsored service projects and are recognized and rewarded for their efforts. In addition, students and faculty members participate in assemblies, dances, multicultural celebrations and activities, and student performances.

Curriculum Standards
The learning outcomes at Pioneer are based upon the standards established by the state and the school district. The school's curriculum, based upon these standards, is well defined and articulated by the school's mission statement—a statement representing the collaborative efforts of teachers, administrators, students, parents, and community members. Teachers demonstrate support of the standards through collaborative planning and by using interdisciplinary units that incorporate several standards into one integrated learning experience for students. Curriculum is aligned with state and district standards through the use of a backward-assessment model. Each department creates notebooks to ensure curricular consistency and student success.

A variety of assessment procedures is used to collect evidence that students are meeting standards. These include backward-assessment tests to check for student understanding of subject material, pre- and posttests to identify areas of need, standardized tests to measure achievement, and an eighth-grade writing test to measure writing proficiency. The results of these assessments, which are disseminated to teachers, parents, and the community, are studied carefully by the principal, teachers, and the parent and community advisory committees, and are used as the basis for program improvement and revision and school-based professional development.

Leadership and Relationships
The principal sets the climate for Pioneer. Her low-key, supportive, collaborative style has enabled her to build strong relationships with students, teachers, parents, and community members. The principal is highly

selective in hiring teachers, insisting that each teacher be knowledgeable about young adolescent learners and middle level practices. In addition, each faculty member is required to make a written commitment to the unique school plan, which reflects the school's philosophy of meeting the intellectual, social, emotional, and physical needs of young adolescents. With this kind of commitment from the teachers, the principal is able to give them a high level of support, collaboration, and acceptance of their ideas for school improvement. As a result of the principal's responsiveness, teachers feel supported, trusted, and appreciated. They feel free to make suggestions about curriculum and instruction and most often see their ideas become part of the school program. They are also significantly involved in the assessment of school practices, decisions for school improvement, and the planning and implementation of school-based professional development. This positive climate has led to the establishment of a strong learning organization that has facilitated programs and practices that are unique to Pioneer.

The principal has been equally open and collaborative with parents and community members. From the very beginning, parents and community members have been involved in the design and life of the school. Their ideas have been welcome, and often their suggestions are implemented. When the school's unique middle level programs were threatened by the year-round-school concept that was being put in place across the district to alleviate problems of overcrowding, the principal worked with parents and supported a successful parent initiative to allow the school to go to double sessions until the overcrowding issue was resolved. On numerous other occasions the principal has worked cooperatively with parents and community members to support the education of young adolescents and the betterment of the community.

Because of the visionary, knowledgeable, responsive, and collaborative leadership of its principal, Pioneer has been able to establish an effective learning community where students and adults can be successful and responsible learners. Pioneer is a successful middle level school because it takes the responsibility of educating young adolescents seriously in an environment that is responsive to students, teachers, parents, and community members.

Southside Intermediate School
Southside Intermediate School is an award-winning middle level school of grades 7–8. It is one of 3 intermediate schools in a district of 19 schools. The Southside community has a population of approxi-

mately 13,000 and is surrounded by several neighboring communities, creating an area population of 72,000 within a county population of nearly 250,000. Situated on the Gulf coast, the Southside community is an hour's drive south of one of the nation's major metropolitan cities and is near the confluence of one of the state's major rivers with the Gulf of Mexico. The community's economy is based primarily on the fishing and petrochemical industries.

The median age of the county's residents is 34. The ethnic distribution in the county is primarily Caucasian (66.2%). Other ethnic populations in the county are Hispanic American (22.8%), African American (8.5%), and Asian American (2%). The ethnic distribution at Southside does not mirror the ethnicity of the county. Of the 575 students at Southside, 37% are Caucasian, 50% are Hispanic American, and 13% are African American. Asian American and African American students make up less than 1% of the student population. Sixty-six percent of the students receive free or reduced-price lunch. The mobility rate of Southside students is 20.5%.

School Development
Southside originated as a 6–8 middle school in the 1980s. It was designated as a "low-performing" school in the 1991–1992 school year. A structural change was initiated in 1992, when the school moved from traditional 45-minute classes to a modified block schedule that included 90-minute classes. In 1995 another structural change moved the sixth-grade students to grade 5–6 centers, creating a 7–8 configuration for Southside.

The structural changes were insignificant compared to the personnel changes during the mid 1990s. In 1995, the current principal arrived and spent her first year "righting the ship." In the 1995–1996 school year, the school consciously established a focus on academic excellence and began to work toward the creation of an environment that was developmentally responsive to young adolescents. The new leader had to convince the faculty that Southside was a place where all students would be academically successful. Staff members who struggled with that concept were encouraged or required to leave. The teacher turnover rate during the principal's first two years was high as she worked to establish a culture of success for all students. Faculty members met regularly to discuss strategies for change, and as the students' state test scores improved, the positive momentum fueled steady increases in academic success. From 1995 to 2001, the school's state assessment scores moved steadily and incrementally from low performing to exemplary in all content areas and

for all social and ethnic subgroups of students in the school. In 1999 the school was designated by the National Forum to Accelerate Middle Grades Reform as one of four national Schools to Watch. In 2001 the school was recognized as a state Five Star School for its academic excellence. In 2002 Southside became a national Blue Ribbon School. The school leaders and faculty members have lived by their motto, The Place Where Great Things Happen, and their mission, Success for All.

School Facilities
In 1998 Southside moved from a two-story, 1940s structure to a new facility less than a mile from the original site. The new facility is a sprawling, one-story structure featuring the school's colors of red, black, and white. Colorful banners of motivational statements are present throughout the building. Many underscore the positive message of Best Students, Best Staff, Best School that is prevalent in the philosophy of the school's leaders and teachers.

The large cafetorium, with elevated ceiling fans, ceramic and tile flooring, and expanses of glass, is a pleasant location for students to eat and socialize. The site includes a main gymnasium, a practice gym, three computer labs, and the traditional array of classrooms for all content areas. The instructional wings of the school are organized by grade level and interdisciplinary teams, creating a "school-within-a-school."

The facility is wired for the Internet and instructional television. Each classroom has a multimedia teaching workstation with television projection capacity. Teachers often use PowerPoint presentations in lieu of overheads. Students can engage in hands-on learning experiences and share those through multimedia presentations. Two classrooms have computers with instructional software to enhance computer literacy. Another classroom is organized for reading acquisition, and online test taking enables teachers to instantly access and analyze student success. A multimedia classroom is used to produce newscasts and announcements that are broadcast schoolwide on a daily basis.

One of the most impressive "classrooms" is the faculty classroom. A regular classroom adjacent to the library/media center is used for faculty and committee meetings and professional development. The walls of the room are replete with oversized charts depicting past and present student achievement results, goals and mission statements, and the school's instructional change processes. On any given month, decorations hang from the ceiling and the walls representing recent faculty "study sessions." In addition to the faculty classroom, a small section of a teacher conference room has been equipped with shelves for sets of "common unit assessments" developed collaboratively by the staff to assess student progress on state standards and goals. At the end of each learning unit, each core-subject teacher collects copies from this room, administers and scores the assessment, and then works with other members of the team to design interventions to ensure that students will be successful. Although these two rooms are not classrooms for learning, their availability directly affects school culture, climate, and academic success.

School Programs

To promote small learning communities, Southside is organized into interdisciplinary teams. Each team is called a tribe and consists of six core-subject teachers (two language arts, two mathematics, one science, and one social studies) who work with approximately 150 students. Teachers of special education and electives are also attached to a tribe to complete the interdisciplinary team. The school day is organized into an alternating-day (A/B) block schedule. Tribe teachers share a common planning period on A days, whereas departments share a common planning period on B days. Each tribe and each department meets weekly. Agendas for the meetings are shared with the principal. The A/B block enables students to receive 90 minutes of *daily* instruction in math and language arts and 90 minutes of time on *alternating* days in science and social studies. Teachers are expected to provide active learning and direct instruction throughout the 90-minute block rather than allowing the second 45 minutes to become "homework time."

An additional "team-time hour" was designed at the end of each day to give teams the opportunity to address individual student needs. Based upon student assessments, the composition of the learning groups for the added instructional hour is changed regularly during interdisciplinary-team planning meetings. Instruction during the team-time program may also include small-group and individual tutoring by teachers. Peers and teacher aides also support students having difficulty understanding new concepts. Teachers also tutor students individually and in groups before and after school.

Limited English proficient (LEP) students at Southside receive extensive support for their development of English competency. Five and one-half percent of the students are classified as LEP and an additional 20% are classified as special education students. Inclusionary practices are the norm, with special education and LEP personnel working with students in the regular classrooms. Southside has a Spanish-speaking classroom staffed by a bilingual teacher and a bilingual aide who help new students develop fluency in English.

The instructional program at Southside is organized around an eight-step process. The first step is analysis and disaggregation of existing state assessment data, with particular attention to problem areas and objectives. The second step is the design of an instructional timeline based upon the data, with additional time and effort given to deficient areas. The third step is for each discipline to develop an instructional focus sheet to ensure attention to the targeted objectives. After instruction has been provided, the fourth step is to administer ongoing assessments and benchmarks to identify students who have achieved mastery with a subject and those who have not. The fifth step is to devote the team-time period as well as before-school and after-school tutorial time to the reteaching of nonmastered objectives. Step six is the provision of enrichment experiences to students who have mastered the objectives to extend their knowledge beyond the minimum objectives. Step seven is maintenance of knowledge developed and includes the use of ongoing activities and some reteaching to ensure that students retain the basic knowledge. The final step is monitoring the success of individual students by anaylzing student profiles. The principal, team leaders, and department chairs meet with teachers and students to review the assessment profiles. The principal visits classrooms regularly to observe and discuss the success of the eight-step process.

Curriculum Standards

The state essential knowledge and skills curriculum is the basis for the curricular standards at Southside. The design and delivery of instructional practices throughout the school are driven by the state objectives. The school leaders and staff members at Southside are dedicated to the success of all students, regardless of socioeconomic status or ethnicity. To realize their goal of equality of success, the data for these subgroups are analyzed and used as a basis for curriculum design, redesign, instruction, and reinstruction.

The success of Southside educators' strategies to achieve academic mastery for all students is evident in the multiyear composite profile of data for Southside. In 1995, 46% of their students passed the state assessment. In 1996 that percentage was 69%, rising the next year to 83%, then increasing to 96% in 2002. For African American students the numbers began at 28% in 1995 and rose to 93% in 2002; for Hispanic American students, 40%–97%; and for economically disadvantaged students, 38%–95%.

To achieve such an impressive record of success requires a constant focus on instruction associated with the state academic standards in language arts, math, science, and social studies. Double periods of instruction in language arts and math produced positive results for Southside, but such intense focus does have its limitations. With the amount of time devoted to the core courses, the opportunities for exploratory and elective offerings at Southside are limited. Each student receives double instructional time in language arts/reading and mathematics, and standard instructional time in science, social studies, physical education, and computers. Students select electives from foreign languages, industrial technology, chorus, and orchestra. Cocurricular offerings include honor societies, publications, service clubs, and varied student clubs. Interscholastic sports include basketball, football, tennis, and track. Volleyball is also provided for girls, and cheerleading is also a part of the sports program.

Leadership and Relationships

Even the most casual observer of life at Southside would make the following conclusions: The school culture at Southside is collaborative, focused, and committed to the academic and social development of young adolescents; the faculty members and administrators function as a family and genuinely care about one another and the students they serve; and the principal is passionate and dedicated to leading a school that ensures success for each student. The principal and the teachers at Southside have transformed the school from the doormat of the district to an award-winning school that meets the needs of all students, regardless of ethnicity or socioeconomic status. Southside has become what writers of school leadership and school improvement would describe as a "caring, collaborative learning organization."

At the heart of the culture and climate that transformed Southside into a learning organization is an aggressive, deeply committed principal with a vision for the school and students. She is a leader who will not accept failure on the issue of student success. Her first two years at Southside were replete with challenge, anxiety, and frustration as she worked to change the school's culture and climate. She had to establish a norm of academic excellence for all students and establish the belief that each child could be successful if given the right type of instruction and support. With an elementary teacher's understanding of learning, a desire to succeed, and keen intuition and basic knowledge about leadership, the principal steadily transformed the staff members, and thus the school, to produce established standards and expectations. She achieved this through genuineness, sensitivity, and caring for those who were committed to the

goals of success for all; an impatience toward those who did not share those goals; and a strength of personality best described as determined and charismatic. Southside faculty and staff members are meaningfully engaged in the process of improvement. The principal uses interdisciplinary teams, content teams, cadres, advisory councils, and campus improvement teams to analyze and design strategies for continuous improvement. The school has a process for instructional improvement that is understood and embraced by all staff members.

Southside has not rested on its laurels. In the 2000–2001 school year, the staff members adopted a slogan, Excellence and Beyond, to reinforce the necessity of maintaining the academic excellence established in the 1990s and define the challenges of how to better serve the comprehensive needs of their students. Southside is located in a high-poverty area and serves the needs of educationally and socially disadvantaged students. The staff members and leaders are committed to continuing their journey of academic excellence, developmental responsiveness, and social equity. As noted by the National Forum in 1999, this truly is a school to watch.

Summary

Each of the six site-visit schools is exemplary in the manner in which it serves its students and community. The profiles presented in this chapter provided the context for the six schools and specific information about the uniqueness of each school. The contextual settings are common to thousands of middle level schools across the country. Conscious efforts are in progress in these schools—rural setting to planned suburb, small poverty to high poverty, small enrollment to massive enrollment—to design and redesign programs that effectively address the needs of their students. The data from teachers, students, and parents affirm that these schools have been successful in that ongoing endeavor.

More-detailed information about the programs, practices, and leadership in the six schools are discussed in chapters 4 and 5. Combined with the understanding of the contexts of the six schools presented in this chapter, the detailed insight presented in the following chapters will provide the opportunity to better understand program design, change practices, and leadership strategies, each a crucial component of successful school reform.

Programs and Practices in Six Highly Successful Schools

Ensuring success for all students, the all-encompassing theme of *Turning Points 2000: Educating Adolescents in the 21st Century* (Jackson & Davis, 2000), has become a major challenge for middle level educators in the 21st century. Meeting this challenge calls for the careful examination of middle level programs and practices and their influence on student learning and success. Although there is evidence that the middle level concept, when highly implemented, leads to increased student achievement (Felner et al., 1997), there still is much left to be learned about *how* successful middle level schools implement the middle level concept and *what* programs and practices contribute to the creation of effective learning environments for young adolescents. To gain new insights on these effective learning environments and their implementation, programs and practices in six highly successful middle level schools were analyzed.

In the six middle level schools selected for site visits, quantitative and qualitative procedures were used to gather information on programs and practices. Quantitative data sources included the online surveys of principals, teachers, and students and the Instructional Practices Inventory (IPI; Painter, Lucas, Wooderson, & Valentine, 2000). Qualitative data were drawn from the previsit interviews with principals; the principal nomination survey (open-ended questions); structured interviews conducted on-site with principals, teachers, assistant principals, counselors, librarians, and parents; informal interviews and conversations with district superintendents, stu-

dents, teachers, and parents; and observations of classrooms and various school activities. These data formed the basis for the information presented in this chapter.

The Six Highly Successful Schools

School Enrollment and Class Size

The six schools selected for visits were representative of middle level schools in urban, suburban, and rural settings and varied in enrollment from 180 to 1,485 students (Table 4.1). Teacher-to-student ratios ranged from 1 teacher for every 11–15 students (Fourstar Middle School) to 1 teacher for every 36–40 students (Pioneer Middle School).

Middle Level Programs

For the most part, the principals of these six schools were very committed to the middle level concept, the success of which has been well documented in research and practice (Jackson & Davis, 2000). Five of the six principals believed that interdisciplinary teaming, exploratory courses, and adviser–advisee programs were very important (Table 4.2). There was also strong support for cocurricular programs that were scheduled during the regular school day, with all but one principal rating them as important or very important. Intramural programs were also considered very important by five of the six principals.

Table 4.1 School Enrollment and Average Class Size

Criteria	Einstein Middle Academy	Fourstar Middle School	Kent Middle School	Mark Twain Middle School	Pioneer Middle School	Southside Intermediate School
School enrollment	550	309	1,046	180	1,485	589
Class size (range)	26–30	11–15	26–30	21–25	36–40	21–25

Table 4.2 Middle Level Programs and Practices: Degree of Importance

Program	Einstein Middle Academy	Fourstar Middle School	Kent Middle School	Mark Twain Middle School[a]	Pioneer Middle School	Southside Intermediate School
Interdisciplinary teaming	Very important	Very important	Very important	Important	Very important	Very important
Exploratory courses	Very important	Very important	Very important	Very important	Very important	Important
Advisor–advisee program	Very important	Very important	Very important	Very important	Very important	Little or no importance
Cocurricular programs[b]	Important	Very important	Very important	Very important	Little or no importance[c]	Important
Intramural activities	Very important	Very important	Very important	Very important	Very important	Little or no importance

aThe enrollment at Mark Twain Middle School averaged 60 students per grade.
bCocurricular program is separate from regular graded courses but occurs during the regular school day.
cCocurricular program occurs after school.

In each of the five schools in which the principal rated interdisciplinary teaming, exploratory courses, and intramural activities as very important, the programs were fully implemented (Table 4.3). However, although adviser–advisee programs were rated as very important by five principals, they were fully implemented in only two of those schools, partially implemented in one school, and not implemented at all in the other two schools. (The sixth principal rated those programs as having little or no importance, and the program was not implemented in her school.) In the three schools where principals rated cocurricular programs as very important, the programs were fully implemented in two schools and partially implemented in a third. (Note that at Pioneer, cocurricular activities were strongly supported by the principal but not during the regularly scheduled day, and an extensive activities program existed after school.)

Program Coherence

Although all six of the principals of these exemplary schools supported the middle level concept and had implemented many of the components, they also looked to other complementary programs to bring instructional and curricular coherence to their schools. Newmann, Smith, Allensworth, and Bryk (2002) suggested that strong program coherence will occur when three conditions exist in a school: a common instructional framework that guides curriculum, instruction, assessment, and learning; a working environment that supports the implementation of the school's instructional framework; and allocation of resources such as materials, time, and staff assignments that advance the school's instructional framework.

In five of the schools, specific frameworks provided program coherence. Pioneer found coherence in Creating Independence through Student-Owned Strategies (CRISS), a comprehensive program of specific instructional and learning strategies, and Accelerated Reader. Kent Middle School adopted the International Baccalaureate Middle Years Programme, and Mark Twain Middle School found coherence in Project ASSIST (Achieving Success through School Improvement Site Teams), a comprehensive middle level reform program developed by the Middle Level Leadership Center. Southside Intermediate School, with its intensive focus on student learning, found support and coherence as part of the Schools to Watch program of the National Forum to Accelerate Middle Grades Reform and the Deming model (Walton, 1986) for leadership, management, and decision making. Fourstar's emphasis on differentiated instruction provided its program coherence.

Einstein Middle Academy found coherence in more subtle ways. With a strong drive for academic excellence and high levels of student achievement, Einstein's teachers built coherence around the school district's core of knowledge and the principal's vision of excellence for the school.

Table 4.3 Middle Level Programs and Practices: Degree of Implementation

Program	Einstein Middle Academy	Fourstar Middle School	Kent Middle School	Mark Twain Middle School[a]	Pioneer Middle School	Southside Intermediate School
Interdisciplinary teaming	Full implementation	Full implementation	Full implementation	No implementation	Full implementation	Full implementation
Exploratory courses	Full implementation	Full implementation	Full implementation	Full implementation	Full implementation	Partial implementation
Advisor-advisee program	Full implementation	Partial implementation	No implementation	No implementation	Full implementation	No implementation
Cocurricular programs[b]	No implementation	Full implementation	Full implementation	Partial implementation	No implementation[c]	No implementation
Intramural activities	Full implementation	Full implementation	Full implementation	Full implementation	Full implementation	No implementation

[a] The enrollment at Mark Twain Middle School averaged 60 students per grade.
[b] Cocurricular program is separate from regular graded courses but occurs during the regular school day.
[c] Cocurricular program occurs after school.

Each school found program coherence in a different way, but there was one constant: Each principal had a strong vision about how young adolescent learners could be successful in their schools. This focused vision, which was shared and adopted by teachers, students, parents, and community members, provided the direction and coherence for the schools.

Student Achievement

The results of emphasis on student learning in supportive and coherent frameworks of curriculum, instruction, assessment, and learning were readily apparent in these six schools. With student scores of 97% in reading, 98% in math, and 96% in writing, Southside received exemplary status for its performance on the state's standardized tests. Einstein reported that its students performed at the top of the schools in its county. Pioneer's students scored in the top 3% of the schools in its district, and Fourstar's students performed above state standards. At Kent student scores continued to show improvement, and Twain was recognized as one of the top-performing schools in its state on the state assessment.

Programs and Practices

The data gathered on the programs and practices in these six schools were organized around categories of curriculum, instruction, staff, relationships, parents and community, and safe and healthy environment. The categories serve as the framework for presenting and discussing the programs and practices in these six outstanding middle level schools.

Curriculum

Curriculum Design

Principals at Fourstar, Kent, and Twain, when asked to identify the curriculum designs used in their schools, identified discipline-centered as the most frequently used design (Table 4.4). Topic-centered design was the most frequently used design at Einstein, Pioneer, and Southside. These same three schools also had the highest percentages of theme-centered design in use in their schools. The principals at Fourstar and Southside also indicated that student-centered design was used in their schools about 20% of the time.

In implementing these various designs, principals and teachers identified the following issues that guided curriculum in their schools: high expectations for all students, education of the whole child, curriculum alignment and assessment, and curricular breadth.

High Expectations for All Students
All six schools were characterized by cultures of high expectations for all students, expectations that typically were reflective of district and state standards and most often measured by standardized tests and/or state criterion-referenced tests. This fact was corroborated by the principal at Southside, who stated, "The num-

Table 4.4 Curriculum Design

Design	Einstein Middle Academy	Fourstar Middle School	Kent Middle School	Mark Twain Middle School	Pioneer Middle School	Southside Intermediate School
Discipline-centered (most instruction in departmentalized settings)	25	40	60	80	5	5
Topic-centered (content linked between disciplines, but instruction is mostly departmentalized)	50	30	40	20	50	50
Theme-centered (interdisciplinary themes; instruction is truly interdisciplinary)	20	20	0	0	45	25
Student-centered (teachers and students identify themes/units; instruction almost entirely in interdisciplinary teams)	5	20	0	0	0	20

ber one piece of data I use is test scores, specifically the state assessment." In other schools, principals also expressed their visions of high expectations—rigorous curriculum for all and standardized-test results—as verification that expectations were being met or that consistent progress was being made in achieving expectations. An example of the emphasis on academics at these schools was the academic pep rallies held at Southside. These pep rallies recognized honor roll students, most spirited students, and most improved (academically) students from each team.

Principals in these six schools appeared to have been very successful in sharing their visions of high expectations with their teachers. Almost all the teachers interviewed talked about their commitment to high expectations. Typical comments from teachers included:

The high expectations make this school different.

The mission of this school is to guide students to achieve at a high level, believing that all kids can achieve at a higher level, and expecting that of all of them.

We have a common goal: high expectations.

We have an expectation that kids will meet standards.

Principals also expressed a strong commitment to ensuring the success of all students by achieving high expectations. When talking about personal commitment to success for all students, the principal of Pioneer reflected her concerns regarding high expectations and student success:

I've been here for nine years and our population is changing a little bit, and people need to know this information. We still need to have high expectations for our children even if the population is changing—the ethnicity is changing. We still expect this kind of rigor. We may change how we deliver, but we aren't going to change our expectations.

Other principals expressed similar concerns about high expectations and ensuring success for all students, which was often achieved by providing extra resources for tutoring programs, summer programs, and special classes that addressed specific learning needs. At Southside and Twain, for example, students not achieving at acceptable levels were required to participate in tutoring programs.

Teachers in these schools were equally committed to all students being successful. "At our school," said one teacher, "if you don't believe that all students have the capacity to learn, you will pretty much be pulling against the wagon." Another teacher stated, "We think every child can succeed because they are given what they need." Other teachers talked about "wanting students to be successful," "meeting kids where they are," and "helping each student to do his or her best." A teacher at Southside captured the commitment of the teachers in the six schools:

> Our faculty believes all students can learn given enough time and resources. I think what we mean by this is "we take no excuses." We don't try to excuse failure because he is from that family or his family uses or he uses drugs. We just don't accept that as a reasonable excuse. We have them for the eight hours and we utilize it, and we do what we can. We stay longer if they need longer. Right now we stay three days a week until 5:00 [to work with kids].

It is clear from the data that there was a congruence of purpose among principals and teachers in these schools. They were committed to high academic expectations for all students, believed that all students could be successful, and were committed to providing the time and resources to ensure student success.

Education of the Whole Child

With the strong commitment to high expectations and student success also came a commitment to educating "the whole child." The teachers and administrators in these schools recognized that they must address the developmental needs of young adolescents. Most acknowledged that their vision was more than just meeting state requirements. Southside's principal restated this belief when he said, "We want kids not to just master a test, but we want them to be proficient in life skills. Proficient, with rigorous curriculum."

At Fourstar the principal stated, "We are not just creating academic machines, we are talking about needs of the whole child at this age and also the unique needs." His beliefs were echoed by teachers at Fourstar who described their mission as a faculty "to foster development of the whole child—physical, emotional, learning."

Other schools were equally committed to educating the whole child. Teachers at Pioneer described the importance of a well-rounded approach and preparation for life—teaching academics, skills for lifelong learners, and good citizenship—to develop young adolescents who feel they have a civic responsibility to the community and country. To do this, teachers "take and apply middle level concepts to students, providing them with a variety of experiences," and "incorporate enough programs and strategies to make kids feel successful." Twain's teachers talked about creating "productive" adults and citizens and "self-directed learners," and developing "social skills." At Southside the principal and teachers described their mission for "all students to succeed academically, socially, and culturally." "Our

vision is that we want all of our students to succeed in the real world beyond our schools." And at Einstein teachers reported that their mission "is for our kids to succeed and for us to have an impact on their future."

At each school there appeared to be a basic understanding of young adolescent development and the middle level concept. In the application of middle level concepts that addressed the issues of educating the whole child, principals and teachers demonstrated their commitment to curricular structures that fostered responsive approaches focused on intellectual, physical, emotional, and social development (Lipsitz, 1984; NASSP Council on Middle Level Education, 1985; National Middle School Association, 1995).

Curriculum Alignment and Assessment

Middle level educators, similar to their colleagues in elementary and high schools, have been struggling with the issues of improved student achievement and the push for accountability. At all six schools, educators dealt with this challenge by using backward mapping (Jackson & Davis, 2000) and various other approaches to align curriculum with school, district, and state standards.

At Pioneer backward-assessment notebooks had been developed for nearly every course in the school, and at Twain backward mapping was used to align the school's curriculum with state standards. Twain also used vertical teams across the district's 6–12 programs to design curriculum. Teachers and administrators at Kent participated in a districtwide effort to backward map and align the curriculum with state standards and to develop the district's own K–12 standards. Teacher teams at Fourstar used mapping to examine the use of thematic teaching. Subject-area teachers at Einstein met regularly to make sure the curriculum was aligned. Southside teachers and administrators made a concerted effort over the past several years to align their curriculum with state assessment measures, for example, by designing learning units to fit grade-level objectives and developing "state-like" unit exams for teachers to use to assess student learning. From these common unit assessments, teachers identified specific students for enrichment and remediation.

The curriculum alignment process provided the basis for assessment in these schools. Using established frameworks, teachers and administrators were able to focus their assessment procedures on student progress and instruction in areas that directly related to school, district, and state standards. Out of necessity, standardized and state criterion-referenced tests were widely used to measure progress. Information from other, often more informal, assessment procedures, however, augmented formal testing data.

Although educators often view standardized and formal testing with a negative opinion, these six principals believed testing could offer valuable insight about student success and program effectiveness. The principal at Pioneer voiced a typical position about standardized testing:

> The fact that there is accountability with testing has always been there. It is nothing new to us. We have always had a really positive approach to testing. From the beginning when we started the school we have approached standardized testing in a positive way. We have assemblies for the kids. We give them a lucky penny and they get their lucky pencil. It is very positive because standardized tests will not go away. I want my children to take different tests all year long, not just when it is standardized test taking time. That has been our approach forever.

At Pioneer the assistant principal disaggregated the data from tests and other sources and distributes the data to teams who use the information to make decisions for program improvement.

Even prior to the No Child Left Behind Act mandates, five of the six principals reported using disaggregated data from standardized test scores and found that the data served a variety of uses. In most of the schools, data were disaggregated by the state or school districts. In addition, at Pioneer, Kent, Southside, and Twain, teachers and leaders disaggregated standardized test data. Twain's principal distributed disaggregated data to teachers on a professional development day, and they examined the data to identify areas of improvement. At Southside and Einstein, disaggregated data were used to identify weaknesses and to focus the entire faculty's efforts on correcting those weaknesses. Disaggregated data at Kent were used to identify achievement gaps among the various ethnic groups enrolled in the school.

In addition to disaggregated data from state assessment measures, these schools gathered and used data from a variety of sources, including standardized and criterion-referenced tests; measurable learning objectives with assessments; portfolios; surveys of students, teachers, and parents; discussions and brainstorming sessions with students, teachers, and parents; comprehensive observations of teachers and students; classroom walk-through observations; attendance rates; and student discipline rates. In some cases data were communicated in formal ways through reports, meetings, and workshops with the expectation that teachers and teams would develop recommendations for school, curricular, or instructional improvement. In other cases, principals would communicate information in informal ways with the expectation that teachers and teams would take the initiative to make appropriate decisions on the basis of the data.

Curriculum Breadth

Although teachers and administrators in these six exemplary schools appeared to be addressing the issues of accountability and high-stakes testing with success, they were concerned about the breadth of curriculum in their schools. The principal of Southside said:

> We have expended so much energy to improve basic skills. We now can begin to focus on expanding our curriculum. We have to move beyond our existing curriculum because children of poverty will not get the exposure if we don't provide it. At the same time we are scared to death what expansion will do to our achievement in basic skills. We are moving in the right direction. We keep incorporating new things like Shop and Spanish II into our curriculum. We are open to change and we are making change.

Teachers at Southside echoed their principal when they said:

> The vision is exemplary and beyond. We have been successful on the basic skills and now we need to focus on the University Scholastic League competition. We are ready to focus on academic competition and challenges beyond the basic skills exams.
>
> We need to incorporate the fine arts and go beyond what we are already doing.
>
> Our vision is "beyond exemplary." We want to move into other areas of success.
>
> Evidence of "beyond exemplary" will be when more and more students excel in music competitions, and other competitions, etc., that go beyond basic skills.

Keeping the focus on academics while still being developmentally responsive, which is also an aspect of curriculum breadth, was the concern of one teacher at Fourstar: "We really do stress academics because I think some middle schools don't. But we also put a premium on socialization, which should be our number one goal—especially for 7th and 8th graders."

Teachers and principals in other schools also talked about having a curriculum "that would prepare students academically, with emphasis placed on life skills and communication skills" and one "that is child-centered [and] student-oriented and considers what is best for each student."

The schools used numerous approaches to add breadth to their curriculum. The most prominent approach was curriculum integration. As a result of curriculum alignment and mapping activities, teachers at Fourstar and Southside found ways to make connections across the curriculum. Teachers reinforced content in one another's classes and helped students see natural connections and the larger picture. Interdisciplinary curriculum and content integration were also found at Pioneer and Kent. At Einstein, where integrated curriculum was encouraged but not forced, a teacher urged caution:

> I was at another school where teachers did themes because they were forced to. It was not a natural fit . . . they forced it to say they had a thematic unit. Here, thematic units are used if they can advance learning.

Curriculum breadth was also addressed by reading and writing programs across the curriculum. At Southside common elements in reading and writing were identified and emphasized across all subject areas. Accelerated Reader provided a framework for reading improvement throughout Pioneer. Kent teachers placed a heavy emphasis on reading across the curriculum, as did those at Twain, where reading was added to the sixth-grade exploratory wheel. Writing across the curriculum was the focus of workshops at Fourstar, and a basic English guide for all students and teachers was developed at Einstein to ensure that all teachers were addressing the same skills. Clearly, literacy was an important component of the programs at each of the six schools.

Several schools also increased the breadth of their curriculum through the use of adviser–advisee programs where emphasis was placed on organizational skills, character education, and community values. Service learning, exploratory courses that often included technology, cocurricular activities, and intramural and interscholastic sports were other ways in which these schools broadened the curricular experiences of their students.

Instruction

Intrinsically, high expectations and a focus on meeting standards do not pose a threat to developmentally responsive middle level programs. It is how those expectations and standards are interpreted and what procedures are put in place to meet them that determine their appropriateness in educating young adolescents (Clark & Clark, 2003c). Standards, contends Mizell (2002), are not the enemy of developmentally appropriate middle level school programs. Nor are they "an excuse for narrowing a teacher's instruction to pre-

pare students to pass a high-stakes test" (Mizell, 2002, pp. 77–78).

Curriculum identifies, organizes, and structures the content expectations that frame school goals and district and state standards, but it is instruction that provides the vehicle for introducing content and engaging young adolescents in the learning process. Drawing from survey and interview data, the purpose of this section is to describe the commitment of principals and teachers to appropriate instructional strategies, the types of instruction found in these schools, the origin and nature of instructional improvement efforts, and the relationship of instruction and assessment.

Commitment to Appropriate Instructional Strategies

Principals and teachers in the six schools were committed to providing instruction that was appropriate for young adolescent learners. This commitment was evident in their interviews and in the data collected from the surveys. The principal at Einstein talked about the importance of making a classroom "an inviting place, a creative place, a place for kids to do projects, where they can solve problems, where they are interested in the curriculum." Southside's principal stated:

> We spent a lot of time discussing what are effective teaching practices; what I like to see. Noise is okay, activities that involve movement are great. We dialogue about what's good teaching at the middle level. What is developmentally responsive to young adolescents? We feel like this is an age group that is very unique and we are constantly trying to grow professionally on how to meet the needs of these students.

Teachers also had a strong commitment to appropriate instruction. At Twain, for example, teachers talked about their active involvement in developing and implementing new strategies. They reported how they "place emphasis on individual needs," "coordinate learning within the classroom," "try new ideas—innovate—trial and error," and were continually "looking at best practice." Teachers at Pioneer gave evidence of their commitment to appropriate instructional approaches when they reported using "cutting-edge strategies," having "the flexibility to try new things," and feeling "the responsibility to teach in ways that children learn." Teachers from the six schools also talked about appropriate instruction with statements such as "you teach on your feet, not on your seat," "you must be having fun in learning," and "you must approach learning differently for various students."

Table 4.5 Planning Strategies

	Einstein Middle Academy	Fourstar Middle School	Kent Middle School	Mark Twain Middle School	Pioneer Middle School	Southside Intermediate School
Percentage of time teachers consciously use planning strategies that reflect the primacy of student needs (average of all responses)	89%	87%	91%	79%	94%	90%

Responses to the teacher survey gave additional evidence of the importance teachers placed on using appropriate instructional practices. On the Planning Strategies Scale of the teacher survey, teachers were asked to indicate the frequency with which they "consciously utilize planning strategies that reflect the primacy of students needs." Teachers in these six schools indicated that most of the time (79%–94%) the primacy of student needs guided their instructional planning (Table 4.5).

Types of Instruction

Principals and teachers were enthusiastic about the variety of instructional approaches in use in their schools. At Twain the principal talked about appropriate instructional programs that supported student learning. He also talked about the importance of focusing on active student engagement in the classroom. Teachers at Twain also stressed the importance of appropriate instruction. During the interviews they mentioned "emphasis on individual needs," "trying new ideas," "using a variety of teaching styles," "student engagement," "looking at best practice," "getting students active in something," "peer tutoring," and the "implementation of fourth-hour study hall/advisory for additional instructional help."

Southside's principal reported that teachers use appropriate instructional strategies to engage students. This was confirmed by one of the teachers who stated, "Our staff will do just about anything to get the students' attention . . . we dress up, we sing and dance . . . we do anything we can to make them want to be here." At Pioneer the principal and teachers were very clear about how they engaged students in learning. They had received training in and embraced the 18 CRISS strategies—an approach that engages teachers and students in a variety of teaching and learning strategies. Because of this commitment, teachers at Pioneer believed that they were on the cutting edge.

Typical comments from them included "no problem with incorporating new ideas and strategies," "we use a variety of different strategies," "lots of options to make it interesting," and "opportunities to be involved in many different activities." These teachers also reported how student learning and instructional strategies were an important part of their planning. "We talk about strategies to help the kids," and "at team meetings we discuss students behaviorally/academically and share what works."

Differentiated instruction provided the focus for planning and instruction at Fourstar. Teachers talked about how they helped students be successful and that much of their instruction occurs in large blocks of time. At Kent integrated instruction was used whenever possible, and the emphasis on appropriate instruction brought coherence by using the multiple, integrated approaches found in the International Baccalaureate Middle Years Programme. Similar to those at Fourstar and Pioneer, teachers at Kent centered their conversations about students on ways in which multiple instructional strategies could help them learn.

In addition to interviewing principals and teachers about their instructional practices, study team members used the IPI, an instrument developed by the Middle Level Leadership Center at the University of Missouri, to systematically assess the nature of classroom instruction in core and noncore classrooms (Figure 4.1)

The IPI has been used in hundreds of schools across the country, but norms have not been established on the basis of data from a random sample of schools. However, the center does provide a range of percentages that is *currently typical* of middle level schools that have used the inventory (Table 4.6).

Teacher-led instruction was the most frequently used strategy in five of the six schools, a finding that corresponds to typical middle level schools. However, with

Figure 4.1 Instructional Practices Inventory

The Instructional Practices Inventory (IPI) is a process and rubric for observing and categorizing the nature of instruction across an entire school. This rubric is used to make repetitive observations of all classrooms over a designated period of time. Data are then used to develop a profile of instruction that informs the school improvement discussions for all faculty members. For specific information about the use of the IPI, see www.MLLC.org.

Student-Engaged Instruction	Student Active Engaged Learning	Active mental engagement such as authentic project work, cooperative learning, hands-on learning, demonstrations, active research. Higher order thinking evident.
	Student Learning Conversations	Active conversation among students with most or all engaged. Teacher initiated but not directed. Higher order thinking evident
Teacher-Directed Instruction	Teacher-Led Instruction	Teacher-led learning experiences such as lecture, question and answer, teacher giving directions, video instruction with teacher interaction. Discussion may occur, but instruction and ideas come primarily from teacher.
	Student Work With Teacher Engaged	Students working on worksheets, book work, tests, video with teacher viewing the video with the students, etc. Teacher assistance or support evident.
Disengagement	Student Work With Teacher Engaged	Students working on worksheets, book work, tests, viewing of video, etc. Teacher assistance or support not evident.
	Complete Disengagement	Neither teacher nor students engaged in learning or teaching, such as watching video or doing activities not directly related to the curriculum.

Note. From Painter and Valentine, 1996, 2002. Reprinted with permission of the author.

the exception of two schools, teachers in these schools tended to use more student active, engaged learning teaching strategies than did typical middle level schools. The active, engaged learning data from Twain were particularly impressive. The staff members at Twain had been collecting and studying their IPI data for two years prior to this study. Their higher IPI scores were probably related to their school goals to use higher-order learning on the basis of findings from their IPI data prior to the study and the related staff development through Project ASSIST, the school's comprehensive school reform initiative. Note also that, with one exception, there was less use of student seatwork while the teacher is disengaged and not as much total disengagement than is typically found in most middle level

schools. In addition, when the data from the six schools were compared with shadow study data from prior studies of middle level schools (Clark & Clark, 1998; Lounsbury & Clark, 1990), these schools showed much less student disengagement.

Origin and Nature of Instructional Improvement Efforts

The strong commitment to providing appropriate instruction that engages young adolescents in learning was demonstrated by the continuing efforts to improve classroom instruction. In all six schools there was strong instructional leadership and the expectation that teachers would use appropriate strategies, and in many instances the instructional improvement

Table 4.6 Types of Instruction in All Classes From the Instructional Practices Inventory*

Type	Typical Range	Einstein Middle Academy	Fourstar Middle School	Kent Middle School	Mark Twain Middle School	Pioneer Middle School	Southside Intermediate School
Student active engaged learning	15–20	27	17	36	55	24	17
Student learning conversations	3–5	4	3	5	5	2	1
Teacher-led instruction	35–45	42	43	45	29	48	36
Student seatwork with teacher engaged	20–30	19	30	13	10	15	17
Student seatwork with teacher not engaged	10–20	8	6	1	1	7	28
Complete disengagement	5–10	0	1	0	0	4	1

Classroom Instructional Practices Inventory developed by the Middle Level Leadership Center–University of Missouri, Columbia. For detailed descriptions of each category, see www.mllc.org and select the MLLC Instruments section of the home page.

effort was generated by committees, teams, and individual teachers. At Pioneer, for example, the principal reported that a learning improvement committee, focused on the changing needs of students, and teachers talked about their continuing emphasis on learning and instruction. Teachers also talked about their team and department planning meetings where discussion of "strategies to help kids" and the integration and use of the CRISS strategies in their classrooms was commonplace.

Teachers at Kent also reported that their teams often focused on instructional improvement. During the teams' common planning time, teachers:

- Collaborated to produce lessons and curriculum
- Talked about how to improve different strategies
- Shared knowledge about best middle level practices
- Focused on ways to help students, including using multiple instructional strategies of the International Baccalaureate Middle Years Programme
- Examined how to accommodate individual learning differences for each student.

Instructional improvement at Twain, reported the principal, was partially driven by the work of district content-area teams that focused on action plans leading to changes in classroom instruction. This district-led effort featured an emphasis on instructional strategies during summer workshops and included follow-up sessions during the school year. Teachers suggested that the principal's strong instructional leadership provided substantial support for instructional improvement and created a positive learning environment.

The culture at Southside expected and supported instructional improvement. The principal talked of "creating a culture of learning." She stated, "We are now a community of learning, we are learners, we became learners." The success of this culture was verified when teachers talked about their personal efforts to improve instruction: One teacher said:

> To improve my instruction, at the end of the day I will try to write down what I did with the lesson . . . were the kids bored, did they grasp it? I try to at least write down those thoughts and then go home and think about how to make the lesson better.

A first-year teacher remarked, "If I am having a problem, I will ask another teacher to come in and observe me and give me some ideas."

With their focus on differentiated instruction, the principal and teachers at Fourstar reported that ideas gathered at conferences and workshops often formed the basis for instructional improvement. The teachers at Fourstar described their climate as supportive of instructional change and improvement.

Instruction and Assessment

In addition to using data for decision making on curriculum and student achievement, principals and teachers at several of the schools talked specifically about how they used assessment to improve instruction. For example, the principal at Kent described efforts to monitor instruction: "I ask each teacher to give me in writing activities tied to rubrics; I want to see one of your (teacher) tests; I want to see Middle Years Programme activities."

Monitoring and assessing instruction were also strongly supported by the principal at Southside:

> You teach a skill, you check for understanding. Right? My check for understanding is called an assessment. An assessment is maybe just a worksheet with maybe five questions on that particular skill. If they get four out of five they have mastered it. I will be looking at your assessment data every time you teach a skill.

Carrying out their principal's desire for assessment data, Southside's core teachers administered common assessments at the completion of a unit and studied the results. They identified students who had not mastered the content and retaught the content using different instructional approaches.

Frequent assessment was also a part of monitoring instruction at Pioneer, where the principal promoted positive approaches to testing and regularly provided feedback to teams and to teachers. The principal also sought to use data to determine the effectiveness of current instructional approaches as the school population changes. The principal asked, "What do we need to change, if anything, to meet the needs of our changing population—whether it is teaching strategies, techniques, or structuring their learning?"

The principal at Twain talked about the school's focused effort to improve instruction through the Project ASSIST program and the use of the IPI. He also described informal use of data in monthly focus-group sessions where teachers talked about what has worked and what has not worked. In addition to these monthly assessments of instruction, "Teachers have measurable learning objectives in which they have an assessment for each objective, on whether a student masters an objective or not." These data were

given to teachers and often served as an impetus for instructional improvement.

Teachers also talked about their efforts to use assessment and feedback to guide their decision making about classroom instruction:

> We know we are doing a good job because students tell us when they come back to visit with us. One of the high school teachers also has students write letters to former teachers. We get a lot of feedback from those letters.
>
> After we get the state test results the principal expects us to follow up.
>
> Teachers are looking at data and best practice.
>
> Research backs up what you do; research and data-driven decision making; action research.
>
> Teachers and counselors identify and coordinate what students need.

Whatever the source—scores from standardized or state tests, common unit assessments, results of informal classroom appraisals, feedback from monitoring and observing in classrooms, teacher information exchanged at team planning meetings, or communication with current and former students—teachers were committed to the use of assessment to enhance instruction to improve the learning of the students in their schools. They made specific decisions about instruction for individuals and groups on the basis of the assessment results.

Staff

As a result of their focused leadership to develop schools that are responsive to the needs of young adolescents, principals have created cultures in their schools that feature common values, collaboration, shared leadership, and communities of learning. In these schools, the professional staff members—administrators, teachers, counselors, librarians, resource teachers—all appeared to work in cultures that positively influenced the ability of the schools to be effective in developing successful young adolescent learners. Typical of these cultures, as reported by principals, was the following statement by Pioneer's principal:

> I think it is the culture of the school that we do whatever it takes and they [teachers] really do embrace new ideas. They are eager to share and do whatever it takes to make this a better learning environment for the kids and make themselves better teachers.

As the study team observed and interviewed various staff members, three factors emerged that characterized the culture and staff at these six outstanding middle level schools: a consensus of values, a commitment to collaboration and shared leadership, and continuing desire for individual and collective learning.

A Consensus of Values

Principals and teachers in these schools shared a core of common values and were unified in their purpose. On the Unity of Purpose section of the teacher survey, teachers across the six schools confirmed that teachers work toward a common goal at their school (Table 4.7).

This unity of purpose was also demonstrated in the teacher interview data. Teachers consistently reported a collective belief that all students could learn and be successful. At Einstein that belief was confirmed by the following teacher statements:

> Everybody here believes that all kids can learn and we have high expectations for our students.

> Faculty collectively believe that all students can learn.

Teachers at Kent also talked about their commitment to the success of all students and their "singleness of purpose" in achieving that goal. That singleness of purpose was also shared by teachers at Pioneer who report-ed that "we share the same philosophy—we are here for the kids." Teacher interviews were filled with such phrases as "students first," we "value students," we "help students do their best," "making sure kids learn," and "student success." Twain teachers also expressed their commitment to student success. They talked about "all students being important," and their belief that "kids come first" and that "all students can learn." Teachers at each of the schools expressed a strong commitment to the learning success of all students.

This collective commitment to success for all students (as reported in the curriculum section) was also rooted in the belief of high expectations. Teachers talked about the importance of "high expectations," "student achievement," and "academic skills to achieve at the next level." In the context of high expectations, they also spoke about their commitment to the "development of the whole child," "helping kids develop comfort in middle school," and "a positive learning environment." Within the context of high expectations there was also a commitment to "care about kids," and a concern for "bringing the grades up for students who are struggling." One teacher stated, "The willingness of teachers to help students sets us apart—that is why we are here."

Table 4.7 Teachers' Perceptions of Other Teachers and School Leaders

Type	Einstein Middle Academy	Fourstar Middle School	Kent Middle School	Mark Twain Middle School	Pioneer Middle School	Southside Intermediate School
Teachers work toward common mission for the school (unity of purpose)	4.87	4.56	4.44	4.80	4.69	4.54
Teachers work together effectively (collegial support)	4.89	4.56	4.39	4.90	4.51	4.53
School leaders establish and maintain collaborative relationships with school staff (collaborative leadership)	4.82	4.63	4.08	4.78	4.53	4.64
Teachers engage in constructive dialogue that furthers the educational vision of the school (teacher collaboration)	4.36	4.00	4.03	3.77	4.27	4.38

Note. 1 = strongly disagree; 5 = strongly agree.

There was also evidence that the teachers in these schools valued collegiality, and data from the teacher survey showed that teachers perceived high levels of beneficial collegial support at their school (Table 4.7).

During the interviews, teachers talked about the respect they had for one another, and several teachers reported the joy of working with highly qualified colleagues who were "committed to working with middle level kids." They also talked about their colleagues as being dedicated, hard working, and willing to help one another. In addition, they reported the importance of friendship, with one teacher stating, "We value friendship and camaraderie and the family of our school." Another said, "We are family, just one big happy family." Teachers also mentioned that teamwork, "working with good teachers toward a common goal," and "a real commitment of teachers working together," were important to them.

Within these schools the researchers found collegial and family-like environments where trust, respect, and collegiality supported and facilitated a culture that was highly focused on student success, high expectations, and student and adult well-being.

A Commitment to Collaboration and Shared Leadership

Studies have indicated that schools organized around democratic and collaborative cultures produce students with higher achievement and better levels of skills and understanding than do traditionally organized schools (Darling-Hammond, 1997). In addition, Fullan (1998) reported:

> Student achievement increases substantially in schools with collaborative work cultures that foster a professional learning community among teachers and others, focus continuously on improving instructional practice in light of student performance data, and link to standards and staff development support. (p. 8)

Collaboration flourished among the collegial culture of these schools. On the teacher survey and in interviews, teachers indicated that their schools were highly collaborative. The six principals viewed themselves as being collaborative. For example, the principal at Einstein said, "I believe that I have built a collaborative culture and one of trust that if I had to make a decision without their input, they [teachers] would be fine with it, and if they were not, then they would come to me and talk about it." Teachers also viewed their principals as being supportive of collaboration. In fact, on the Collaborative Leadership section of the teacher survey, teachers strongly agreed that their principals had established and maintained collaborative relationships (Table 4.7).

Strong teacher support for collaboration was found at all six schools, where teachers most often collaborated in teams, department meetings, and advisory groups. Teachers reported collaborating with their principal in making important decisions about their school, including class schedules, curriculum issues, school rules, dress codes and uniforms, year-round school versus double sessions, cocurricular activities, and professional development.

Teachers indicated their strong support for collaboration on the teacher survey and in the on-site interviews. In most cases teachers felt strongly that the collaboration in their schools supported the educational vision of the school (Table 4.7).

At Pioneer every teacher interviewed believed that the school had a very collaborative culture, and many teachers attributed that culture to the principal. Typical comments included "we are constantly interacting and sharing," "teams collaborate, departments collaborate—share lesson plans and bounce ideas," and "we have team meetings daily, department meetings monthly, and inservice across grade levels." One teacher said, "We hope the kids see collaboration in us and learn from that." Another teacher stated, "You don't belong in this school if you cannot collaborate and work with other people." Teachers at Pioneer also emphasized the importance of teaming. For them, "teaming was important in developing and sustaining collaborative relationships."

Teachers at other schools were equally supportive of the collaborative culture. "Our faculty has a collaborative culture," stated one Southside teacher. Another Southside teacher reported:

> We have input on decisions around school. We also have Cadres where teachers meet in little groups so the principal is not doing everything. In the old days [before the current principal] the principal did everything and a lot did not get done.

At Einstein teachers described one of their most important successes as being able "to come together and share our concerns." "Just about everything we do as a school we get together on," another teacher said.

When principals described how they share leadership, they identified a variety of approaches. Most commonly they relied on team leaders, department leaders, committee leaders, and leadership and advisory committee members. In some cases principals used resource teachers to augment their instructional leadership.

At Kent teachers viewed teacher leadership as a major force in change and identified formal teacher leadership in terms of team leaders and committee chairs. They also stated said that "other faculty can stand up and lead almost any time." Pioneer teachers credited the principal with encouraging leadership and that, as a result, there "was a huge latitude for leadership" and "there were lots of leaders on campus." Teacher-leaders serve as team leaders who "help make decisions for the school" and as members of various committees. Department chairs play the role of curriculum facilitators and are responsible for taking care of "anything that has to be done in regards to curriculum, like the faculty assessment notebooks and attending district inservices." Fourstar teachers reported that "faculty exercise leadership within the teams and that everyone really feels that they have a voice," and at Twain teachers provided leadership on focus teams, content-area teams, and vertical teams.

Resource teachers also provided leadership in these schools. A special education teacher at Fourstar accepted an expanded role of responsibility to help teachers with differentiated instruction, and reading teachers and consultants assumed new leadership responsibilities at Kent and Einstein. At Pioneer a learning strategist worked with teachers to implement the CRISS strategies and worked with the professional development committee to coordinate teacher-learning activities.

In all six schools, principals valued and supported teacher collaboration and teacher leadership. The principals provided a variety of opportunities for teachers to share their expertise, to exercise leadership, and to participate in collaborative decision making. They had created cultures in which teachers felt safe and where widespread involvement was expected. Teachers appreciated the opportunities and responded by becoming involved in a variety of leadership and decision-making capacities.

A Continuing Desire for Individual and Collective Learning

It was clear that the principals and teachers in these six highly successful schools had created a culture that was conducive to continual learning. Teachers at Einstein expressed a commitment to the culture when they said, "Our faculty believes in continual staff development," and, "Professional development is very important to the principal and staff—every week it seems like there is a new professional development program or conference." At Kent teachers portrayed their colleagues as "highly qualified and continuous learners." They also talked about a "professional development plan required of all teachers" and "multiple opportunities to grow professionally."

Principals also commented on the importance of continual learning and professional development in their schools. Two principals characterized their schools as learning communities. Another principal described professional development as part of school values and beliefs. One principal talked about the importance of professional development in enhancing the middle level concept:

> I wanted to get proactive about it as we started designing staff development days. . . . From the very beginning we were going back to middle school 101 because the feeling was, they thought as a staff they understood middle school and they thought that we were already a middle school because we already had the name. We needed to go back to that.

Another principal talked about the lack of teachers specifically prepared to teach at the middle level and the need for a professional development program at her school to retrain newly hired teachers:

> We are dealing with people who move in who are probably secondary people who need a job so I have to grow these teachers at the middle level. I've got elementary teachers and I've got to grow them for this level, too. So I think our focus is professional development—all the things that tie in to being developmentally responsive, what is unique about the middle level, and what are we going to provide for kids that works.

Principals reported that they supported professional development in a number of ways. At Fourstar, Pioneer, and Kent, principals hired or identified specific people to coordinate professional development activities. At other schools, principals used district and county consultants and university faculty members to aid them with professional development. In addition, most of the schools had professional development committees that worked with teachers, principals, and professional development coordinators to plan the schools' professional development programs and keep the activities focused on the vision and mission of the school. Several principals described their efforts to finance professional development, including applying for grants, using regional center resources, and arranging school fundraising activities.

Professional development in these schools was approached in a variety of ways that are supported by research and recommended professional development practices (Clark & Clark, 2004; Elmore, 2002; National Partnership for Excellence and Accountability in Teaching—NPEAT, 1999; Sparks & Hirsh, 1997). For the most part, the professional development was embedded at the site level and consisted of formal and informal activities. All schools were allocated professional development days, and all schools had some latitude in determining how those days would be used.

Some preferred to use whole days whereas others broke their allocated time into half days, which gave them the opportunity to meet more frequently. Even with district requirements for specific professional development activities, principals appeared to be very diligent in seeing that their teachers participated in activities that related to the school's specific curricular and instructional needs. For example, Southside teachers reported:

> Normally the school district provides so many days per school year for professional development. Our principal has made a point to get us to our own meetings. Before that we might have [had] to go to something that might not be of value.

> We do building inservice that addresses specific needs and issues. For example, the principal gathered all the new teachers to address a specific topic.

Teachers and principals reported a variety of ways that professional development supported the specific needs of their school. At Kent, with a focus on the International Baccalaureate Middle Years Programme's multiple approaches to instruction, the principal required teachers to do peer observations. In addition, new teachers must observe the department head. The professional development person also observes and works with individual teachers but does not evaluate.

Twain's teachers had annual summer workshops with follow-up sessions during the school year. They were heavily involved with Project ASSIST, a comprehensive school improvement program. They also spent time during districtwide differentiated contract days to conduct schoolwide discussions, review disaggregated achievement data, and identify and revise building goals. Focus, content, and vertical teams also enabled Twain teachers to study and expand their knowledge in curriculum, instruction, and school organization.

Data about student learning provide the focus for professional development at Southside. The principal and teachers continually looked at how their students were progressing and then adjusted their curriculum and instruction to improve student learning. In addition to professional development that centered on continual monitoring, reflection about, and modification of student instruction, the principal and teachers also focused their learning on the middle level concept and the building of developmentally responsive environments. To do this, the principal encouraged attendance at state and national conferences where teachers not only attended but often participated by making presentations. The Southside principal said, "If you don't go, you don't grow," and:

> We have little traveling teams that do a lot of consultations and presentations. Every time we go

somewhere we always learn. We have a little saying that goes, "All ideas are stolen, modified to look like they're not stolen, and shared among thieves.

Fourstar's principal indicated a "great deal of professional development" at school, which placed an emphasis on "what's good for kids" and differentiated instruction. To improve the quality of professional development, he designed a new role for the special education teacher in which the teacher worked as a consulting teacher to help other teachers implement differentiated instruction. Much of the professional development at Fourstar occurred on a very informal basis, including sharing information and "exploring ideas for instructional and curriculum development in team meetings." As resources were available, the principal also supported the idea of teachers attending conferences and workshops to augment their ongoing professional development.

Similar to the other five schools, the professional development activities at Pioneer were built on a culture of collaborative learning. Teachers who had visited other schools or attended conferences often generated the ideas for school improvement. In fact, when teachers were given resources to attend conferences, they were required to report back to their colleagues any ideas that might be successful at Pioneer. This was the process by which the CRISS instructional strategies program became part of the school, and as a result much of the professional development at the school focused on the implementation of these strategies. Data also drove the professional development at Pioneer. With the support and direction of the principal, teams appeared to be central to the school's professional development efforts. Teachers in teams were expected to become knowledgeable of best practices, to use formal and informal data, and to collaborate in using that knowledge and information to adjust curriculum and instruction. In addition, the alignment of curriculum (backward mapping) with district and state standards afforded the teachers and administrators the opportunity to participate in focused professional development. At Pioneer professional development was planned and coordinated by a professional development committee who worked with the learning specialist and the principal to address the learning needs of the faculty and individual teachers.

Einstein's teachers described their principal as being very committed to professional development. Similar to Pioneer, teaching teams that met weekly—and subject-matter teams that met less frequently—formed learning communities. According to the principal, these learning communities were not only responsible for improving instruction and assuring curriculum alignment but also "making sure we communicate." As in the other five schools, professional development at Einstein was closely connected to school improvement efforts.

The interviewers found a strong teacher commitment to professional development in all of the schools. In discussing this commitment, teachers described ways in which the faculty learned as a whole and how they advanced their own individual learning. The following activities were used to keep the faculty current:

• Districtwide contract days
• Summer workshops
• Team and department meetings
• Brainstorming
• Talking with other teachers
• Group book studies (e.g., *Turning Points 2000*)
• Conferences and workshops
• Discussions with the principal
• District and county courses and workshops.

In describing their own efforts to advance their own knowledge, teachers most frequently used:

• Districtwide staff development
• Journals, books, Internet articles
• School-based professional development
• Conferences
• Professional memberships and conferences
• Building and district committee meetings
• Team meetings
• College courses
• Talking with other teachers.

The teachers in these schools had numerous opportunities to learn. The opportunities emphasized collaborative and individual learning, were formal or informal in nature, and supported school and individual needs.

Principals were successful in creating learning communities in these schools. For the most part, professional development was embedded at the school site, provided for individual and collaborative learning, and was congruent with the school improvement plans.

Relationships

Southside's principal said, "The number one thing is relationships," which is a belief that all six principals shared. These principals took the building and nurturing of relationships with and among students and teachers very seriously. The results of their efforts were evident in the respect and trust the teachers had for their principals and for one another, their strong consensus of values that centered on high student expectations and student success, their belief in the efficacy of collaboration and shared decision making, and their commitment to colle-

gial and individual learning. These schools were places where students and adults felt valued and where strong, positive relationships enhanced learning.

In this section, the findings on relationships are reported in the following categories: relationships with students, principal–teacher relationships, and teacher–teacher relationships.

Relationships with Students

In *Turning Points 2000*, Jackson and Davis (2000) stated, "For young adolescents, relationships with adults form critical pathways for their learning; education 'happens' through relationships" (p. 121). Principals and teachers at all six schools reported strong, positive relationships with their students that were built around values of caring and individual worth and a belief that all students could be successful. A teacher at Fourstar stated, "We genuinely do care about kids and want to do what is best for them," and teachers at Kent reported that they "care deeply about students." At Twain the principal reported positive student relationships and attributed that to teachers taking ownership to ensure that all students are successful. Teachers at Twain spoke of "caring and the desire to help each kid," of being "concerned and compassionate," and of commitment— "students come first." In addition, they talked about the school being small enough to get to know each student and about the respect that students and teachers had for one another.

Teachers at Pioneer, similarly to teachers in the other five schools, exhibited care and concern for students by their commitment to student success. Teachers reported team discussions that included "talk about strategies to help kids," a "focus on students who need assistance," and "recognition of student success." In addition, to ensure a continuing emphasis on positive adult–student relationships, the principal regularly monitored team activities.

> We look at the teams to see if they are doing activities with children . . . and if I have a team . . . that is doing nothing, I will look at that to see if they are working hard enough on relationships with children.

At Einstein teachers demonstrated their support for student success by organizing a specialized class for sixth-grade students who were not successful. In this class, sixth-grade students received special help studying for tests and doing homework, and other academic help as needed. The success of this special "helping class" prompted the teachers to consider a similar class for seventh-grade students.

Another example of a school's commitment to positive student relationships was at Southside, where the principal met periodically with a group of students to ascertain their feelings about school. The principal described these meetings:

> I meet with a panel of kids and we do a chart . . . about what would be some of the things you would change about our school. It is a powerful thing I do and I learn so much. I have my secretary type up the notes I take and we put it in everyone's box so they can read it.

The teachers' and principals' commitment to positive relationships with students was evident when teachers relayed comments made by students who returned to visit their school after having gone on to high school. Students typically talked about the support they got from their teachers, how much they appreciated the teams, the good times they had with their teachers, and how their experiences at the middle school were much more rewarding than at the high school. They also talked about their positive relationships with teachers and how they had influenced them. One student told her former middle school teacher, "I want to become a teacher because of you." In addition, students talked about how their experiences had prepared them for the hard work and academic rigor of high school.

Principal–Teacher Relationships

Principals reported a variety of factors that were crucial to building and maintaining positive relationships in their school. Most of them shared the opinion that, after students, teachers were most important. "I need them, they don't need me. I treat them right," stated one principal. "Make them feel valued," suggested another principal. That principal went on to say:

> I know how I felt as a teacher. I didn't always feel valued. I try to make sure that I tell them as regularly as I can. One teacher came in and told me I hadn't been telling them enough so I have to make sure I don't take them for granted either or get caught up in what I am doing.

Principals showed how they valued teachers in various ways. They used informal compliments, were approachable and accessible, and were open to ideas and suggestions. They also empowered teachers to collaboratively make decisions and to share leadership responsibilities. In addition, principals described their efforts to recognize teachers through celebrations that honored teams and individuals, through conferences and presentations where they received validation of what they were doing in their classrooms, and through school-recognition awards (e.g., Blue Ribbon and other state or national awards).

Several principals talked about knowing teachers individually. One principal spoke about recognizing individual problems and giving specific individualized support. Another principal suggested:

> Just remember some people need a pat on the back, some people need a kick in the pants, some people need both . . . . Different people need different things. Some people need to be celebrated for the smallest strides and other people need to be challenged.

A third principal stated:

> I just think it is important that they realize I know them as individuals. I treat them the same way I expect them to treat children. [We are] like a family. I value their opinions. We are going to work very hard and play hard. I have always tried to remember what it was like as a teacher so I can make sure they have everything they need.

Part of knowing teachers individually was determining issues that were of importance to them. One principal reported, "I met with each team individually and I met with each person individually to talk about what we needed to do. A lot of it was just sitting down and talking about what was needed."

Two principals spoke about summer meetings with teachers where they had the opportunity to identify and talk about issues of mutual concern. Another principal took a much more formal approach to ascertaining teachers' issues and concerns:

> I ask them what their needs are formally every year. I want to make sure they are happy with the team they work with. I want to make sure they are happy with their classroom, with the grade level they teach, with the subject they teach. I want to know, Do you want to change next year? Are you going to stay here next year? What do you need to make your job better? What will improve our school?

The principal went on to say, "Those [responses] are confidential. They know they can write anything there. We take that kind of input."

Part of the process of receiving valuable, honest feedback from teachers was the high degree of receptiveness and accessibility of the principals. Each principal talked about being available, walking the halls, sitting in classrooms, and meeting with teams. One said, "You never see me in my office." Another reported, "I don't care what I am doing, I will stop to take care of their needs. . . . If they see me, they can say something."

These principals were not only available to receive input from their teachers, but also were diligent in acting upon the information they received. In most instances they did not view themselves as problem-solvers but as facilitators and enablers. They empowered teachers, facilitated collaborative decision making, and shared leadership.

Teachers were very satisfied with the relationships they had with their principal. For the most part, they confirmed what the principals had reported. Teachers at one school reported that their principal had built strong sharing relationships with the faculty members, was approachable, and appreciated and valued teachers. They characterized their principal as being very "open to ideas," a "listener," and a person who "gives teachers freedom to help kids." At another school the teachers reported that their principal "encourages teachers to use techniques from all sources," "says you're doing a good job," and "is an excellent instructional leader, and that sets us apart."

Teachers at other schools were equally appreciative of their principal. "I truly believe in the principal and his leadership," reported one teacher. Other teachers found the principal to be "very approachable and a good listener," "top-notch, concerned about students and faculty," and "a wonderful instructional leader." In addition, many teachers were very positive about their principals who would "listen and then make decisions on what's best for kids," were "approachable and supportive," and were "upfront and honest."

Principals of the six site-visit schools created cultures that were built on strong, positive relationships. The principals valued the teachers in their schools, knew each teacher individually and collectively, trusted the faculty members to do what's best for students, and enabled teachers to be active participants in decision making and leadership. The teachers responded positively and viewed themselves as important partners in establishing learning environments where all students could be successful.

Teacher–Teacher Relationships

Three words best describe the relationships that teachers have with one another in these schools: collaborative, family, and community. The teachers liked one another, enjoyed working with one another, and appreciated the collegial support of their colleagues. Comments from the teachers at Twain were representative of the responses of teachers in other schools:

Good place for students and teachers.

Dedicated, hard working staff.

Collegial faculty.

Staff—best people I've ever worked with.

For many of the teachers, collaboration was the vehicle that was responsible for building these strong, positive relationships, and teaming made collaboration possible. While talking about collaboration, teachers often mentioned sharing—sharing knowledge, sharing ideas, sharing concerns about students, sharing instructional strategies, and sharing the joy of success. One teacher at Pioneer confirmed the power of sharing when she stated, "When we meet as a team, it's awesome to talk about a success story. We can ask what you are doing in the classroom that makes the light go on for a child."

Teachers also talked about the caring and helping relationships and the respect that emerged when they were afforded the opportunity of working with other teachers. Their comments were characterized by statements such as "we care about each other," we "work together and give each other help," we have "respect for one another as teachers," and "faculty [members] definitely support one another . . . they value that." A Southside teacher captured this strong sense of caring that existed in these schools: "I think that love and concern is so evident between teachers and kids. It is also evident in the way teachers demonstrate care and concern for one another."

When teachers were asked to describe the relationships of teachers in the school, a Fourstar teacher responded, "All of us here view our school as a family." A Southside teacher stated, "We work as a family within our team. We are very bonded within our team." At Twain teachers talked about "a sense of community" and said that their school was "more like a family."

In addition to talking about a sense of family and community, teachers also talked about friendship. Most often these were friendships had been built through teams by teachers who collaborated together, planned together, taught together, and worked together on a shared, common purpose. Some of the friendships had been formed over long years of teaching together. Teachers at Pioneer talked about a strong core of teachers that had remained the same over a period of years; teachers who had learned and grown with the school. In fact, many of the teachers had been at the school since its establishment nine years ago. A teacher at Twain remarked, "Teachers have worked together for a long time. I feel really fortunate to have been here for 19 years."

It was clear that the teachers had strong, positive relationships with one another. They valued one another and often classified the faculty as a community or a family. They were committed to collaboration, enjoyed collegial relationships, and cared for and assisted one another.

Parents and Community Members

When schools and parents work together, children tend to succeed. In fact, "studies conducted over the past 30 years have identified a relationship between parental involvement and increased student achievement, enhanced self-esteem, improved behavior, and student attendance" (Mapp, 1997, p. 1).

Principals and teachers in these six highly successful schools made major efforts to build strong relationships with parents and community members. In this section the information collected by the study team is organized and reported in the following categories: involving parents and community members, building parental and community awareness, and communicating with parents and community.

Parental and Community Member Involvement

Parents reported that each of the six principals was highly accessible and promoted parental involvement in their school. Typical comments from parents included, "an open-door school for parents . . . encourages parent involvement at all levels," "the principal is always open to comments and suggestions," and the principal "listens with understanding to students, parents, and staff as well as community." At Southside the principal reported, "We really got parents on board because they felt welcome to come and collaborate," and Pioneer's principal said, "Parents are here all the time." At Einstein the principal stated, "Our parents are very involved. I think that it is just the nature of a parent who wants their child in a magnet school."

For the most part, teachers also supported their principals' openness and encouragement of parental and community participation. "Parents are part of the mission," stated a teacher from Kent. Teachers at Einstein reported, "Our faculty believe in parent involvement," and "Our parents are very involved."

The type of parental and community involvement varied in each of the schools. Several schools reported that parents and community members were active participants on their school advisory or leadership council. At Pioneer, for example, the principal reported that parents and community members, along with teachers and administrators, had been involved in collaborative decision making since before the school opened. The principal said, "We started the school and determined the philosophy, mission, and vision by including the teachers I had hired at that point, the administrators, counselors, support staff, and parents from the community."

That pattern of involvement at Pioneer was established early, has continued, and was endorsed by parents. One parent said, "Committees of parents, teachers, administrators, and community leaders serve the school. They develop unique school plans and school improvement plans." Parents of students at Einstein reported involvement in school decision making as members of their school's advisory council. A parent stated, "Change comes from three sources—parents, teachers, and administrators." At other schools, in addition to participation on school leadership teams and school advisory councils, parents and community members were involved in the schools through informal dialogues and had the opportunity to provide input through surveys.

Parent–teacher–student organizations were another way that parents and community members became involved in the school. The principals at Kent, Einstein, and Pioneer reported that their schools had particularly active parent–teacher–student organizations. In addition, principals and teachers reported that parents and community members volunteered in the office, the library, and classrooms. At Southside, for example, parents were encouraged to come to school and have lunch with their sons or daughters (with permission of the child) and to attend school functions. Parents and community members also served as mentors, guest speakers, and chaperones at school events. In some schools, local businesses participated in mentoring programs and provided long-term tutoring and mentoring to students.

Schools and students also made significant contributions to the community. A community service program at Kent "encourages each student to go out into the community and find ways to help." Teachers at Twain reported that positive relationships were built with the community as a result of service-learning projects and teacher visits to community businesses.

Principals also reported cooperative efforts by schools and community groups to share facilities and to sponsor activities that benefited students. An example of this was a Pioneer community group that provided support to keep the computer lab open after school and sponsored family nights and classes on school practices.

Not all schools were satisfied with the level of parental and community involvement. Looking toward the future, Southside teachers suggested, "Our school could become a better school with even more parental involvement," and "Our vision should include involving our community more." The principal agreed:

> I would enhance our current vision by getting us out more into the community. We have been real site-focused, but there is a need for more parental and community involvement. I feel like this is an area where we need to greatly improve.

Teachers and principals in other schools also talked about having higher levels of involvement and were committed to improvement. In a few relatively infrequent cases, teachers mentioned that they felt the parents in their schools were uninvolved and not supportive.

Building Parental and Community Awareness

Although involvement by parents and community members in the schools' programs was an effective way of building awareness, principals also used a variety of other strategies to assist parents and community members in becoming more knowledgeable about their schools. At Southside parents were invited to spend a day watching teachers, and parents had the opportunity to attend special parent meetings. At Pioneer the principal reported that each year the school had a "new-parents night." At these sessions the principal and a group of teachers talked about school programs—how the program was set up and how it met the needs of young adolescents. Kent's principal also organized a number of activities to build parental and community awareness of the school. Each fall, to orient new students to the school, there was a spaghetti dinner for sixth-grade students and their parents. Throughout the year Kent administrators scheduled other events—meetings, dinners, and so forth—with other groups of parents and community members. Twain's principal said that he tried to build community awareness on the basis of students' accomplishments: "The students have been really excelling and helping us to meet that goal. So we try to do a newspaper article or that sort of thing."

Parent–teacher–student organizations provided an opportunity for parental and community involvement and were identified by principals as useful in building awareness. In addition to general meetings, board meetings, and other functions, most of the parent–teacher–student organizations sent out monthly newsletters that provided information about the schools and special school activities. In addition, open houses, parent conferences, student performance nights, and sports events provided teachers and administrators with opportunities to build parental and community awareness about their schools.

Awareness is a two-way street, and several of the principals made a concerted effort to personally understand and become more aware of the needs of parents and community members from the various, divergent groups in their school's community. Principals at Einstein and Kent discussed the challenges of trying to meet the varying expectations of parents. Both principals reported that, at times, programs developed to assist students who were having difficulty learning were often interpreted by parents of high-achieving students as a diversion of effort from their children's education. Einstein's principal stated:

> We have some advanced kids and the parents of those kids have high expectations. They think you are not meeting their kids' needs, so you have to make sure you are meeting their needs while you are meeting the needs of low performers.

The principal addressed this perception by implementing programs directed specifically at each group of students, which seemed to satisfy parents.

Understanding parents was an especially important issue at Southside, and the principal addressed it as follows:

> I have to look at the community I am working with. I am not teaching college professors' kids. What I am teaching are people who are trusting the school to do their job because they are working. In some form or fashion they are trying to make ends meet. So, no they are not going to come flocking to the PTA meeting—they will come if their kid is doing a performance. They will come to the [academic] Pep Rally. These parents have barriers in their lives, be it poverty, be it language, be it they are on shift work and must sleep during the day and work at night. We cannot use parents as our excuse why Johnny can't learn…What we can do is work internally and create success so parents want to trust the school factor. At this school, I can't use parents as an excuse because they are working night and day to make ends meet.

The schools took several approaches to understanding and meeting the needs of divergent communities. Pioneer's teachers and administrators spent a day examining the implications of poverty on learning, and they continued their efforts to develop programs and strategies that would be responsive to this special group of students. The principal at Kent was particularly committed to serving the various ethnic groups within the school. In addition to involving the faculty members in human relations activities that familiarized them with the community, the principal met frequently with parents and representatives of various ethnic groups to determine ways in which the school could help children be successful. Because of the principal's concern and awareness of community needs, the school, on several occasions, was able to assist disadvantaged and bereaved families.

In their efforts to understand their parents and communities, four of the six principals used formal surveys. These surveys provided a variety of information about parents' opinions regarding school programs, school strengths and weaknesses, and parents' satisfaction regarding their children's school experiences. These four schools used the data not only to build their awareness of parents' opinions but also as a basis for school improvement.

Communicating With Parents and Community Members

Building positive relationships with parents, as exemplified by the principals' openness and accessibility, was an important factor in communication. As a result, much of the communication at these schools was often conducted on a face-to-face basis or by telephone. Because of a strong belief in personal communication with parents, the principal at Kent initiated a major effort over the past two years to encourage teachers to call parents on a regular basis. Teachers at Southside and Pioneer also reported that they frequently called parents to talk about a variety of issues concerning their children.

Teachers at Pioneer stated that the main reasons they called parents was to "report on the strengths of their child, what they were good at—then go on to areas needing improvement" and to "help parents be aware of what was going on at all times." The teachers also talked with parents about "strategies for helping kids at home," "working together to help their child make the transition," and "what's available for additional help." At Southside teachers reported, "We are very comfortable with calling parents," "My discussions with parents are about helping their children," and "If I see a need, I feel free to call a parent. Our parents work and cannot get off work so I call them at night."

Principals and teachers also used a variety of fairly common approaches to communicate with parents, including scheduled parent–teacher conferences, face-to-face meetings to resolve problems and issues, and notices and newsletters prepared by individual teams. At Einstein the principal reported that e-mail was used to communicate with parents. In addition, she posted information and data about test and survey results on the Internet. The principal at Einstein remarked, "Some of the parents feel it is too much information, and other parents just love every bit of it."

A strong commitment to parental and community involvement was evident across the six schools. In some cases an acknowledged need to improve was expressed. Principals worked hard to build parental and community awareness in their schools, and most of them reported a personal commitment to understand and work with the divergent groups within their communities. Special attention was paid to effective communication with parents; communication that often emphasized the "personal touch" of a telephone call or a face-to-face meeting.

Safe and Healthy Environment

The six highly successful schools also had safe and healthy environments. In each school there was a commitment to safe emotional and physical environments. A Kent teacher stated, "A safe place to learn is part of what we believe." At Twain and Pioneer, teachers reported that their schools' mission/vision included "the creation of a safe environment" and to "provide a safe environment."

It was evident to the researchers that the educators in these schools valued safety and that the schools were places where adults and children could work and learn in a supportive climate. Parents and teachers often reported that "a safe environment exists," "we have a very clean, very safe, and very comfortable environment," and "what I like most [about this school] is that this is really a safe environment for my child."

Although these schools, on a day-to-day basis, provided safe and healthy environments, the caring, nurturing cultures also gave educators a foundation to deal with more difficult problems presented by out-of-school conditions. Southside's principal and teachers discussed the recurring problem of gang affiliation; "We address our issues; we don't ignore them," reported a teacher, who went on to say:

> Sometimes it's just impossible to eliminate them because it [the problem] is so pervasive. I think gang affiliation is one of those items. We have dealt with it time after time and it is hard to convince our students that that is not the way it has to be. I think that the [interdisciplinary] teams replace some of the identity with the gang. When they [student gang members] are on our campus we don't have problems. When they leave our school, they have a problem.

Another Southside teacher expressed a similar thought: "We have some people [students] who are associated with gang elements in the community. They are totally different people when they leave school than when they are here." It appeared that teachers, even with the frustration they felt about gang activity, have created an environment that was safe for students who were and who were not gang members.

A safe and healthy environment also provided the foundation for one of the schools to deal effectively with the September 11, 2001, crisis. A parent at the school that morning reported on how effectively the principal, other administrators, counselors, and teachers supported and helped students, many of whom had relatives who worked at the Pentagon, cope with this tragedy. One of the teachers noted that the way the school dealt with September 11 was one of the most significant accomplishments of the school year.

Although principals used multiple approaches to build these safe environments, several factors were apparent. At Pioneer the principal expressed the importance of "using positive approaches," "making teachers feel valued," and "creating environments where all children can learn." In addition, other principals discussed their commitment to the success and well-being of all students and adults in their school and their belief in the value of engaging teachers in leadership and decision making.

Principals also believed that what they did in their schools made a difference in creating safe environments. Southside's principal discussed her first year at the school:

> I remember a cartoon that said you must be the climate creator. So I remember the first year we could either sob in our beer or roll up our sleeves and say if it is going to be, it is up to me. I wouldn't ask the staff to do anything that I wouldn't do. I try to model behavior and I give them enough autonomy where I don't stifle their spirit. At the same time I have to channel their energies toward a goal . . . .
>
> What did I do to shape the culture? Well, easy things like letting them go to conferences and not worrying about how much paper they used in the copy machine. . . . Really praising what I valued and creating a community of learners.

Teachers also talked about things they and their schools did to create a safe and healthy climate. At Kent teachers mentioned an antibullying program and teachers who were "being more proactive." Teachers at Fourstar talked about the "importance of the learning atmosphere" and the leadership of the principal, who had created more "stability and cohesiveness in the faculty." Teachers at Pioneer reported that "looking more at problems/safety net/prevention" issues had helped them create a culture of safety at their school. They discussed their much more aggressive approach to "identifying needs," "working with counselors and administrators," "working on helpful strategies," and "establishing early contact with parents."

Safe and healthy environments were the norm in these schools. A commitment to student and adult emotional and physical safety was part of the mission/vision of these schools, and that commitment was acted on in many ways and in many situations. Within these safe environments, cultures were created that emphasized supportive relationships, effective communication, and successful learning.

Summary

This chapter described the programs and practices of six highly successful middle level schools. There are many factors that contributed to the successes of these schools, and four important cornerstones provided the foundation on which the programs and practices of these six schools were built and sustained: a consensus of values and beliefs, a commitment to collaboration and shared leadership, a continuing desire for individual and collective learning, and a culture of respect and support.

Consensus of Values and Beliefs

The principals and teachers in these schools shared a common core of values and beliefs that guided programs and practices: high expectations for all students, educate the whole child, all students will be successful, and curriculum breadth.

The commitment to these four shared beliefs was evident in the programs and practices of these schools. The curriculum was aligned with state and district standards through the use of back-mapping and other curriculum alignment strategies, and all students were expected to meet those standards. Curriculum and instruction were designed with the needs of young adolescents in mind and included opportunities for students to participate in interdisciplinary units, exploratory classes, and cocurricular activities. Educators promoted student success by continually monitoring student progress, modifying instruction, and providing specialized activities for students who were having difficulty. The learning opportunities provided for the students underscored the importance of each child being exposed to a core of common learning and the opportunity to explore noncore areas of content.

Commitment to Collaboration and Shared Leadership

Collegial cultures existed in these schools, and collaboration was valued and flourished. Principals viewed themselves as collaborative and provided teachers with the time and opportunity to work together. Teachers were also strongly committed to collaboration and collaborated with their principals in making a variety of important decisions. In addition, teachers were involved in school leadership. They commonly served as team leaders, department leaders, committee leaders, and school leadership team and advisory council members. They also coordinated professional development and directed efforts to improve classroom instruction.

Continuing Desire for Individual and Collective Learning

Learning was the focus of the schools—student *and* adult learning. It was evident that the principals and teachers had created cultures that were committed to continual learning. Principals characterized their schools as learning communities, and teachers talked about their commitment to learning and of their multiple opportunities to grow professionally. Professional development was embedded with a focus on the acquisition of new skills and the improvement of instruction. When teachers lacked knowledge about middle level programs and practices, their professional development concentrated on building an understanding of young adolescents and of the middle level concept.

Teachers participated in planning formal professional development activities and appreciated that the learning experiences were relevant and helpful in meeting the challenges they faced. In addition, collaborative team-planning activities provided a powerful learning opportunity for teachers. In these informal meetings, they focused on student learning, exchanged ideas, reviewed assessment data, and planned and modified curriculum and classroom instruction. Many teachers also committed their own time and resources to advance their learning by attending conferences and workshops, attending university classes, and obtaining advanced degrees.

Cultures of Respect and Support

The principals of these six schools believed that "the number one thing is relationships," and they worked very hard at building relationships with and among students and teachers. "Students are first" was a common theme in these schools, a theme that set the tone for student–adult relationships. Students were valued, and decision making was always predicated on "what's best for kids." The adults had positive relationships with the students, which helped create climates of physical and emotional safety and cultures of support and learning.

Teachers were valued by the principals who made special efforts to know them personally and provide them with appropriate support. The results of these efforts were evident in the respect and trust that the teachers had for their principals. In these six schools, teachers and principals shared strong, positive relationships. They valued one another, they trusted one another, they enjoyed the collegial relationships fostered by collaboration, and they cared for and assisted one another.

One other factor greatly influenced the programs and practices of these six highly successful schools: teaming. Although all of the schools had implemented many of the programs and practices typically found in middle level schools and recommended by current research, it was teachers working together in teams who appeared to provide the most powerful influence on curriculum, instruction, and school improvement. Teaming, which was supported by scheduled planning time, provided teachers with opportunities to collaborate and reflect on curriculum standards, appropriate instruction, and student learning. Teaming enabled teachers to share and discuss data, participate in collaborative decision making, and take on additional leadership roles within the school. Teaming, with its focus on learning, also facilitated a culture of learning where a community of learners could regularly engage in a variety of formal and informal continuous learning activities. The process of teaming allowed teachers to build strong relationships of trust, to create cultures of collegiality and support, and to develop core values and beliefs that led to successful student and adult learning.

CHAPTER 5

Leadership in Six Highly Successful Middle Level Schools

Leadership and learning are indispensable to each other.

—*President John F. Kennedy*

Had President John F. Kennedy been able to deliver this message in the speech he had prepared for the November 22, 1963, meeting of the Dallas Citizens Council, the link between leadership and learning may have become universally accepted earlier in the culture of educational reform. As the middle level movement has evolved over the past four decades, education researchers have confirmed that school-site leadership is directly related to effective schooling experiences for students (Cotton, 2003; Marzano, 2000; Waters, Marzano, & McNulty, 2003). This chapter describes the leadership of the principals of the six site-visit schools and their personal leadership qualities, skills as change agents, leadership for teaching and learning, and expertise in resource management. Each of the six schools was highly successful, in large part, because of the leadership of its principal. Significant insight about the nature of effective school-level leadership that can transform a school into a high-quality learning organization can be gleaned from this analysis.

Personal Leadership Qualities

The personal and professional backgrounds of the six principals were as diverse as the schools they led. They ranged in age from late 20s to late 50s, had 4 to 11 years of experience as a principal, and each had a graduate degree, including a master's degree in education and a doctorate. There were three women and three men. Each had taught for fewer than 10 years before becoming an assistant principal or a principal; most were appointed to their first principalship or assistant principalship before the age of 35, and all but one intended to remain a principal in the same school for the next five years. What is perhaps most striking in the analysis is how each principal, in a unique and

powerful way, exemplified a fundamental belief that principals are charged with doing everything possible to ensure that the students in their school show maximum academic, social, and emotional growth.

Profiles of the Six Principals

Einstein Middle Academy

The principal at Einstein Middle Academy was an elementary classroom teacher for eight years before being appointed as an elementary assistant principal. She served in that position for three years, became the assistant principal at Einstein for one year, and then assumed the principalship. In her first eight years at Einstein, she successfully led the school through an accreditation process and established it as a highly successful magnet school. She stated that the most important challenge that Einstein will face in the future will be to maintain its magnet status while also meeting desegregation requirements.

Fourstar Middle School

The principal at Fourstar Middle School had been in his position for two years at the time of the site visit. He had six years of experience as a middle level teacher before coming to Fourstar. He had also served for two years as a middle level assistant principal, and had been appointed to a middle level principalship in another district prior to the age of 30. He has a master's degree with certification in counseling and educational administration. He said that Fourstar must make steady improvement in student achievement data while providing comprehensive opportunities for students in the relatively small school. Another challenge will be the relocation in fall 2004 from the very old, current middle school facility to a remodeled facility that was once the district's high school.

Kent Middle School

The principal at Kent Middle School had been an assistant principal in the school for 11 years and was named as its principal 4 years prior to the site visit. He also had 5 years of teaching experience at the middle level and 1 year at the high school level. After becoming an assistant principal prior to the age of 30 and serving as an assistant for 9 years at the high school level, he left education for a period of time. He then returned to the field as an assistant principal at Kent. His graduate major was secondary administration, and his graduate coursework included a number of classes specific to middle level education and all the required coursework toward a doctorate. The significant challenge in the immediate future for Kent is to fully implement the International Baccalaureate Middle Years Programme (MYP) for all students in a school that is not a magnet school and whose student body represents enormous economic, ethnic, linguistic, and social diversity. Upon retirement from the principalship, this principal would like to return to the classroom to teach and work with young adolescents.

Mark Twain Middle School

The principal at Mark Twain Middle School presents a striking contrast to the other principals. He was in his late 20s and in his third year as principal at Twain at the time of the study. He taught for five years at the middle level, has not served as an assistant principal at any level, and was an elementary principal for one year before being appointed principal at Twain. He has a master's degree and an education specialist degree in secondary school leadership and an endorsement in middle school administration. Future challenges at Twain include providing quality and comprehensive programs in an era of declining enrollment, associated revenue declines, and a struggling local agricultural economy.

Pioneer Middle School

The principal of Pioneer Middle School has the most middle level experience of all six principals. She has taught middle school for seven years, served as a high school assistant principal for three years, and has been Pioneer's principal since it opened in 1993. She holds a doctorate in education with a focus on middle level education and administration. She brought a strong commitment to middle level concepts and best practices to the school, basing much of the school's plan and philosophy on the recommendations from *Turning Points: Preparing American Youth for the 21st Century* (Carnegie Council on Adolescent Development [CCAD], 1989). Maintaining high levels of student achievement with rapidly changing demographics and unprecedented growth in the district are significant challenges for Pioneer.

Southside Intermediate School

In the seven years since assuming the principalship at Southside, the principal has helped the school evolve from a low-performing school into one with sustained exemplary performance. Prior to being named principal at Southside, she was an elementary school principal for two years and an assistant principal at the elementary level for four years. Similar to the other principals in this group, she has had relatively few years of teaching experience (six at the elementary level) and was named to an administrative position shortly after turning 30. She has an undergraduate major in elementary education, a master's degree in educational administration, and coursework specific to the middle level. She is the only principal in the group whose salary is linked to school and student performance. Future challenges for Southside include maintaining the student achievement level at above 95% at a time when the state is changing the high-stakes assessment tests.

Moral and Visionary Leadership

In *The Human Side of School Change*, Robert Evans (1996) maintained that leaders who are followed are *authentic,* meaning that they are distinguished not only by their techniques and styles but also by their integrity and savvy. He stated, "Integrity is a fundamental consistency between personal beliefs, organizational aims, and working behavior . . . savvy is a practical competence, a hard-to-quantify cluster of qualities that includes craft knowledge, life experience, native intelligence, common sense, intuition, courage, and the capacity to 'handle things'" (p. 184). This section examines the six principals by analyzing their integrity and savvy—their competencies as moral and visionary leaders.

Despite differences in background and career development, the six site-visit principals share a bedrock belief that each student in their school can be successful and that they must do whatever they can to ensure that each student is given every opportunity to grow academically, socially, and emotionally. They demonstrate this core value as moral leaders, social leaders, and intellectual leaders. The variations within each category are as creative and unique as are the individuals; however, the significance of "students first" resonates throughout the narrative that describes their personal leadership characteristics.

As moral leaders, all six principals established the importance of a focus on the individual student, thus fostering a set of beliefs and values based on the core concept that "all students can learn." When questioned about what they meant by the term "all," it was clear that the term was used synonymously with "every." "Every single one," "every last one," "every student," and "each student" were phrases used by the principals. These principals were not promoting a vision of success defined by an *average* increase in a school performance; they were striving for an increase in *every* student's performance, and they expected the same of their teachers. The principal of Pioneer portrayed that expectation in a visual manner by stating:

> I used to tell my teachers "Don't tell me a child can't learn until you have done everything, including standing on your head and spitting quarters, to get their attention. Then maybe you can tell me that you haven't gotten to that child."

Teachers rated each of the six principals highly as moral leaders—as a provider of vision, as one who models what needs to be done to approach that vision, and as one who fosters the commitment of others to that vision (Table 5.1).

The vision of "success for all" governed all six schools, but it was expressed differently in each case. The principal and teachers at Southside work under the belief that all students can behave and achieve. It is no longer acceptable within the school culture to make excuses for why a student cannot learn. Failure is not an option at Southside. At Pioneer and Twain, teachers described their moral purpose as doing what is best for kids. At Kent, it was explained as "closing the achievement gap." Teachers at Einstein reiterated the importance in their beliefs that all students can learn and that high expectations are important for each student. The principal at Fourstar summed up the criteria for vision-based decision making by stating, "We have to ask ourselves constantly, is it good for kids?"

In addition to a commitment to focus on success for each student, the principals of these schools validated the importance of caring for each child as a human being. It was not enough that each student learned and

achieved; each should be cared about and valued as an individual and a person. Teachers at the schools talked about looking at the development of the "whole child" and using a holistic approach to student development. A teacher at Fourstar said that the faculty members viewed "the student" as the center of everything they did and that they needed to deal with students' emotional and social self for them to be successful. The principal at Kent illustrated this value with the following statement:

> When you look out there I want you to see your child, or if you don't have children I want you to see yourself and how you would want to be treated. This is our value: We are going to treat every one of them the same. I don't care if he has a hole in his coat or his nose is running or not, we are going to support them.

The notion of closing the achievement gap was significant in the beliefs and values about student achievement. There was a genuine agreement that "success for all" did not refer to a good or even exemplary average of scores, but rather for each student to be successful. At Einstein, a magnet school, teachers would put a student on probation if his or her GPA dropped below a certain point or if behavior was a problem. They used weekly interventions and multiple strategies to improve performance and ensure that students met the standard required to stay in school. "Dismissing" a student and requiring him or her to return to his or her zoned school was not taken lightly. One teacher stated, "We always strive to find out what we can do better."

At Kent, where the diversity of the student population was significant, the teachers also knew the importance of success for each student. Joking that data were disaggregated "down to their shoe size," Kent's principal said that the school's primary focus was to "improve their reading skills and close the gap." At Pioneer the issue of disparity in student achievement was centered on a changing student population. The principal and

Table 5.1 Teacher Perceptions of the Principal for Variables Associated With Moral Leadership

Trait	HS	Einstein	Fourstar	Kent	Mark Twain	Pioneer	Southside
Provides vision	4.10	4.96	4.87	4.21	4.92	4.68	4.46
Models behavior	4.12	5.00	5.00	4.12	5.00	4.53	4.87
Fosters commitment	4.19	4.96	4.69	4.04	4.88	4.58	4.74

Note. 1 = strongly disagree; 5 = strongly agree; HS = highly successful schools (n = 98)

teachers acknowledged that the student population would be changing due to the unprecedented rapid growth in the community and that new strategies and skills would be needed to continue to meet the needs of all students. The school staff members recognized that their moral purpose was to focus on doing what was best for each student, and, as the student population changed, teaching strategies and programs would have to be added to continue to meet the needs of every student. A teacher at Southside made the following comment, exemplifying the kind of vision and values and beliefs that are representative of these schools and their leaders and teachers:

> We will do damn near anything to get these kids on board. We will do whatever it takes if it means going to their house, facing a SWAT team because someone does not like your opinion, whatever it is we are going to do what is best for the kids. Every decision, after the emotion is set aside, the final bottom line is "what is best for the kids."

The principals' ability to foster commitment to the school vision and goals—and their capacity to model that commitment—is another form of moral leadership. As with other leadership behaviors, each principal was unique in his or her way of approaching these issues, and each was successful.

The principal at Twain talked about the importance of being true to one's personal values and of modeling the establishment of measurable goals and working toward their accomplishment. Pioneer's principal said it was important that she treat the school's teachers the way she wanted them to treat the students and that it was important to remember what it was like to be a teacher so she could try to provide what the teachers needed to be successful. A teacher at Southside described the importance of the principal as a model: "You get the feeling that teachers genuinely care for the students, and that starts at the top." The principal agreed, reflecting that the principal's behavior does reflect the school's vision and that the teachers and the administrators are working harder than they have ever worked in their lives. She compared it to service organizations such as United Way or the Salvation Army, where participants work hard but it is what they love to do. "I haven't forced anyone to stay until 6:00 working," she said.

The comment of a teacher from Fourstar explained what it looked like when the principal was a master at fostering commitment:

> If I make a statement to our team that our principal really wants this, then everybody feels like it should be looked at. It does not matter how long

they have been teaching or how much more they think they know than him, they just believe that he is sincere enough about his goals that if he values it, it is worthy of their time.

Evans (1996) stated, "It is increasingly clear that leadership rests on values, that commitment among constituents can only be mobilized by leaders who themselves have strong commitments, who preach what they believe and practice what they preach" (p. 184). The principal at Southside described teaching a class of disruptive students during her first year and sending a message to the faculty: "This elementary cream puff was going to endure in the 'hood.'" They saw that:

> My priorities were teaching and learning. I value that [teaching and learning] more than discipline. Let's get the discipline under control . . . now we have a system for discipline, now let's value teaching and learning. You know what? We started laughing and having fun.

Each of the principals demonstrated distinctive aspects of authentic leadership. Regardless of their style, each inspired the faculty members to work to accomplish goals that were grounded in a set of beliefs and values that put students first. They were able to accomplish this through some combination and creative application of providing vision, supporting teachers, modeling what they believed, and fostering commitment. The principal at Twain expressed perhaps the ultimate moral leadership when he stated, "I am not afraid to put my kid in any one of those classrooms out there."

Social Leadership

In *Improving Schools from Within*, Barth (1990) asserted that no relationship in a school has a greater effect on the quality of that school than the relationship between teacher and principal, and the key to improving schools lies within the improvement of those relationships. Bolman and Deal (1993) concurred with that statement, stating, "The quality of a principal's leadership depends on the quality of his or her relationships with the entire school community" (p. 10). These writers considered such relationships to be indicators of social leadership, defined as the qualities associated with trust and support.

The significance of trust emerged at each site but within different contexts. In some schools it was defined with reference to the principal's support; in other schools trust was more closely aligned with the principal's consistency of expectations. Other definitions included trust as indicated by the presence of a safety net, or the ability to take risks and experiment with instructional strategies

Table 5.2 Teacher Perceptions of Principal Support and Communication

Trait	HS	Einstein	Fourstar	Kent	Mark Twain	Pioneer	Southside
Provides individualized support	4.21	4.95	4.89	4.42	4.92	4.71	4.78
Communicates effectively	4.03	4.86	4.53	4.12	4.97	4.49	4.70

Note. 1 = strongly disagree; 5 = strongly agree; HS = highly successful schools (n = 98)

fundamental to the improvement of instruction. The principal at Pioneer said it was important that each teacher feels valued and to regularly confirm that appreciation. Teacher survey data from each school (Table 5.2) indicated extremely high levels of individualized support provided by the principal to the teachers of their respective schools.

The concept of trust also included the ability to demonstrate the integrity and courage to follow through on what was stated as important. It was particularly evident within the context of teacher performance and contract continuance. One principal acknowledged that some teachers were "leery of me," stating, "They know that if they are not doing their job, I will get rid of them." The principal also spoke of the value of flexibility, stating, "I will give anyone a break but will also come down hard on them as well." Another principal agreed that integrity did not require that all persons be treated alike in all situations by saying, "Some teachers need a pat on the back, some need a kick in the pants, and some need both." The principal at Southside told a story about her initial year as principal:

> My first year, 12 people left. They hated my guts. One threatened to kill me and had to be escorted out by a SWAT team. They did not want to be accountable, they hated the state tests, and by damn, they were not going to teach in this wretched place. I let them go. I only want people here who want to be here. . . . Now I say we average one [contract nonrenewal] every two years.

One of the principals best captured the integrity and courage required of a highly successful principal by explaining:

> There is a group of teachers that really struggles, and a group that are superstars, and probably most teachers fall somewhere in between. I have to make sure I support those who are struggling and kind of push the ones who are doing OK and want to do good. And it is my job to make sure the ones that don't want to improve are not here.

The ability of the principal to develop and sustain positive connections with parents is an additional part of Bolman and Deal's (1993) statement about relationships. Jackson and Davis (2000) concur: "Working together, parents and schools can strengthen the tie between home and school and, in doing so, can promote higher academic achievement in every student" (p. 209). Several teachers talked about the value they placed on their principal's ability to communicate and work with parents. One principal said that in the past there had not been a lot of parental support at the school and that the teachers had not felt comfortable with parents in the building. The principal told teachers, "If you don't feel comfortable, then you must be hiding something," and invited parents into the classrooms to watch teachers teach. The importance of telephoning parents or contacting them with a concern was mentioned at several schools, and one principal said, "Giving a failing grade without warning is like an eviction with no notice." Another concurred:

> My biggest [parental] complaint at the beginning of my career was that the parent didn't know her kid was failing until she got the report card. I feel that one of the strengths of our school is that we keep parents informed regardless of their education level, regardless of whether they can read or write, regardless of if they can speak English. . . . We have to keep the parents on board.

The exact definition of the relationship between parents and the school was not as important as was its existence, and, regardless of the format it took in each school, it was positive, open, and focused on what was best for the student. The principal at Kent, a school located adjacent to a 10-lane commuter highway, created a visual image of how parents and school personnel worked together for the best interests of students:

> I tell parents that we are like guardrails on that highway; we are one set, the parents are the other; they [students] go across all kinds of lanes and bounce off all sorts of things, but the students are the ones who have to find the lane, we just help them.

Communication and Approachability

The ability to engage in two-way communication has long been recognized as a hallmark of effective leadership and an absolute necessity as a change agent. It is a skill to be discussed not only as a personal quality but as an essential component of a principal's ability to lead change and to serve as an instructional leader. "Communication is the lifeblood of the school; it is the process that links the individual, the group, and the organization" (Lunenburg & Ornstein, 1997, p. 176). Studies indicate that school leaders spend up to 80% of their time in communication with other members of the school community (Green, 2001).

The six principals provided excellent examples of the consequence of being able to communicate effectively, engage in professional dialogue and debate, and invite and respond to feedback. Each of the six principals was rated highly by teachers for communication (Table 5.2), which included the ability to speak and write clearly, engage in conflict management, facilitate groups in problem-solving techniques, use group process skills, and work effectively as a team member.

Parents and teachers confirmed the high level of communication skills of these principals. Parents described their principals as generally available, accessible, seeking input, open to comments and suggestions, and willing to provide feedback. A parent of a student at Twain said the principal was able to listen with understanding to parents, students, and staff members as well as to community members; a parent at Fourstar said that the principal really listened to parents and tried to do whatever he could to improve the school. A parent from Einstein identified an admirable balance of skills, explaining that, "Although our principal is very good at seeing possibilities and trends, she does not mandate changes with a top-down attitude. Our principal is very good at building consensus and allowing parent-led organizations to provide input."

Approachability and listening skills were also closely aligned in the comments of teachers at several schools, one of whom said, "Our principal's door is always open and [the principal] is open to suggestions." One teacher compared the culture of communication to that of a family, saying that she could tell the principal when she was mad and then fix it or agree to move on. One principal described it as follows:

> I am never in my office; I get out and am talking to you. I tell my assistants: that person's problem is the only problem in the world to that person right now. You have got to stop and talk to them.

The willingness to listen to suggestions, have a conversation, discuss differences of opinion, and work for a resolution were consistently identified as characteristics of principals of highly successful schools.

Intellectual Leadership

It is difficult to draw a definitive line between the principal as an intellectual leader, which is a personal characteristic, and as a facilitator of staff development, which is an indicator of instructional leadership. For purposes of this research, being an intellectual leader was inherent in what the principal did to "sharpen his or her personal saw" (Covey, 1989), the latter in what he or she did to enhance and further develop the knowledge and skills of the teachers in the school. The fact is that significant overlap exists, with numerous indications that there may be a high correlation between the two qualities and that much of the "saw sharpening" occurs jointly between principal and teachers.

The principal at Southside offered perhaps the best example of the importance of intellectual leadership when she recalled what a former superintendent had said: "The difference between a good leader and a great leader is that a great leader reads." In all six schools, principals and teachers talked about the importance of reading professional literature and the value of sharing and studying it with teachers. Additionally, they emphasized the importance of reflective thinking, acknowledged that networking with other middle level principals was invaluable, and spoke about the importance of maintaining contact with experts in the field and using regional resources.

The Pioneer principal's qualifications as an intellectual leader were genuinely exemplary, with substantial expertise and knowledge in school improvement and middle level education. Her dissertation was about the implementation of the *Turning Points* recommendations, and she had developed the expertise and credibility needed to advocate for specific programs and practices at Pioneer. She became a voice for middle school best practices across the district. She addressed her school's success:

> Well, if you ask me why we were successful from anything I have done, I would say it is three things I have done. First, my knowledge about middle level practices so I can tell people. And then getting people in the school to understand it and stick to it, too. And the third is enthusiasm. I think that is a biggie.

The importance of lifelong learning and its value to establishing a learning community was a common factor for success as an intellectual leader. The leaders of the six highly successful schools acknowledged the importance of a continuous improvement model. They were constantly striving to increase their own knowledge and skills and enhance the knowledge and skills of their teachers, thus advancing student achievement and development. These six schools were unmistakably characterized as "learning organizations."

Leadership for Change

John Kotter's (1999) representation of the difference between leadership and management lends insight to the analysis of principals as change agents. Kotter maintained that leadership is the force behind successful change, and management is the force behind maintaining the status quo. Thus, it is axiomatic that principals of highly successful schools must be both sensitive to the complexities of any change in their school as well as become skillful facilitators of change processes.

This study indicated that this is, in fact, the case. As presented in chapter 2, when the 98 highly successful school principals were asked about roadblocks to success in their schools, 46% identified resistance to change as *not* a factor, and only 2% of the highly successful school principals saw resistance as a serious roadblock to success. This was a striking contrast to the national sample of principals, where only 22% identified such resistance as *not* a factor, and 16% saw it as a serious roadblock. An analysis of the leadership of the six site-visit schools clarified what leaders in highly successful schools do to successfully implement change and demonstrated that the processes used by these six principals varied but had common threads. Processes for collaboration and formats for decision making differed by school as well as by issue. Predominant across all six schools, however, was the recognition that change happened successfully when it was linked to the school's vision and beliefs and when the need for change was established through analysis of student performance data. Fourstar's principal said, "We have to ask ourselves constantly, is it good for kids? If it is good for staff too, that is great, but somehow it has to come back and be in the best interests of kids."

Change Processes, Collaboration, and Teacher Leadership

Education literature is consistent about the importance of stakeholder participation as a necessary ingredient of successful change. *Turning Points* (CCAD, 1989) and *Turning Points 2000: Educating Adolescents in the 21st Century* (Jackson & Davis, 2000) recommend that middle level schools operate with a democratic governance structure that is collaborative and focused on student learning. The involvement of teachers as well as parents contributes to a reduction of resistance to change, an increase in the quality of decision making, and an enhancement of successful program implementation (Green, 2001). Principals who adopt a model of shared leadership and decision making realize that a change is likely to be improved when staff members who have to carry out a decision also have a voice in making that decision. The principals and schools visited provided excellent proof of this.

As noted, the specific change processes used varied across schools. Formal and informal processes were practiced, and the source of initiation varied by school and with each specific event. Twain used the most formal approach, applying the Project ASSIST school reform framework to lead the enhancement of school culture and climate, pedagogy, leadership, and organizational structure. Einstein had recently been involved in a regional accreditation process that required the development of a comprehensive school improvement plan. Kent was in the process of applying for accreditation as an International Baccalaureate MYP school, and, once that direction was determined, strategies were designed to meet specific requirements. Southside based its approach on the Deming model (Walton, 1986) of gathering data and having stakeholders involved in decision making. The principal and staff members at Southside developed and implemented an eight-step process for instructional improvement.

What was most striking, however, was not the specific processes used or even the range of approaches used across the six schools but the underlying significance of extensive collaboration in each situation. Each school implemented change through a course of communication and collaboration that was consistent with the norms of its particular culture. One principal emphasized the importance of teachers being able to collaborate: "I hire personality first; we can teach you how to teach, but first you have to get along with people." The Pioneer principal expressed what others also believed:

> I don't have all the answers and ideas. I mean, I have this faculty that has tremendous ideas and they want to be included. I can't imagine if I had to make all the decisions. I don't think that would work well at all . . . they are knowledgeable and always make me proud of what they are doing. They articulate what we do well, and they are usually right on target with their assessments. They are really good people.

The faculty members at Twain, the smallest of the schools, used various devices such as a school improvement team, a building leadership team, focus groups, vertical teams, committees, and district high-performance collaborative teams. The result was the sense that *everyone* is involved in any change event. At Fourstar the teachers and the principal said that initial change was accomplished by the principal meeting separately with each team and each faculty member to discuss what was needed. Committees and discussions have since become part of the ongoing collaborative effort. Southside's system was to use the campus advisory team, in conjunction with content-area teams, grade-level teams, interdisciplinary teams, and cadres. One teacher noted, "Everyone is involved somehow." Another teacher commented, "The principal gives everybody a say, even sometimes giving too much opportunity for input." Einstein's process was similarly layered: There was a school advisory council that included faculty and community members, a faculty advisory committee, and a team leader structure. Pilot programs were often used to assess alternatives. A teacher at Einstein described teacher collaboration:

> Just about anything we do as a school we get together on. We either meet as a faculty or we start out in teams; maybe they have a team leader meeting with the administration and they bring it to us. We definitely collaborate on almost everything.

Pioneer and Kent, the largest site-visit schools, gave clear evidence that big schools were not incompatible with collaborative change processes. Kent used an instructional leadership team, consisting of department heads, team leaders, and the MYP coordinators. Kent also had a staff development teacher who was responsible for working with faculty members to communicate needed change and processes for change and for bringing all faculty members together to discuss how to implement change. At Pioneer there was a general agreement that some sequence of meetings with team leaders, department chairs, committees, and the faculty as a whole would lead to a decision or solution. There was room for individual innovation as well: After attending a reading workshop, one teacher started a committee at the school that began to study a specific approach that was addressed at the workshop. As one teacher noted, "People take the initiative here to do things. . . . They don't need to be told." It was evident that the school's collaborative culture was key to successful change, and although many of the teachers attributed this to the principal, the principal credited the teachers. One teacher's simple and absolute response to the question, Do you have a collaborative

culture? represented the replies of many others: "Definitely. The principal created it . . . we are constantly interacting and sharing." The principal said, "It is the culture of our school that we do whatever it takes, and we really do embrace new things. They [teachers] are eager to share and to do whatever it takes to make this a better learning environment."

Principal and teacher collaboration was the most obvious force behind continual growth, yet the principals also spoke to the reality of external pressure for change. They noted the need to address district and state mandates and expectations. One principal said, "I am not a rebel. I do what the big guy [superintendent] tells me. . . . I tell the teachers, 'This is what we have to do. How should we go about doing it?'" Another said that when it looked like a directive was coming from "above," their school liked to be proactive and start a pilot project. "I don't want to wait and have them tell us that we are going to have to do it. I want to start doing those things and see how it works for us. Then I can give them feedback on how *we* do it."

Not every change event was perfectly collaborative, even in highly successful schools. Several schools noted that change sometimes started at the bottom, and other times, at the top, and sometimes by people outside of the school. A teacher at Kent said, "Some change is top-down, some is bottom-up; some is democratic, some unilateral. But regardless of the decision, there is always opportunity to be heard and to understand the reasoning." The principal's perception of the implementation of the MYP at Kent illustrated the limits of collaboration:

> From the beginning, the MYP involved not only the Instructional Leadership Team but also the established folks who had been here the longest. We ran a lot of trial balloons, asking, "what would you think if we did . . . ?" and then we made it very, very clear that MYP was coming—period. That was not the point of discussion; the discussion was how were we going to implement it. I met with them to help them understand, sent them to staff development all over the country. I would meet with each grade level team. We never got to shouting, but there was some resistance. It finally got to "I guess you are telling us that if we don't like it, we can leave." I said, "yes." No one left.

Leaders of highly successful schools need to be collaborative as well as decisive, and the artistry of knowing when to do what is a hallmark of excellence in leadership. A teacher at Fourstar said:

> At this school, we have a lot of committees and a lot of discussion about most major decisions. But the principal is not a spineless person who will not make

a decision when it is needed. If he has to make a decision without the discussions or after the discussions and you disagree with it, he will tell you why that decision was made.

Clearly, the principals in these schools were collaborative. They also understood the needs of their schools and the context of why changes were essential. They balanced collaboration, trust, respect, and decisiveness, and with faculty support they produced changes to fit the unique needs of their respective students.

Parent Involvement

Collaboration was not limited to the faculty and staff members. Each school also involved parents in change efforts, formally or informally. The opportunity to be heard, give input, and be included as part of a decision-making process was important to the parents in each school. Most of the schools recognized the importance of using surveys to gain input and feedback from a wide variety of parents. In some cases the major involvement was within a formal parent organization, but parents also emphasized that they could express themselves as individuals and school officials would listen. Teachers talked about their principal's ability to form positive relationships with parents and how this skill had been a definitive factor in implementing change. A parent's vote of confidence at Fourstar was typical: The principal "listens to parents and really tries to do whatever he can to improve our school."

Use of Data in the Change Process

Kotter (1996) maintains that one of the biggest mistakes people make when trying to change organizations is to plunge ahead without establishing a high enough sense of urgency. "People will find a thousand ingenious ways to withhold cooperation from a process that they sincerely think is unnecessary or wrongheaded" (p. 36). The principals and teachers of the site-visit schools consistently used data to understand the crucial need for change, to help others see the need for change, and to monitor the implementation of change.

Effective data analysis was a leadership skill observed in every school. The Southside principal said, "You measure what you treasure," and, "You monitor what you measure." The principal at Kent clearly articulated what the principals and teachers of the six exemplary schools often said: "We don't make change for the sake of change. Show me some data that indicates that this is better for kids, and we will do it."

In these schools the term *data* was not synonymous with *standardized-test scores*. *Data* included attendance information; discipline records; failure rates; teacher-made assessments; and survey information about school climate, culture, leadership, and instructional practices. At Twain *data* also included the use of an instructional profile to stimulate conversations about needed change.

Pioneer's principal clarified what was also evident at the other schools by stating:

> It is from teacher observation, from analyzing data we have, talking to one another, analyzing reading scores…we talk about these things. From that, we analyze the programs we have and say, "Okay, this one is working well or this one isn't." Then we ask how we are going to get there as a faculty. Staff development goes hand in hand with that too.

The other principals concurred. Twain's principal said, "Data inform our goals." The principal at Kent stated: "I show them the data that in our situation present a problem and ask, 'How are we going to deal with this?' " Einstein's principal illustrated the point:

> With everything we do, we evaluate it to see if it was worth it, should we continue it, is it something we want to do again next year? Did it make a difference in student outcomes? And we shouldn't do it if it doesn't affect student outcomes or student success.

The Fourstar principal expanded on that concept:

> Whatever the results, the numbers, I share it with the staff . . . personally. The day the numbers come in, I would share them, and then we would follow that up with specific information . . . I don't tell them, "This is what you need to do." I think with professional people, you bring them to the doorstep and they come up with the ideas.

Data analysis was also used in a manner consistent with and illustrative of the vision of the schools. Data were disaggregated and reevaluated to determine if, in fact, *all* students were learning, the Kent principal said. Pioneer's principal discussed the value of disaggregating achievement data to determine the performance levels of the most transient students. Fourstar's principal talked about the importance of conducting item analyses on test data to determine specific curricular and instructional strengths and deficits. The schools looked at grade distributions, failure rates, and achievement gaps. They included attendance and discipline data in their ongoing analyses. It was not enough for the schools to see an *overall* increase in student achievement. They were seeking an increase for *all* students. When asked what she dreamed about regarding her school, a teacher at Einstein said, "I dream that every child will find his or her own personal success."

The Southside principal vividly described the school's use of data in the mid 1990s as the faculty members began to reform the low-achieving school:

> We started looking at our data; we started being data driven. Our tears aren't going to solve it. We had been crying in our beers all those years and nothing had happened. So, we started looking at our data to fine tune what it was we needed to work on by target objective, and once we started looking at our data, we looked at what groups of kids did poorly on this objective and what groups of kids did well on this objective. We became more data-driven.

Finally, it is important to note that the ability of these six principals to effect learning and foster change was not limited to these six schools. The Southside principal explained how one principal influences life in many other schools: "Some teachers have left because they have gone on to become administrators, and I am real proud of that. I hate it when they leave me; I cry, but I am proud that they are burning the torch somewhere else."

Leadership for Teaching and Learning

Instructional leadership has been repeatedly identified as a competence that differentiates effective principals from other principals. Many of the competencies already discussed in this chapter (moral leadership, vision, ability to communicate and collaborate, and skills as a change agent) are often associated with the capacity of the principal to be an effective instructional leader. But it is the leader's direct effect on instruction and learning that is the focus of this section. The quantitative and qualitative data from this study were analyzed to ascertain what these six principals did on a regular basis to enhance teaching and learning in their schools. As with the other areas, there was much to learn from these principals, both individually and collectively.

The teacher survey provided data on each principal as a resource provider, an instructional resource, and a visual presence in the school. Whether a principal was considered a resource provider was assessed by evaluating his or her value as an instructional resource, promotion of staff development, ability to mobilize support to achieve school goals, and knowledge of instructional resources. A principal was identified as an instructional resource through his or her ability to evaluate and reinforce effective instructional strategies, provide feedback to improve instruction, apply student performance data to instructional issues, and address instructional concerns or problems with teachers. Visible presence was measured through behaviors such as frequent classroom observations, accessibility, active participation in staff development, and a presence throughout the school that was recognized by staff members as well as students (Andrews & Soder, 1987; Smith & Andrews, 1989).

In each category, teachers from the six site-visit schools rated their principals above the average of the 98 highly successful school principals (Table 5.3). The principals' skills and abilities in all three areas were rated as strong, and these ratings were confirmed in the interviews. A synthesis of the skills and abilities of these six highly successful principals as evidence of their capacity to lead teaching and learning are presented in the following section.

The Principal's Role in the Improvement of Instruction

The principal's ability to evaluate and reinforce effective instructional strategies and provide feedback to enhance the improvement of instruction is a crucial component of instructional leadership. Frequent classroom observations are an important requirement, but they are often not sufficient to improve instruction in isolation. The ability to use formal and informal observations to provide meaningful feedback to teachers is a characteristic and a skill important to instructional leadership. Most of the

Table 5.3 Teacher Perceptions of Principal Instructional Leadership Variables

Trait	HS	Einstein	Fourstar	Kent	Mark Twain	Pioneer	Southside
Resource provider	4.14	4.86	4.81	4.34	4.90	4.67	4.88
Instructional resource	4.06	4.89	4.61	4.28	5.00	4.61	4.73
Visible presence	4.01	4.84	4.75	4.33	4.95	4.19	4.75

Note. 1 = strongly disagree; 5 = strongly agree; HS = highly successful schools (n = 98)

principals interviewed in this study talked about informal processes more than formal processes. They provided feedback by discussing data and specific students, by answering teachers' questions, and by being available for teachers when they needed help with something. The principal at Pioneer said, "I am going to be in classes, see lesson plans, look at improvement. I want to see 10% more differentiating instruction." The Southside principal talked about walkthrough data as part of the bigger picture of the data used to evaluate teacher and student performance. At Twain the principal believed that observations were another way to model the importance of maintaining a focus on school goals, especially when accompanied by the monthly assessment results each teacher submitted. One principal described how he hand-delivered messages, and another told of how she personally delivered paychecks as a way to drop into a classroom and observe teaching and learning in action. Informal observation practices were clearly an important and a valid way for these six leaders to gain important information about their schools.

The formal observation procedures, which differed by state and district, were also important in the improvement of teaching and learning. The Kent principal had a unique manner of conducting classroom observations. The principal observes in a specific class for three days in a row.

> When I come in and observe you the first day, I do script taking. I want to see what is going on. . . . When I come in the next two days, I am looking for the types of questions you ask and where you are taking them. I am looking for the type of follow-up you are doing with your discussions, the kind of assignments you are giving. So I know from being in your classroom what kind of rigor you are providing. . . . Within three days, I should see something, shouldn't I? That is how I know what they are doing and how I give them feedback.

High Expectations for Teachers

In a manner consistent with having high expectations for students, the principals held exceedingly high expectations for teachers. At Pioneer newly hired teachers were required to sign a statement in support of the school's vision, values, and beliefs. They were told by the principal, "I expect your best; you are to do everything you can to achieve the goals of the school. If you are going to come here, I will expect 110% of you and we will all work together to make sure this is a place that does the right things for children." The principal at Southside stated that the word got out quickly regarding the high expectations for teachers and lack of tolerance for ineffective teaching. The principal at Twain clarified the importance of high peer expectations as well:

> When we have had discussions [about values and beliefs] it has really helped the expectations of the teachers for each other. I see some of that happening per person, and some in teams. Because the teams have said, "We agreed to do this . . . we agreed to do this assessment . . . we agreed to use this teaching strategy," that has upped the pressure more than anything I have done individually.

Support for Continuous Improvement and Professional Development

Along with high expectations for teachers, each of these principals had fully embraced a belief in continual improvement and had inspired the faculty members to do the same. They regularly reviewed data, identified successes, analyzed weak areas, and set new goals. Nearly every conversation about the schools' vision and goal-setting processes included the concept of "raising the bar." The Southside principal explained what the process had been at her school:

> Once you taste success, you never go back [to the way it was]. The first year was survival, crowd control. The second year we got the taste of success. The third year we nailed success. Then we started asking, "What else can we do?" So, for the last four years, we have been going beyond what the test measured. Exemplary is top notch according to our state, but we have learned that there is so much more to measure students by than a standardized test.

In each school it was strikingly evident that if a model of continual improvement was followed, it would succeed only through the constant enhancement of teacher skills. "An effective school principal keeps a school focused on student learning by ensuring that the faculty members have the professional development opportunities they need to improve practice and that they make good use of them" (Jackson & Davis, 2000, p. 158). Teachers in every school commended the quantity, quality, and variety of professional development activities available to them. They presented at and attended conferences, took classes, participated in seminars, attended workshops, engaged in book studies, and read and discussed professional journals and articles. Not only was there schoolwide commitment to professional development, new strategies and approaches were regularly brought back to the school and actively implemented by groups of teachers. The conventional model of "sit and get" or "hear it today and file it tomorrow" was not present in these schools. Teachers worked together to improve teaching strategies and thus enhance student achievement. One school was able to use state money for differentiated contract days in the summer when the staff members could come together for professional development activities. One principal explained the importance of providing professional development regarding middle level concepts and developmentally appropriate practices, noting that most of her teachers came to the middle school with a high school background. The importance of focus was noted by the Kent principal, who said, "I can't remember one inservice we have had recently that did not focus on reading. . . . We focus and we make sure you understand one thing before moving on to the next." The principal at Twain highlighted the importance of teacher self-assessment:

> I guess my job is not to have a whole bunch of answers for teachers but to keep asking questions about their work . . . to really keep asking critical questions and to try not to become predicable. It is important that they are quality questions so that the teachers start asking them [the questions] of themselves.

Twain's principal also summarized the principal's role in professional development: "I am making sure that I am leading instructionally, that I am giving them the professional development they need."

The two largest schools had a staff development faculty member who focused on enhancing teaching strategies. The primary role of the learning specialist at Pioneer was to train teachers to implement reading and other learning strategies across the curriculum. The specialist said that whereas teams had previously used 6 strategies, now they were applying as many as 18. The learning specialists in both schools were expected to be knowledgeable about effective instructional processes and to implement professional development that supported instructional improvement. At Kent the position was held by a teacher on special assignment. The individual worked closely with the MYP coordinators as well as with the instructional leadership team to instruct teachers in how to implement new strategies. The in-house staff development person was highly respected and perceived as a tremendous resource to the advancement of teaching skills. The principal emphasized that the role of the staff development faculty member was not an evaluative one: "He works with them individually . . . he does sample lessons. He will work with them as a department, a team, and an individual. He does not report back to me." The role of an in-house teacher trainer was not limited, however, to large schools. At Fourstar, a school of about 300 students, the role of the special education teacher was beginning to incorporate that role. The principal explained how the role was in transition:

> We had a very old fashioned view of special education, where . . . these people were popping in and out all day long versus putting them on the team and working directly with teachers. We are moving [him] more toward a consulting teacher [role] now. My goal eventually is that he is not teaching classes much but is working with all the other teachers to show them differentiation in action and ways they can do it all the time.

The motivation and stimuli for professional development were not always external. Teachers at these six schools showed an inherent drive to advance their knowledge and learn teaching strategies. A teacher at Kent characterized the faculty members as very professional, dedicated, and very interested in improving their skills, which was representative of the findings in each school. Teachers were empowered and acted as leaders in professional development in a manner similar to the way they approached change and decision making. Ideas for teacher growth and teaching strategies were as likely to come from teachers as they were from administrators. A teacher at one school made it clear that this was a part of the culture of teacher growth and development at the school. The teacher said, "When we go to a conference, we come back and present [materials] to the faculty." Another described it as "a group of people become experts and build training for all faculty; the administration gives the resources and support to make it happen." Several schools used teacher study groups or brown-bag lunches to examine new concepts and strategies, begin implementation of strategies, and engage in reflective observation and evaluation. Professional development was also not limited to formal presentations or expert knowledge. Teachers stressed the value of peer observations and working with a mentor, a protégé, or a team.

The support of the principals of these schools was invaluable to the professional growth and development processes for teachers. Their enthusiasm, knowledge, and ability to provide teachers with everything they need to be the best they can be were cardinal elements in the culture of continual improvement.

Leadership for Resource Management

The almost universal emphasis on the importance of the principal as a visionary, a change agent, and an instructional leader has somewhat minimized the value of skills in managing, procuring, and strengthening resources. However, the ability to actually work toward a vision, implement a change, and improve instructional strategies is often ultimately dependent on those exact skills. Resource management is a key factor that enables great leaders to produce extraordinary results. In many cases, that factor can make the difference between a leader and a dreamer.

The six principals demonstrated and illustrated excellence in every skill area addressed thus far, and the management of resources was no exception. They used a combination of social leadership, communication skills, vision, commitment, and the ability to empower and engage others to garner resources and then distribute them in accordance with the school vision.

Several of these principals were excellent examples of managers of time, as particularly evidenced by their delegation of responsibilities to assistant principals and empowerment of teachers. Teachers at Kent said their principal "is not a micromanager," and, "Our administration gives you the direction and then leaves you alone." A teacher at Southside said, "Our school is broken into tribes [teams]. A lot of the administrative work is handled in the tribes. The teachers in the tribes like the responsibility for scheduling and discipline and they handle it very well." Assistant principals reported significant autonomy. Statements typical across the schools included: "Once he hands me something, he expects me to run with it. But if I have questions, he is there," and, "She trusts me to get the job done." However, the same assistant principals also spoke about how they worked together with the principal, filling in the gaps and picking up the pieces as a team. As one assistant concluded, "We complement each other well." One principal spoke about a unified approach to keep the delicate balance of autonomy for members of the administrative team: "Two are strong, but when you braid three, there is some real strength. Every time we are up against some big fight, I say, 'OK, the braided cord.' They know it is all of us together."

The principals were also skillful at appropriating resources for professional development. Following are typical comments from teachers: "Our principal is good at getting grants, money, funds, to help with staff development beyond our five [district] staff development days," and, "If you want to go to a workshop, he will find the money." One school was even able to get school board members to supervise the students so the teachers could engage in a training session. Among the six schools, there was a clear commitment to do whatever was necessary to carry out the staff development plan: One of the principals said, "If we run out of budget, we are going to sell pickles at lunch to the kids so we can pay for our gas [to go to professional development]."

Summary

Research has demonstrated that the process of becoming a highly successful school is exceedingly complex and that consummate leadership is required for substantive and continuous improvement. The study of the leadership in these six highly successful schools provided insights to and examples of how varied personalities and differing circumstances can each produce extraordinary results. The six principals have confirmed that there is no one route to success in middle level schools, nor is there any one prescribed style of leadership. They have, however, individually and with other staff members, established and emphasized that the following four key leadership themes are crucial to the process of ongoing school reform.

Students First

At each site-visit school, the principal and the teachers jointly embraced a vision that put students first and ensured that decisions were made in alignment with that vision. The term *students* was used synonymously for *every student, each student,* and *every single one,* as opposed to *most students.* The notion that the school's faculty members, as well as its programs and practices, had to focus on the success of *every* student in the school was fundamental to the shared vision of these highly successful schools.

Professional Learning Communities

Each principal guided the evolution of his or her school into a professional learning community. For learning to steadily improve, it was evident that the teachers and principal had to be engaged in a process of continual professional development. Improved student achievement was directly linked to enhanced teaching strategies and highly competent teachers. The principals modeled the importance of professional development, were respected as facilitators in the improvement of instruction, and held their teachers to incredibly high standards. Each principal knew how and when to appreciate, motivate, coach, correct, and confront teachers. Each was committed to shepherding resources to support the school's professional development plan. Each principal was a courageous leader who made it clear that excellence in achievement would only occur as the result of excellence in instruction.

The Change Process

The six principals were outstanding examples of leaders who deeply understood successful change and whose mastery of the intricate change processes allowed their schools to warrant identification as "highly successful." They helped their schools establish collaborative visions and related action plans, and they engaged stakeholders, especially teachers, in learning-related decision making.

In essence, each principal created a school culture that not only accepted continuous change but also embraced it.

Commitment and Passion

Throughout the site visits; the interviews; and the review, analysis, and synthesis of qualitative data it was evident that these six principals truly believed in what they were doing. They were committed to young adolescents and middle level education and were dedicated professionals who cared deeply for the students and the staff members. Working an inordinate number of hours and facing extraordinary challenges did not daunt their enthusiasm or passion. They had, in fact, shaped their schools into quintessential examples of what President Kennedy would have described as that indispensable combination of leadership and learning.

CHAPTER 6

Understanding Highly Successful Schools and Leaders: Implications for Practice

The purpose of this study is to provide principals, teachers, policymakers, researchers, other educators, and members of the public with insight about the programs and practices of highly successful middle level schools and the leaders who helped establish and maintain those programs. A highly successful school was defined as one in which the principal and the teachers consciously work together to effectively meet the needs of the young adolescents they serve. The schools selected for this study were identified as highly successful because they were effectively meeting unique student needs through a variety of developmentally appropriate programs and practices. They were (1) implementing middle level programs representative of the current research and literature about effective middle level schools, (2) making a conscientious effort to improve their programs as that knowledge evolved, and (3) studying and using student achievement data as well as other forms of student and school data to inform their purposeful changes. All data collected on these schools indicated that they were making a positive difference in the educational lives of the students they served.

The highly successful schools in this study were selected from an initial pool of 273 schools nominated by more than 200 education leaders from across the country. From that pool, 100 "highly successful schools" were invited to participate in the study, and 98 accepted. Quantitative and qualitative data about the 98 schools were collected from the schools' principals, teachers, students, and parents. The findings from that portion of the study are detailed in chapter 2. After studying the data from the 98 schools, a set of 6 schools was identified for more extensive study. The 6 schools were demographically representative of the 98 schools but, more important, they were among the most impressive schools because of the educational programs and practices they had developed and implemented for their students. The detailed study of the 6 schools provided important insights about the manner in which the programs and the personnel in the six schools addressed

the unique needs of the students they served and each school's ability to evolve to best meet students' needs. Descriptions of the 6 schools are provided in chapter 3. The programs and practices implemented in the 6 schools are described in chapter 4 and the leadership practices of the schools are presented in chapter 5.

This chapter provides a set of brief discussions of the more significant findings from the study. The discussions are followed by a list of implications for middle level principals and teachers. Five themes serve as the basis for the discussions and implications: (1) academic excellence for all students, (2) educational core knowledge, (3) relationships, (4) communities of learning, and (5) leadership.

Expectations of Academic Excellence for All Students

The mission of this school is to guide students to achieve at a high level, believing that all kids can achieve at a higher level, and expecting that of all of them.

—Teacher at a highly successful school

The highly successful schools in this study had cultures of high expectations and success for all students. One teacher said, "Our faculty believes that all students can learn, given enough time and resources. I think what that means is, 'We take no excuses.'" Those words echoed throughout the discussions and interviews at the 6 site-visit schools, and the same philosophy was evident in the written responses from the other 92 schools. Establishing a culture of excellence and success requires the deep level of commitment found at all of the site-visit schools.

A commitment to excellence and success for all depends on the values and beliefs of the members of the organization. The teachers and principals in the highly successful schools worked together to clarify what they valued—what they considered "very important"—in the overall process of schooling. They also articulated what they believed—what they considered to be truths—about the schooling process.

Do these educators truly value success for all? Do they really believe that each student can learn, given adequate time and resources? Or have such statements become the politically correct response? The faculty members of these highly successful schools regularly discussed and articulated their values, beliefs, and commitment. They did so within the small-group work of their teams, committees, cadres, and councils. They did so in whole-group faculty meetings, as they discussed the directions and challenges of their schools. And they did so because their principals had established an environment in which such discussions were possible and expected. In each site-visit school, the principal was described repeatedly as espousing the positive values and beliefs that permitted faculty members to safely join in and build that collective voice for excellence and success. Teachers lacking in their level of commitment to excellence and success for all were on the outside looking in. As one teacher noted, "At our school, if you don't believe that all students have the capacity to learn, you will pretty much be pulling against the wagon."

A level of commitment to success is usually present to some degree in all schools. In the six site-visit schools, that level was given the opportunity to emerge and grow much deeper through the leadership of the six principals. The principals had to find the key to unlock the commitment and instill it as a part of the school's culture and they had to have the courage to establish and maintain high expectations. The principals met such challenges head on. They described the struggles they faced upon accepting their position, and the principals and their teachers articulated the commitment necessary to transform their schools into settings of excellence. The statement of one principal was typical of the commitment of the principals and the principals' willingness to face the challenge with their teachers: "When you look out there I want you to see your child, or if you don't have children, I want you to see yourself and how you want to be treated. This is our value: We are going to treat every one of them the same." Another principal described that it is important for principals to model their values and to treat teachers in the same manner in which teachers should treat students. Another was more direct: "It is my job to make sure that the ones [teachers] who don't want to improve are not here."

A school's vision guides the decisions and work of the school. The visions of the highly successful schools were based upon an understanding of current research that defines best practices; these visions reflect the values, beliefs, and commitments of the education communities they serve. The highly successful schools each had a vision that was student-centered. The visions were developmentally appropriate, yet challenging. They reflected an understanding of the maturation levels of each school's students. Each school's principal and teachers spoke frequently of high expectations for all students and of finding ways to foster success without compromising those expectations.

Implications for Practice

Academic excellence for all students was more than just a phrase in the highly successful schools. The principals and teachers translated that statement into action. They moved from talking about to trusting to acting on their beliefs about excellence. From the work of the highly successful schools, the following implications for practice in all middle level schools are offered for consideration to principals and teachers:

- Engage in purposeful discussions and staff development activities to establish a set of shared values, beliefs, and commitments about key aspects of the schooling process, including student learning, curriculum, instructional practices, and assessment practices
- Maintain ongoing dialogue about the values, beliefs, and commitments to internalize those into the daily life of the school
- Take a stand on what you believe is right for students and do everything possible to maintain that stance
- Accept the fact that faculty members who do not share the commitment to excellence should work somewhere else
- Engage in purposeful discussions and professional development activities to establish a collaborative vision of what the school will need to look like in the future to achieve and maintain a high level of excellence
- Build knowledge about best practices and apply that knowledge to the development of values, beliefs, and commitments and to the development of the vision and the goals necessary to accomplish school improvement.

Educational Core Knowledge

We spend a lot of time discussing what are effective teaching practices . . . what is developmentally responsive to young adolescents. We feel like this is an age group that is very unique and we are constantly trying to grow professionally on how to meet the needs of these students.

—*Principal of a highly successful school*

There is a significant difference between the existence of programs commonly recommended for practice in middle level literature and a thorough understanding of that literature coupled with the effective implementation of the programs. The schools selected for this study had high degrees of implementation of the programs because they were nominated and reviewed in part on the basis of their correspondence with the key indicators from *Turning Points: Preparing American Youth for the 21st Century* (Carnegie Council on Adolescent Development, 1989) and *Turning Points 2000: Educating Adolescents in the 21st Century* (Jackson & Davis, 2000). However, what was impressive about the schools, particularly the six site-visit schools, was the degree of knowledge and understanding that principals and teachers had about the research and literature on best programmatic practices in the middle level. They expressed strong support for middle level programs such as interdisciplinary teaming, exploratory courses, and advisory opportunities; they implemented those programs very effectively; and they articulated why they implemented the programs and how the programs were effective for their students. As one teacher noted, "[We] take and apply middle level concepts to students," and "incorporate enough programs and strategies to make kids feel successful." The site-visit schools established small learning communities for their students. Each school had an exploratory program that fit the needs of their respective students. These schools did not just implement the programs, they implemented them well and with a purpose. One teacher spoke for others at her school when she indicated that faculty members did not integrate curriculum across disciplines just to do so, they did it when there was a "natural" fit. The teacher continued, "Here, thematic units are used if they can advance learning."

As is evident in the opening quotation of this section, teachers in highly successful schools are committed to effective teaching practices. The data from the observations in the six site-visit schools revealed relatively high levels of students actively engaged in learning and low levels of disengagement. "We use a variety of different strategies," one teacher reported. Another stated, "At team meetings we discuss students behaviorally/academically and share what works."

Each school had an instructional improvement process in place, typically led by teacher cadres, committees, or teams. The principals usually established the structures for these groups, but the groups still functioned effectively because teachers accepted the responsibility of analyzing their instructional strategies. The teachers described their principals as strong and effective instructional leaders, but the processes the principals used would best be described as "shared." The teachers accepted leadership roles on committees and teams. They studied together and they learned from each other. They designed curriculum and instruction and assessment together and shared their work with their colleagues. The teachers "stepped up" and challenged their colleagues when challenges were necessary, and they complimented and celebrated one another over their successes.

The use of data to inform changes in curriculum and instruction and to promote student success was evident in the highly successful schools. Teachers administered common unit assessments to identify students who were in need of remediation or ready for enrichment. They observed one another and used a common language to discuss teaching practices. They studied schoolwide instructional profiles and developed strategies for improving practices. The data they used directly affected the way they worked with students on daily and weekly bases.

Implications for Practice
The depth of understanding and use of the core knowledge of middle level education, in particular, the design, development, and implementation of the curricular, instructional, and assessment programs, provide the basis for several implications for practice:

- Share the responsibility for instructional leadership, realizing that the paradigm of the principal as the sole instructional leader is questionable because, in highly successful schools, teachers with instructional expertise accept the responsibility of leadership among their peers
- Use small groups, whole-faculty groups, and individual sessions to study the current research about best programs and practices in middle level schools, including student learning, curricular programs, instructional practices, and assessment practices
- In formal settings, such as faculty meetings, team meetings, and committee meetings, discuss best teaching practices and share ideas and strategies for working with specific students
- Use interdisciplinary teams or some form of organizational structure to create small learning communities where students experience identity and personal attention as well as involvement and belonging, and where teachers accept responsibility for the success of each student in the team
- Use common planning times among team members, even if there is not a separate team planning time, to discuss student needs, design programs and instruction, meet with parents, and find methods to meet students' needs
- Use a variety of instructional strategies to engage students actively in the learning process
- Align curriculum, instruction, and assessment and

monitor the teaching of the curriculum to ensure that the "written" curriculum is the "taught" curriculum

- Use formative assessments on a regular basis to identify concepts for reteaching and enrichment, then adjust schedules and instruction to accommodate remediation and enrichment experiences on the basis of the assessments.

Relationships, Relationships, Relationships

If I am having a problem, I will ask another teacher to come and observe me and give me some ideas.
—A first-year teacher at a highly successful school

The number one thing is relationships.
—Principal of a highly successful school

The level of openness described by the first-year teacher exemplifies the collaborative culture found in the highly successful schools. The principal's statement shows the emphasis that leaders placed on establishing relationships within the highly successful schools. The word *relationships* appeared continually throughout the study. The extent of high-quality relationships was evident in the survey data and the interview transcripts. The principals and teachers spoke most frequently about the positive teacher–student relationships, teacher–teacher relationships, and teacher–principal relationships. Parent-teacher, parent–principal, and student–principal relationships were also described, but with less frequency. It was evident that the daily environment in the highly successful schools was characterized by positive interpersonal relationships among those working together. It also was evident that the principal established the norm for those relationships in the manner in which he or she worked with others in the school setting and that teachers understood the importance of relationships, particularly relationships with one another and their students.

In the classrooms, teachers talked about the importance of being attentive to students' needs, attending school functions, and understanding students' home life. They worked at getting to know their students and building a personal bond with them. That bond enabled teachers to push students academically, reduced discipline problems and increased student responses to teacher requests to control their behavior, and increased students' admiration of teachers. One student said, "I want to become a teacher because of [my teacher]." A teacher summed it up by stating, "The willingness to help students sets us apart—that is why we are here."

The organizational structures in the highly successful schools were designed to foster positive teacher–student relationships. Teachers in all of the site-visit schools spoke of the importance of getting to know each of their students personally, and teachers in the larger schools described how teaming provided the structure for positive teacher–student relationships. One principal addressed the importance of leaders monitoring the team's ability to build relationships. She said, "I will look at the team to see if they are doing activities with children. . . . I look to see if they are working hard enough on relationships with children."

Teachers viewed their schools as collegial and collaborative work environments. They frequently talked about sharing knowledge, strategies, and ideas for working with students. They spoke of caring for one another and of being a family. Friendships evolved because the teachers worked together toward a shared, common purpose. Many spoke of the amount of time they had worked together and the relationships they had formed over those years. The teachers in the highly successful schools had established a personal and professional bond with each other, not because they were close friends and then began to work together, but because they began to work together toward the common purpose of student success and then, over time, the personal and professional bond evolved.

The relationships among the principals and teachers in the highly successful schools could be characterized as outstanding. The survey data affirmed those positive relationships, and the interview data collected in the six site-visit schools provided a depth of understanding about the relationships. Principals seemed to take the initiative to build the relationships. They looked for genuine ways to compliment the work of the teachers. They described how they had felt as teachers and the importance of the principal valuing the work of teachers. The principals expressed understanding of the challenging role of the teacher and provided support to accomplish that role. They empowered their teachers and thus gained their respect and admiration. They also knew their teachers personally and provided support in times of personal problems and compliments in times of personal successes. They understood each teacher's individual personality and knew when to compliment, when to cajole, and when to challenge.

These principals valued parents and community members, and it was evident that the principals had been successful in building strong and supportive relationships with them. Strong efforts were made to involve parents and community members in the life of the school, and those efforts facilitated involvement in a variety of decision-making, instructional, and student support activities. Awareness was an important issue to these principals, and they provided numerous opportunities for parents and community members to learn about adolescent development and middle level programs. In addition, these principals demonstrated a commitment to understand and work with the various groups within their school communities. As a result, their schools were able to contribute positively to their communities and address significant community and multicultural issues. Principals also gave special attention to effective communication with parents, communication that often emphasized the "personal touch" of a telephone call or face-to-face meeting.

Implications for Practice

The relationships among teachers and students, teachers and teachers, and teachers and principals did more than enhance the capacity for each group to work together effectively on a daily basis. These strong relationships made it possible for faculty members to trust one another and meet the challenges necessary for excellence. Each site-visit school had a climate of trust and respect, which provided the basis for strong relationships with parents and community members. To establish that kind of environment takes time, purposeful effort, and commitment:

- Maintain ongoing discussions throughout the school year about the importance of behaviors that build and that destroy relationships
- Engage in study groups about the challenges inherent among the students the school serves, and design strategies to work more effectively to meet those challenges
- Accept personal responsibility to serve as a role model who exhibits the type of behavior from which students and other adults can learn
- Collect data about teachers' perception of the school's climate and culture, and discuss those data in small groups and as a whole faculty
- Engage in staff retreats away from the school setting at least once a year so school issues and challenges can be discussed or resolved, where planning can involve all teachers, and where relationships can be developed and nurtured
- Establish school structures that create small learning communities where relationships can become meaningful, including small interdisciplinary learning teams
- Build and maintain strong relationships with parents and community members and involve them in the life of the school; focus on building school and community awareness, and emphasize effective personal, two-way communication.

Communities of Learning

Our faculty believes in continual staff development.
　　　　　　　—*Teacher at a highly successful school*

Just about everything we do as a school we get together on. . . . We definitely collaborate on almost everything.
　　　　　　　—*Teacher at a highly successful school*

The concept of being a continual learner as an individual, a team or small group, and as a school was evident throughout this study. Learning was continually occurring throughout the highly successful site-visit schools and, more important, it was being shared, discussed, and applied. Graduate study and individual reading were common, as were small study groups. Teachers and principals at the site-visit schools frequently shared their experiences and knowledge beyond the bounds of their schools, making presentations and leading staff development in other schools and at state and national meetings.

The culture for continual learning was established by the principals of the highly successful schools and permeated the school community. The principals modeled learning as readers, participants in conferences and staff development, graduate students, and presenters. Teachers modeled continual learning for their students through continuing graduate studies, readings, and small-group and whole-faculty study sessions. With continual learning being modeled throughout the school, the opportunity was present for students to develop an understanding that learning never ends.

Teachers in the highly successful schools were given and accepted the responsibility to design their own professional development. The teachers and principals worked collaboratively to design professional development that supported their visions and goals. They were impatient with professional development that was not relevant or transferable to their work, and they were aggressive in reducing nonrelevant professional development.

There was a sense of purposefulness within the work of the highly successful schools. The schools' visions and goals provided that purpose, and the structures within the schools provided the framework for change. Change processes played a vital role in the development of these learning communities. Each school had at least one specific process for change, and those processes brought coherence to each school's improvement efforts. In each of the site-visit schools, the staff knew and appreciated the processes. In each case, the processes engaged teachers and often other stakeholders in the work of school improvement and change. And in each school, the changes correlated with the vision and goals of the schools.

Implications for Practice

When the culture of a school enables individuals, groups, and the whole faculty to identify the issues and challenges of the school and then design effective strategies to meet those needs, the school is well on its way to becoming an effective setting for the students it serves. The creation of that culture and the resultant community of learning require time to evolve. The six site-visit schools were excellent examples of organizations in which the culture of the school fostered a collective community of learning. The following implications for practice in all middle level schools are offered to principals and teachers:

- Establish "big picture" processes for change that are known by all staff members and are used as the format for continual growth and improvement so everyone in the school understands the importance of the change and the relationship of the change to the school's vision and goals
- Use small study groups to build knowledge and translate that knowledge into practice
- Be patient, because changing the culture of a school into a continual learning community usually takes multiple years
- Be impatient and be aggressive in the effort to move a school into a culture of continual learning; it does not happen by chance, it happens by design
- Use the current knowledge about the most-effective practices for professional development, including stakeholder design and delivery, relevance, application to practice, and follow-up support.

Leadership Makes a Difference

Every student can learn.
—*Principals at all six site-visit schools*

We have to ask ourselves, is it good for kids?
—*Principal of a highly successful school*

You get the feeling teachers genuinely care about students, and that starts at the top.
—*A teacher at a highly successful school*

Whether middle level principals make a difference in the quality of the school and the effect of the school on students is no longer a question for debate. For more than three decades, educators have surmised that principals do make such a difference. Recent meta-analyses (Cotton, 2003; Marzano, 2000; Waters, Marzano, & McNulty, 2003) confirm that, albeit the relationship may be more indirect than direct (Witziers, Bosker, & Kruger, 2003). Principals can positively influence the schools' curricular, instructional, and assessment pro-

grams. They can shape the organizational structures used to deliver the programs of the school. And principals can significantly influence the relationships among staff members within the school and the norms and values that form the basic culture. In essence, the principal is probably the most essential element in a highly successful school. The principal is necessary to set change into motion, to establish the culture of change and a learning organization, and to provide the support and energy to maintain the change over time until it becomes a way of life in the school. Over time, the principal's leadership will shape the school, positively or negatively. Without high-quality leadership, high-quality schools cannot exist. This was affirmed throughout the course of this study. The significance of leadership was found in the data from the 98 highly successful schools and it was even more apparent in the in-depth study of the 6 site-visit schools.

The personal characteristics of passion and commitment were evident in each of the site-visit principals. They had the passion to provide a high-quality learning experience for all students and a commitment to that goal that did not waiver. The site-visit principals and their teachers affirmed the belief that "students can learn." The performance of the principals modeled that belief. They communicated that belief in their behavior; their decisions; and the expectations they placed on individuals, small groups, and the whole faculty. They led conversations about success for each student, and they challenged their teachers to meet that expectation. They hired individuals who shared that belief and took a stand against those who did not share it, either working to change that individual's stance or by removing that person from the school setting. They understood the importance of literacy and mathematics in the lives of their students, and they designed programs and practices to address those needs. The principals demonstrated the moral backbone to lead a school that was just and equitable for all students.

The highly successful principals were knowledgeable of best educational practices, including curricular and instructional practices, change processes, and middle level programs. They shared that knowledge, and they articulated it in a manner that conveyed the expectation that everyone should understand it. To foster that knowledge, they encouraged individual development, small-group study sessions, and whole-faculty conversations. They participated in professional development with their teachers and frequently led professional development activities in their schools—and other schools. Their influence on effective middle level practices reached well beyond their respective schools.

Data from the 98 schools and the 6 site-visit schools confirmed that the highly successful schools were very well organized and operated efficiently on a daily basis. In the site-visit schools, established operational procedures provided security of mind about the day-to-day life in the school. As teachers became confident in the daily routines, they became able and willing to devote mental and physical energy to best pedagogical practices for students, to creative problem solving, and to risk taking. This managerial effectiveness was a direct result of the leadership of the principals and their understanding that daily life must go smoothly before teachers can expend effort on changes that will make the school an academically effective setting for all students.

The personalities and leadership styles of the principals in the six site-visit schools were different. However, an important common thread among the principals was their ability to distribute the roles and responsibilities of leadership among faculty members. In most instances the distribution was purposeful and included formal leadership roles and related decision making by individuals, committees, cadres, councils, advisory teams, interdisciplinary teams, school improvement teams, and task forces. The principals understood the relationship between involvement in and opportunity to make a decision and the teachers' commitment to implementing that decision. They understood the significance of sharing responsibility and creating a nucleus of leaders among the staff—rather than having a centralized leader responsible for every decision. They understood the value of grooming teacher-leaders, assistant principals, and administrative assistants for formal leadership roles. The schools were collaborative communities where issues, no matter how difficult, could be discussed openly and where individuals of strength and character could step up and be heard and lead the school to make good decisions for students. The principals not only provided that leadership when necessary, they also prepared others to provide that leadership. The collaborative cultures in the six site-visit schools were direct results of the leadership of the principals of each school.

Implications for Practice

Collectively, the principals in the set of 98 highly successful schools were an impressive group. The data about their schools and their leadership confirmed that their schools were exceptional and that their leadership was an integral part of why the schools were exceptional. The detailed study of the 6 site-visit schools provided specific insight about the performance of the principals that enabled them to make such a significant difference in their schools:

- Wear the mantle of leadership with conviction because, in today's education environment, the principal, more than any other individual within the school, will make a difference in the quality of the educational experiences students receive
- Be aggressive in articulating and modeling personal beliefs about the success of each student because few others will have the courage to do so and the school will not serve the needs of all students
- Understand that the teachers are the key individuals who collectively determine the school's quality and that they need involvement, the opportunity for leadership, encouragement, support, and a standard of high expectations for the way they think and behave toward the students they teach
- Establish formal structures, such as committees, cadres, vertical teams, advisory teams, school improvement teams, and task forces, to engage teachers and other stakeholders in the decision-making processes
- Identify potential leaders among faculty members and nurture their leadership talent by providing opportunities for them to become teacher-leaders and have other formal leadership roles, eventually leading to the principalship
- Read and build knowledge of best practices in middle level education, school improvement, change processes, collaborative and distributive leadership, and efficient daily management
- Develop confidence among faculty members, students, and parents that the daily operations of the school will go smoothly; implement effective daily operational routines throughout the school; and maintain communication with staff members so they know and follow those routines
- Implement organizational structures that enhance the academic and social success of middle level students, such as flexible schedules, interdisciplinary teaming, common planning times for team teachers, advisory classes, and extended academic opportunities for remediation and enrichment
- Understand the importance of literacy and mathematics as foundational skills of all middle level students, and do whatever is necessary to provide learning opportunities that prevent students from leaving school without those skills
- Collect and analyze data that will move the school toward accomplishing its vision and goals, including data about students; the school's environment; the instructional practices present throughout the school; the attitudes of parents, students, and teachers; and the integrity of the written and taught curriculum.

In *Turning Points 2000*, Jackson and Davis (2000) urged educators to design middle level schools that meet the needs of the "whole child." Such schools challenge students to think critically, work industriously, contribute to their communities, care about others, and care about their own physical and mental health. Young adolescents with those competencies "become adults whose beliefs, attitudes, and behavior contribute to the success of our democratic society" (Jackson & Davis, 2000, p. 23). The highly successful schools in this study demonstrated their commitment to developing the whole child, and they did so with an understanding of what was developmentally appropriate while maintaining high expectations for academic excellence. That understanding and a dedication to excellence were evident in the values, beliefs, and commitments the principals articulated and in the visions that guided their decisions. The principals implemented effective curricular programs and practices using organizational structures that fit their goals, and they used data as a basis for continual refinement of their work. Teachers and principals understood the importance of positive personal relationships among teachers, principals, students, parents, and community members. Effective leadership was a crucial factor for the success of each school. The leaders were instrumental in establishing a school culture of collaboration and morality. They created work environments where relationships were trusting and respectful. The principals used formal and informal change processes to establish professional learning communities that supported their commitment to success for each student. They created ways to personalize the educational experiences for their students.

The highly successful schools in this study were as diverse as the middle level schools across the nation. Some had large enrollments, others, small; some served urban and suburban communities whereas others served small towns and rural communities; and some were configured with grades 6–8 and others had grades 5–8 or 7–8. However, collectively the schools provided a preponderance of evidence that they were effectively meeting the unique needs of their students through a variety of developmentally appropriate programs and practices. Leaders, particularly principals, set the bar high and would not accept anything but excellence in the programs within their schools. Principals and teachers studied the existing knowledge, analyzed their schools, developed positive solutions to the same types of problems all schools face, and worked collaboratively to create schools that would make a difference in the educational lives of their students. Their level of commitment resulted in the success of the school and the success of their students.

Aikin, W. (1942). *The story of the eight-year study.* New York: Harper.

Alexander, W. (1984). The middle school emerges and flourishes. In J. Lounsbury (Ed.), *Perspectives: Middle school education, 1964–1984* (pp. 14–29). Columbus, OH: National Middle School Association.

Alexander, W., & George, P. (1981). *The exemplary middle school.* New York: Holt, Reinhart, and Winston.

Alexander, W., & McEwin, K. (1989, September). Schools in the middle: Progress 1968–1988. *Schools in the middle: A report on trends and practices.* Reston, VA: National Association of Secondary School Principals.

Alexander, W., & Williams, E. (1965). Schools for the middle years. *Educational Leadership, 23*(3), 217–223.

Andrews, R., & Soder, R. (1987). Principal instructional leadership and student achievement. *Educational Leadership, 44*(6), 9–11.

Anfara, V. A., Jr., & Waks, L. (2001). Resolving the tension between academic rigor and developmental appropriateness (Pt. 2). *Middle School Journal, 32*(3), 25–30.

Arnold, J., & Stevenson, C. (1998). *Teachers' teaming handbook: A middle level planning guide.* Orlando, FL: Harcourt Brace.

Baker, J. (1913). *Report of the Committee on the National Council of Education on Economy of Time in Education* (Bulletin 1913, No. 38). Washington, DC: Department of Interior, Bureau of Education.

Balfanz, R., & MacIver, D. J. (2000). Transforming high-poverty urban middle schools into strong learning institutions: Lessons from the first five years of the Talent Development Middle School. *Journal of Education for Students Placed at Risk, 5*(1/2), 137–158.

Barth, R. (1990). *Improving schools from within.* San Francisco: Jossey-Bass.

Bartlett, L. D., Weisenstein, G. R., & Etscheidt, S. (2002). *Successful inclusion for educational leaders.* Upper Saddle River, NJ: Merrill/Prentice Hall.

Bass, B. M. (1998). *Transformational leadership: Industrial, military, and educational impact.* Mahwah, NJ: Erlbaum Associates.

Beane, J. A. (1993). *A middle school curriculum: From rhetoric to reality* (2nd ed.). Columbus, OH: National Middle School Association.

Beane, J. A. (Ed.). (1995). *Toward a coherent curriculum.* Alexandria, VA: Association for Supervision and Curriculum Development.

Beane, J. A. (1997). *Curriculum integration: Designing the core of democratic education.* New York: Teachers College Press.

Beck, L. G., & Foster, W. (1999). Administration and community: Considering challenges, exploring possibilities. In J. Murphy & K. S. Louis (Eds.), *Handbook of research on educational administration* (2nd ed., pp. 337–358). San Francisco: Jossey-Bass.

Beck, L. G., & Murphy. J. (1994). *Ethics in educational leadership programs: An expanding role.* Thousand Oaks, CA: Corwin Press.

Becker, H. (1990). Curriculum and instruction in middle grades schools. *Phi Delta Kappan, 71*, 450–457.

Blase, J., & Blase, J. (1998). *Handbook of instructional leadership: How really good principals promote teaching and learning.* Thousand Oaks, CA: Corwin Press.

Blase, J., & Blase, J. (1999). Principals' instructional leadership and teacher development: Teacher perspectives. *Educational Administration Quarterly, 35,* 349–378.

Blase, J., & Blase, J. (2000). Principals' perspectives on shared governance leadership. *Journal of School Leadership, 10,* 9–39.

Bolman, L. G., & Deal, T. E. (1993). *The path to school leadership: A portable mentor.* Newbury Park, CA: Corwin Press.

Bough, M. (1969). Theoretical and practical aspects of the middle school. *Bulletin of the National Association of Secondary School Principals, 53*(335), 8–13.

Braddock, J. (1990). Tracking in the middle grades: National patterns of grouping for instruction. *Phi Delta Kappan, 71*, 445–449.

Briggs, T. (1920). *The junior high school.* Boston: Houghton Mifflin.

Brown, K. M., & Anfara, V. A., Jr. (2003). Paving the way for change: Visionary leadership in action at the middle level. *NASSP Bulletin, 87*(635), 16–34.

Carnegie Council on Adolescent Development. (1989). *Turning points: Preparing American youth for the 21st century.* Report of the Task Force on Education of Young Adolescents. New York: Carnegie Corporation of New York.

Cawelti, G. (1988, November). Middle schools a better match with early adolescent needs. ASCD survey finds. In *ASCD Curriculum Update.* Alexandria, VA: Association for Supervision and Curriculum Development.

Clark, D., & Valentine, J. (1981, June). Middle level educational programs: Making the ideal a reality. *NASSP schools in the middle: A report on trends and practices.*

Clark, D., & Valentine, J. (1992). Middle level programs: Making the ideal a reality. In S. Clark & D. Clark (Eds.), *Schools in the middle: A decade of growth and change* (pp. 149–156). Reston, VA: National Association of Secondary School Principals.

Clark, S., & Clark, D. (1990). *Arizona middle schools: A survey report.* Phoenix: Arizona Department of Education.

Clark, S., & Clark, D. (1992). Restructuring middle level schools: Strategies for using *Turning Points.* In S. Clark & D. Clark (Eds.), *Schools in the middle: A decade of growth and change* (pp. 177–189). Reston, VA: National Association of Secondary School Principals.

Clark, S., & Clark, D. (1993). Middle level school reform: The rhetoric and the reality. *Elementary School Journal, 93*(5), 448–460.

Clark, S., & Clark, D. (1994). *Restructuring the middle level school: Implications for school leaders.* Albany, NY: State University of New York Press.

Clark, S., & Clark, D. (1997). Implementation of authentic assessment programs: Issues, concerns, and guidelines. *Middle Level Educator, 6*(1), 10–13.

Clark, S., & Clark, D. (1998). *Program for student achievement, Phase I: School surveys, structured interviews, and shadow studies.* Unpublished report, University of Arizona, Tucson.

Clark, S., & Clark, D. (2000). Appropriate assessment strategies for young adolescents in an era of standards-based reform. *Clearing House, 73*, 201–204.

Clark S., & Clark, D. (2001). The challenge of curricular and instructional improvement in an era of high stakes testing. *Middle School Journal, 33*(2), 52–56.

Clark, S. N., & Clark, D. C. (2002a). Collaborative decision making: A promising but underused strategy for middle school improvement. *Middle School Journal, 33*(4), 52–57.

Clark, S. N., & Clark, D. C. (2002b). Making leadership for learning the top priority. *Middle School Journal, 34*(2), 50–55.

Clark, S., & Clark, D. (2003a). The middle school achievement project: Involving parents and community in school improvement. *Middle School Journal, 34*(3), 12–19.

Clark, S., & Clark, D. (2003b). Standards, accountability, and developmental appropriateness: A leadership challenge for middle school principals. *Middle School Journal, 34*(4), 56–61.

Clark, S., & Clark, D. (2003c). Perspective on three decades of the middle level principalship. *Middle School Journal, 35*(2), 48–54.

Clark, S. & Clark, D. (2004). Expert leadership and comprehensive professional development: A key to quality educators in middle schools. *Middle School Journal, 35*(4), 47–53.

Commission on the Reorganization of Secondary Education. (1918). *Cardinal principles of secondary education* (Bulletin 1918, No. 35). Washington, DC: Department of Interior, Bureau of Education.

Cooney, S. (2000). *A middle grades message: A well qualified teacher in every classroom matters.* Atlanta, GA: Southern Regional Education Board.

Cotton, K. (2003). *Principals and student achievement: What the research says.* Alexandria, VA: Association for Supervision and Curriculum Development.

Council of Chief State School Officers. (1992). *Turning points in action*. Washington, DC: Author.

Covey, S. (1989). *The 7 habits of highly effective people*. New York: Fireside Press, Simon and Schuster.

Danielson, C. (2002). *Enhancing student achievement: A framework for school improvement*. Alexandria, VA: Association for Supervision and Curriculum Development.

Darling-Hammond, L. (1997). *The right to learn: A blueprint for creating schools that work*. San Francisco: Jossey-Bass.

Davis, C. (1924). *Junior high school education*. Yonkers-on-Hudson, NY: World Book.

Deitte, D. (2002). Character education provides focus for advisory. *Middle School Journal, 34*(1), 21–26.

Dryfoos, J. G., & Maguire, S. (2002). *Inside full-service community schools*. Thousand Oaks, CA: Corwin Press.

DuFour, R. (2002). The learning-centered principal. *Educational Leadership, 59*(8), 12–15.

Eichhorn, D. (1966). *The middle school*. New York: Center for Applied Research.

Eichhorn, D. (1973). Middle school in the making. *Educational Leadership, 32*(3), 195–197.

Elmore, R. (1995a). Structural reform and educational practice. *Educational Researcher, 24*(9), 23–26.

Elmore, R. F. (1995b). Teaching, learning, and school organization: Principles of practice and the regularities of schooling. *Educational Administration Quarterly, 31*, 355–374.

Elmore, R. F. (1999). *Leadership of large-scale improvement in American education*. Cambridge, MA: Graduate School of Education, Harvard University.

Elmore, R. F. (2000, Winter). *Building a new structure for school leadership*. Washington, DC: Albert Shanker Institute.

Elmore, R. (2002). *Bridging the gap between standards and achievement: The imperative for professional development in education*. Washington, DC: Albert Shanker Institute.

English, F. W. (2000). *Deciding what to teach and test: Developing, aligning, and auditing the curriculum* (Millennium ed.). Thousand Oaks, CA: Corwin Press.

English, F. W., & Larson, R. L. (1996). *Curriculum management for educational and social service organizations* (2nd ed.). Springfield, IL: Charles C. Thomas.

Epstein, J., & MacIver, D. (1990). *Education in the middle grades*. Columbus, OH: National Middle School Association.

Epstein, J. L., Coates, L., Salinas, K. C., Sanders, M. G., & Simon, B. S. (1997). *School, family, and community partnerships: Your handbook for action*. Thousand Oaks, CA: Corwin Press.

Evans, R. (1996). *The human side of school change: Reform, resistance, and the real-life problems of innovation*. San Francisco: Jossey-Bass.

Felner, R., Jackson, A., Kasak, D., Mulhall, P., Brand, S., & Flowers, N. (1997). The impact of school reform for the middle years: A longitudinal study of a network engaged in *Turning Points*-based comprehensive school transformation. *Phi Delta Kappan, 78*, 528–532, 541–550.

Flowers, N., Mertens, S. B., & Mulhall, P. F. (1999). The impact of teaming: Five research-based outcomes. *Middle School Journal, 31*(2), 57–60.

Flowers, N., Mertens, S. B., & Mulhall, P. F. (2000a). How teaming influences classroom practices. *Middle School Journal, 32*(2), 52–59.

Flowers, N., Mertens, S. B., & Mulhall, P. F. (2000b). What makes interdisciplinary teams effective? *Middle School Journal, 31*(4), 53–56.

Flowers, N., Mertens, S. B., & Mulhall, P. F. (2002). Four important lessons about teacher professional development. *Middle School Journal, 33*(5), 57–63.

Fosnot, C. T. (1996). Constructivism: A psychological theory of learning. In C. A. Fosnot (Ed.), *Constructivism: Theory, perspectives, and practice* (pp. 8–33). New York: Teachers College Press.

Fullan, M. (1993). *Change forces: Probing the depths of educational reform*. London: Falmer Press.

Fullan, M. (1998). Leadership for the 21st century—breaking the bonds of dependency. *Educational Leadership 55*(7), 6–10.

Fullan, M. (2001). *Leading in a culture of change*. San Francisco: Jossey-Bass.

Fullan, M. (2002). The change leader. *Educational Leadership, 58*(8), 16–20.

Fullan, M. (2003a). *Change forces with a vengeance.* New York: RoutledgeFalmer.

Fullan, M. (2003b). *The moral imperative of school leadership.* Thousand Oaks, CA: Sage.

Gatewood, T. (1973). What research says about the middle school. *Educational Leadership, 31*(3), 221–224.

George, P. S., & Alexander, W. M. (1993). *The exemplary middle school* (2nd ed.). Orlando, FL: Harcourt Brace.

George, P., & Oldaker, L. (1985). *Evidence for the middle school.* Columbus, OH: National Middle School Association.

George, P., & Shewey, K. (1995). *New evidence for the middle school.* Columbus, OH: National Middle School Association.

Gilles, C., Cramer, M., & Hwang, S. (2001). Beginning teacher perception: A longitudinal look at teacher development. *Action in Teacher Education, 13*(3), 89–96.

Glatthorn, A. A. (1997). *The principal as curriculum leader: Shaping what is taught and tested.* Thousand Oaks, CA: Corwin Press.

Glickman, C. D. (2002). *Leadership for learning: How to help teachers succeed.* Alexandria, VA: Association for Supervision and Curriculum Development.

Goldring, E. B., & Sullivan, A. V. (1996). Beyond the boundaries: Principals, parents and communities shaping the school environment. In K. Leithwood, J. Chapman, D. Corson, P. Hallinger, & A. Hart (Eds.), *International handbook of educational leadership and administration* (pp. 195–222). Dordrecht, The Netherlands: Kluwer Academic.

Grambs, J., Noyce, F., & Robertson, J. (1961). *The junior high school we need.* Washington, DC: Association for Supervision and Curriculum Development.

Green, R. L. (2001). *Practicing the art of leadership: A problem–based approach to implementing the ISLLC standards.* Upper Saddle River, NJ: Merrill/Prentice Hall.

Grogan, M., & Andrews, R. (2002). Defining preparation and professional development for the future. *Educational Administration Quarterly, 38,* 233–256.

Grooms, M. (1967). *Perspectives on the middle school.* Columbus, OH: Merrill Books.

Gruhn, W., & Douglass, H. (1947). *The modern junior high school.* New York: Ronald.

Hackmann, D. G., & Valentine, J. W. (1998). Designing an effective middle level schedule. *Middle School Journal, 29*(5), 3–13.

Hansen, J., & Hern, A. (1971). *The middle school program.* Chicago: Rand McNally.

Hipp, K. A. (1997). The impact of principals in sustaining middle school change. *Middle School Journal, 28*(5), 42–45.

Huelskamp, R. M. (1993). Perspectives on education in America. *Phi Delta Kappan, 74,* 718–721.

Institute for Educational Leadership. (2000). *Leadership for student learning: Reinventing the principalship. A report of the task force on the principalship.* Washington, DC: Author.

Interstate School Leaders Licensure Consortium. (1996). *Standards for school leaders.* Washington, DC: Council of Chief State School Officers.

Irvin, J. L. (1992). Developmentally appropriate instruction: The heart of the middle school. In J. L. Irvin (Ed.), *Transforming middle level education: Perspectives and possibilities* (pp. 295–313). Needham Heights, MA: Allyn and Bacon.

Irvin, J. (Ed.). (1997). *What current research says to the middle level practitioner.* Columbus, OH: National Middle School Association.

Jackson, A. (1990). From knowledge to practice: Implementing the recommendations of *Turning Points. Middle School Journal, 21*(3), 1–3.

Jackson, A., & Davis, G. (2000). *Turning points 2000: Educating adolescents for the 21st century.* New York: Teachers College Press.

Jenkins, J. M., & Weldon, J. (1999). Reflections on retention and social promotion. *International Journal of Educational Reform, 8,* 308–311.

Keefe, J., Clark, D., Nickerson, N., & Valentine, J. (1983). *The middle level principalship: Vol. 2. The effective middle level principal.* Reston, VA: National Association of Secondary School Principals.

Keefe, J. W., & Jenkins, J. M. (2002). Personalized instruction. *Phi Delta Kappan, 83,* 440–448.

Keefe, J., Valentine, J. Clark, D., & Irvin, J. (1994). *Leadership in middle level education: Vol. 2. Leadership in successfully restructuring middle level schools.* Reston, VA: National Association of Secondary School Principals.

Kennedy, J. F. (2003). Remarks prepared by President Kennedy for delivery to the annual meeting of the Dallas Citizens Council, November 22, 1963. Retrieved May 22, 2004, from John Fitzgerald Kennedy Library Web site, www.cs.umb.edu/jfklibrary/j112263b.htm

Kettler, R., & Valentine, J. (2000). *Parent involvement and student achievement at the middle level* (NMSA Research Summary No. 18). Retrieved March 25, 2004, from National Middle School Association Web site; www.nmsa.org

Koos, L. (1927). *The junior high school.* Boston: Ginn.

Kotter, J. (1996). *Leading change.* Boston: Harvard Business Review Press.

Kotter, J. (1999). *What leaders really do.* Boston: Harvard Business Review Press.

Kruse, S. D. (2001). Creating communities of reform: Continuous improvement planning teams. *Journal of Educational Administration, 39,* 359–383.

Lambert, L., Walker, D., Zimmerman, D. E., & Cooper, J. E. (2002). *The constructivist leader* (2nd ed.). New York: Teachers College Press.

Leithwood, K., & Jantzi, D. (2000). The effects of transformational leadership on organizational conditions and student engagement with school. *Journal of Educational Administration, 38*(2), 112–129.

Leithwood, K., Jantzi, D., & Steinbach, R. (1999). *Changing leadership for changing times.* Buckingham, England: Open University Press.

Lipka, R., Lounsbury, J., Toepfer, C., Vars, G., Alessi, S., & Kridel, C. (1998). *The eight-year study revisited: Lesson from the past for the present.* Columbus, OH: National Middle School Association.

Lipsitz, J. (1984). *Successful schools for young adolescents.* New Brunswick, NJ: Transaction Books.

Lipsitz, J., Mizell, H., Jackson, J., & Austin, L. (1997). Speaking with one voice: A manifesto for middle grades reform. *Phi Delta Kappan, 78,* 533–540.

Lockwood, A. T. (1997). *Character education: Controversy and consensus.* Thousand Oaks, CA: Sage.

Louis, K. S., & Murphy, J. (1994). The evolving role of the principal: Some concluding thoughts. In J. Murphy & K. S. Louis (Eds.), *Reshaping the principalship: Insights from transformational reform efforts* (pp. 265–281). Thousand Oaks, CA: Corwin Press.

Lounsbury, J. (1954). *The role and status of the junior high school.* Unpublished doctoral dissertation, George Peabody College for Teachers, Nashville, TN.

Lounsbury, J. (1991). *As I see it.* Columbus, OH: National Middle School Association.

Lounsbury, J., & Clark, D. (1990). *Inside grade eight: From apathy to excitement.* Reston, VA: National Association of Secondary School Principals.

Lounsbury, J., & Johnston, J. H. (1985). *How fares the ninth grade.* Reston, VA: National Association of Secondary School Principals.

Lounsbury, J., & Johnston, J. H. (1988). *Life in the three sixth grades.* Reston, VA: National Association of Secondary School Principals.

Lunenburg, F. C., & Ornstein, A. C. (1997). *Educational administration: Concepts and practices.* Belmont, CA: Wadsworth.

MacIver, D. (1990). Meeting the needs of young adolescents: Advisory groups, interdisciplinary teaching teams, and school transition programs. *Phi Delta Kappan, 71,* 458–464.

MacIver, D. J., & Epstein, J. L. (1993). Middle grades research: Not yet mature, but no longer a child. *Elementary School Journal, 93,* 519–533.

Mapp, K. (1997). Making the connection between families and schools. *Harvard Education Letter, XIII*(5), 1–3.

Marks, H. M., & Louis, K. S. (1999). Teacher empowerment and the capacity for organizational learning. *Educational Administration Quarterly, 35,* 707–750.

Marks, H. M., & Printy, S. M. (2003). Principal leadership and school performance: An integration of transformational and instructional leadership. *Educational Administration Quarterly, 39*(3), 370–397.

Marshall, C., & McCarthy, M. (2002). School leadership reforms: Filtering social justice through dominant discourses. *Journal of School Leadership, 12,* 480–502.

Marzano, R. J. (2000). *A new era of school reform: Going where the research takes us.* Aurora, CO: Mid-continent Research for Education and Learning.

Marzano, R. J., Pickering, D. J., & Pollock, J. E. (2001). *Classroom instruction that works: Research-based strategies for increasing student achievement.* Alexandria, VA: Association for Supervision and Curriculum Development.

Mayer, D. (1998). Do new teaching standards undermine performance on old tests? *Educational Evaluation and Policy Analysis, 20*(2), 53–73.

McCarthy, M. M. (2002). Educational leadership preparation programs: A glance at the past with an eye toward the future. *Leadership and Policy in Schools, 1,* 201–221.

McCarthy, M. M., & Kuh, G. D. (1997). *Continuity and change: The educational leadership professorate.* Columbia, MO: University Council for Educational Administration.

McEwin, K., & Dickinson, T. (1996). *Forgotten youth, forgotten teachers: Transformation of the professional preparation of teachers for young adolescents.* New York: Middle Grades School State Policy Initiative, Carnegie Corporation of New York.

McEwin, K., Dickinson, T., Erb, T., & Scales, P. (1995). *A vision of excellence: Organizing principles for middle grades teacher preparation.* Columbus, OH: National Middle School Association.

McEwin, C. K., Dickinson, T. S., & Jenkins, D. M. (1996). *America's middle schools: Practices and progress. A 25 year perspective.* Columbus, OH: National Middle School Association.

McLaughlin, J. H., & Doda, N. M. (1997). Teaching with time on your side: Developing long-term relationships in schools. In J. Irvin (Ed.), *What current research says to the middle level practitioner* (pp. 57–71). Columbus, OH: National Middle School Association.

Midgley, C., & Edelin, K. (1998). Middle school reform and early adolescent well-being: The good news and the bad. *Educational Psychologist, 33,* 195–206.

Miller, E. (1995, November/December). Shared decision-making by itself doesn't make for better decisions. *Harvard Education Letter, 11,* 1–4.

Mizell, H. (2002). *Shooting for the sun: The message of middle school reform.* New York: Edna McConnell Clark Foundation.

Monk, D. H., & Plecki, M. L. (1999). Generating and managing resources for school improvement. In J. Murphy & K. S. Louis (Eds.), *Handbook of research on educational administration* (2nd ed., pp. 491–509). San Francisco: Jossey-Bass.

Mullen, C. A., Gordon, S. P., Greenlee, B. J., & Anderson, R. H. (2002). Capacities for school leadership: Emerging trends in the literature. *International Journal of Educational Reform, 11,* 158–198.

Mullins, E. R., & Irvin, J. L. (2000). Transition into middle school. *Middle School Journal, 3*(3), 57–60.

Murphy, M. M. (1998). *Character education in America's Blue Ribbon Schools: Best practices for meeting the challenge.* Lancaster, PA: Technomic.

Murphy, J. (1999). *The quest for a center: Notes on the state of the profession of educational leadership.* Columbia, MO: University Council for Educational Administration.

Murphy, J. (2002). Reculturing the profession of educational leadership: New blueprints. *Educational Administration Quarterly, 38,* 176–191.

NASSP Council on Middle Level Education. (1985). *An agenda for excellence at the middle level.* Reston, VA: National Association of Secondary School Principals.

National Association of Elementary School Principals. (1991). *Proficiencies for principals: Elementary and middle schools.* Alexandria, VA: Author.

National Association of State Directors of Teacher Education and Certification. (1994). *NASDTEC outcome-based standards and portfolio assessment: Outcome-based teacher education standards for elementary, middle and high school levels.* Mashpee, MA: Author

National Center for Education Statistics. (1999, September). *Service-learning and community service in K-12 public schools.* Washington, DC: U.S. Department of Education.

National Center for Education Statistics. (2002). *Digest of education statistics, 2002.* Washington, DC: U.S. Department of Education, Office of Educational Research and Improvement.

National Commission on Excellence in Education. (1983). *A nation at risk: The imperative for educational reform. A report to the nation and the Secretary of Education, United States Department of Education.* Washington, DC: Author.

National Middle School Association. (1982). *This we believe.* Columbus, OH: Author.

National Middle School Association. (1995). *This we believe: Developmentally responsive middle level schools.* Columbus, OH: Author.

National Middle School Association. (2003). *This we believe: Successful schools for young adolescents.* Columbus, OH: Author.

National Partnership for Excellence and Accountability in Teaching. (1999). Characteristics of effective professional development. Retrieved August 23, 2002, from www.ericsp.org/pages/digests/NPEAT.htm.

Newmann, F., & Wehlage, G. (1995). *Successful school restructuring: A report to the public and educators by the Center on Organization and Restructuring of Schools.* Madison, WI: University of Wisconsin, Center on Organization and Restructuring of Schools, School of Education, Wisconsin Center for Education Research.

Newmann, F., Smith, B., Allensworth, E., & Bryk, A. (2002). Improving Chicago's schools: School instructional program coherence. *ERS Spectrum, 20*(2), 38–46.

No Child Left Behind Act of 2001, 115 Stat. 1425 (2002).

Noddings, N. (1988). An ethic of caring and its implications for instructional arrangements. *American Journal of Education, 96*(2), 215–231.

Oakes, J., Quartz, K. H., Ryan, S., & Lipton, M. (2000). *Becoming good American schools: The struggle for civic virtue in education reform.* San Francisco: Jossey-Bass.

Painter, B., Lucas, S., Wooderson, M., & Valentine, J. (2000). *The use of teams in school improvement processes.* Reston, VA: National Association of Secondary School Principals.

Painter, B., & Valentine, J. (1996). Instructional Practices Inventory. Columbia, MO: University of Missouri Center for School Improvement.

Painter, B., & Valentine, J. (2002). Instructional Practices Inventory (revised). Columbia, MO: University of Missouri Middle Level Leadership Center.

Prawat, R. W., & Peterson, P. L. (1999). Social constructivist views of learning. In J. Murphy & K. S. Louis (Eds.), *Handbook of research on educational administration* (2nd ed., pp. 203–226). San Francisco: Jossey-Bass.

Pringle, R. (1937). *The junior high school: A psychological approach.* New York: McGraw-Hill.

Quinn, D., Greunert, S., & Valentine, J. (1999). *Using data for school improvement.* Reston, VA: National Association of Secondary School Principals.

Reyes, P., Wagstaff, L. H., & Fusarelli, L. D. (1999). Delta forces: The changing fabric of American society and education. In J. Murphy & K. S. Louis (Eds.), *Handbook of research on educational administration* (2nd ed., pp. 183–201). San Francisco: Jossey-Bass.

Rock, D., & Hemphill, J. (1966). *The junior high school principalship.* Reston, VA: National Association of Secondary School Principals.

Rosenholtz, S. (1991). *Teachers' workplace: The social organization of school.* New York: Teachers College Press.

Rosselli, H. C., & Irvin, J. L. (2001). Differing perspectives, common ground: The middle school and gifted education relationship. *Middle School Journal, 32*(3), 57–62.

Rowan, B. (1995). Research on learning and teaching in K-12 schools: Implications for the field of educational administration. *Educational Administration Quarterly, 31,* 115–133.

Sale, L. (1979). *Introduction to middle school teaching.* Columbus, OH: Charles E. Merrill.

Scales, P. C. (1992). *Windows of opportunity: Improving middle grades teacher preparation.* Chapel Hill: University of North Carolina, Center for Early Adolescence.

Scales, P. C., & McEwin, C. K. (1994). *Growing pains: The making of America's middle school teachers.* Columbus, OH: National Middle School Association.

Schlechty, P. C. (1997). *Inventing better schools: An action plan for educational reform.* San Francisco: Jossey-Bass.

Schmoker, M., & Marzano, R. (1999). Realizing the promise of standards-based education. *Educational Leadership, 56*(6), 17–21.

Schön, D. A. (1987). *Educating the reflective practitioner.* San Francisco: Jossey-Bass.

Shapiro, S., & Klemp, R. (1996). The interdisciplinary team organization: Promoting teacher efficacy and collaboration. *Michigan Middle School Journal, 20*(2), 26–32.

Short, P. M., & Greer, J. T. (1997). *Leadership in empowered schools: Themes from innovative efforts.* Upper Saddle River, NJ: Prentice-Hall.

Smith, W., & Andrews, R. (1989) *Instructional leadership: How principals make a difference.* Alexandria, VA: ASCD.

Smrekar, C. E., & Mawhinney, H. B. (1999). Integrated services: Challenges in linking schools, families, and communities. In J. Murphy & K. S. Louis (Eds.), *Handbook of research on educational administration* (2nd ed., pp. 443–461). San Francisco: Jossey-Bass.

Smylie, M. A., & Hart, A. W. (1999). School leadership for teacher learning and change: A human and social capital development perspective. In J. Murphy & K. S. Louis (Eds.), *Handbook of research on educational administration* (2nd ed., pp. 421–441). San Francisco: Jossey-Bass.

Smyth, J. (1996). The socially just alternative to the "self-managing school." In K. Leithwood, J. Chapman, D. Corson, P. Hallinger, & A. Hart (Eds.), *International handbook of educational leadership and administration* (pp. 1097–1131). Dordrecht, The Netherlands: Kluwer Academic.

Sparks, D., & Hirsh, S. (1997). *A new vision for staff development.* Alexandria, VA: Association for Supervision and Curriculum Development.

Sparks, D., & Hirsh, S. (2000). *Learning to lead, leading to learn.* Oxford, OH: National Staff Development Council.

Stake, R. (1999). The goods on American education. *Phi Delta Kappan, 80,* 668–670, 672.

Starratt, R. J. (1996). *Transforming educational administration: Meaning, community, and excellence.* New York: McGraw-Hill.

Stigler, J. W., & Hiebert, J. (1999). *The teaching gap: Best ideas from the world's teachers for improving education in the classroom.* New York: The Free Press.

Strike, K. A. (1999). Can schools be communities? The tension between shared values and inclusion. *Educational Administration Quarterly, 35,* 46–70.

Sykes, G. (1995). Learning, teaching, and administering: A response to Rowan. *Educational Administration Quarterly, 31,* 143–150.

Thomason, J., & Thompson, M. (1992). Motivation: Moving, learning, mastering, and sharing. In J. L. Irvin (Ed.), *Transforming middle level education: Perspectives and possibilities* (pp. 275–294). Needham Heights, MA: Allyn and Bacon.

Thomson, S. (Ed.). (1993). *Principals for our changing schools: Knowledge and skill base.* Lancaster, PA: Technomic.

Tomlinson, C. (1999). *The differentiated classroom: Responding to the needs of all learners.* Alexandria, VA: Association for Supervision and Curriculum Development.

Tomlinson, C. A. (2001a). Grading for success. *Educational Leadership, 58*(6), 12–15.

Tomlinson, C. A. (2001b). How to differentiate instruction in mixed-ability classrooms (2nd ed.). Alexandria, VA: Association for Supervision and Curriculum Development.

Trimble, S. (2003). Research-based classroom practices and student achievement. *Middle School Journal, 35*(1), 52–58.

Trump, J. L. (1969). Changes needed for the further improvement of secondary education in the United States. *The Bulletin of the National Association of Secondary School Principals, 53*(333), 117–133.

Trump, J. L., & Baynham, D. (1961). *Focus on change: Guide to better schools.* Chicago: Rand-McNally.

Trump, J. L., & Georgiades, W. (1970). Doing better with what you have—N.A.S.S.P. Model Schools Program. *The Bulletin of the National Association of Secondary School Principals, 54*(346), 106–133.

U.S. Department of Labor. (2002–2003). *Occupational outlook handbook, 2002–2003 edition.* Washington, DC: U. S. Department of Labor, Bureau of Labor Statistics. Retrieved January 29, 2003, from U. S. Department of Labor Web site: http://stats.bls.gov/oco/home.htm.

Valentine, J., Clark, D., Hackmann, D., & Petzko, V. (2002). *A national study of leadership in middle level schools: Vol. 1. A national study of middle level leaders and school programs.* Reston, VA: National Association of Secondary School Principals.

Valentine, J., Clark, D., Irvin, J., Keefe, J., & Melton, G. (1993). *Leadership in middle level education: Vol. 1. A national survey of middle level leaders in schools.* Reston, VA: National Association of Secondary School Principals.

Valentine, J., Clark, D., Nickerson, N., & Keefe, J. (1981). *The middle level principalship: Vol. 1. A survey of middle level principals and programs.* Reston, VA: National Association of Secondary School Principals.

Valentine, J. W., Maher, M. C., Quinn, D. M., & Irvin, J. L. (1999). The changing roles of effective middle level principals. *Middle School Journal, 30*(5), 53–56.

Vars, G. (1969). *Common learnings: Core and interdisciplinary teaming approaches.* Scranton, PA: Intext.

Van Til, W., Vars, G., & Lounsbury, J. (1961). *Modern education for the junior high years.* Indianapolis, IN: Bobbs-Merrill.

Walton, M. (1986). *The Deming management method.* New York: Penguin Putnam.

Waters, J. T., Marzano, R. J., & McNulty, B. A. (2003). *Balanced leadership: What 30 years of research tells us about the effect of leadership on student achievement.* Aurora, CO: Mid-Continent Research for Education and Learning.

Wehlage, G., Newmann, F., & Secada, W. (1996). Standards for authentic achievement and pedagogy. In F. Newmann & Associates (Eds.), *Authentic achievement: Restructuring schools for intellectual quality* (pp. 21–48). San Francisco: Jossey-Bass.

Weick, K. E. (1976). Educational organizations as loosely-coupled systems. *Administrative Science Quarterly, 21*(1), 1–19.

Wheelock, A. (1998). *Safe to be smart: Building a culture for standards-based reform in the middle grades.* Columbus, OH: National Middle School Association.

Whitaker, K. S. (2003). Principal role changes and influence on principal recruitment and selection. *Journal of Educational Administration, 41,* 37–54.

Wiggins, G. (1996). Honesty and fairness: Toward better grading and reporting. In T. R. Guskey (Ed.), *ASCD Yearbook 1996: Communicating student learning* (pp. 141–177). Alexandria, VA: Association for Supervision and Curriculum Development.

Wiggins, G., & McTighe, J. (1998). *Understanding by design.* Alexandria, VA: Association for Supervision and Curriculum Development.

Windschitl, M. (1999). The challenges of sustaining a constructivist classroom culture. *Phi Delta Kappan, 80,* 751–755.

Witziers, B., Bosker, R., & Kruger, M. (2003). Educational leadership and student achievement: The elusive search for an association. *Educational Administration Quarterly, 39*(3), 398–425.

Wright, G., & Greer, E. (1963). *The junior high school: A survey of grades 7-8-9 in junior and senior high schools—1959–60.* Washington, DC: U.S. Department of Health, Education, and Welfare, Office of Education.

Youngs, P., & King, M. B. (2002). Principal leadership for professional development to build school capacity. *Educational Administration Quarterly, 38,* 643–670.

Zemelman, S., Daniels, H., & Hyde, A. (1998). *Best practice: New standards for teaching and learning in America's schools* (2nd ed.). Portsmouth, NH: Heinemann.

Appendix A:

A-1
Nominator Letters, Form, and Criteria

Name _____ Date _____

Address _____

City, State, ZIP _____

Dear (Name):

At the beginning of each of the past two decades the National Association of Secondary School Principals (NASSP) sponsored a National Study of Middle Level Principals and Schools. The 1980 and 1990 studies provided significant information about developments in middle level education and the principalship. As we move through the year 2000, we are again in the midst of this "decade" study.

We recently concluded the data collection for the <u>first phase</u> of this current three-year study of middle level principals and programs. The information from that phase will establish a "state of the art" image of middle level leadership and school practices in the year 2000.

We are now beginning the <u>second phase</u> of the study, which is where your participation is important. This phase includes a study of 100 successful middle level principals and schools across the nation. We are asking middle level leaders from throughout the United States to submit nominations of middle schools that they consider to be exemplary according to the principles of *Turning Points* (attached). Because we are seeking a geographically representative sample of 100 successful schools, we are asking you to restrict your nominations to schools in your state. For your state, we are asking you to nominate no more than (number specified per state) schools.

To facilitate your participation in this process, we have established a website for you to electronically submit your nominations. The website contains the directions you will need to make your nominations. It will take but a few moments. Please use the following web address to access the website:

Website address: <u>web address specified</u>

We know you are certainly busy. We truly appreciate the time you can take to help us in this next phase of the study. Your nominations provide the opportunity for highly successful middle level schools to be recognized. In addition, the information gleaned from the 100 selected schools will provide a database of best practices in a relatively large set of highly successful middle level schools. Practitioners and researchers will benefit from such a knowledge base.

If you have any questions, please contact me by email at <u>ValentineJ@missouri.edu</u>. Thank you for your time and help in this portion of the study.

Jerry Valentine
National Study Research Team Chair
Director, Middle Level Leadership Center
University of Missouri

Research Team Members:
Donald C. Clark, University of Arizona
Vicki Petzko, University of Tennessee–Chattanooga
Donald Hackmann, Iowa State University
John Nori, NASSP

A-2

National Study of Leadership in Middle Level Schools
NOMINATOR FORM

Please use this form to submit the names of middle level schools and principals who are, in your opinion, highly successful at meeting the needs of middle level students. To be deemed "successful" a middle school must be addressing each of the eight principles from *Turning Points: Preparing American Youth for the 21st Century.*

A summary of the *Turning Points* principles may be found by clicking <u>here</u>.

Please provide support for your nomination by completing at least two of the sections below that ask for detailed evidence about how this school is meeting the *Turning Points* principles. While this will require some additional time and effort on your part, we are asking you to do this so that the nominations you make are based on the actual goodness of the schools' programs rather than on reputation alone.

Click the "submit" button at the bottom of the form when you have completed it. To make each additional nomination, return to this page after you have "submitted" the prior nomination.

If you have any difficulty in completing this form, please e-mail me at <u>nationalstudy@coe.missouri.edu</u>.

Thank you,
Jerry Valentine
Middle Level Leadership Center, University of Missouri

The NASSP Research Team
Donald Clark (University of Arizona)
Vicki Petzko (University of Tennessee–Chattanooga)
Donald Hackmann (Iowa State University)
John Nori (NASSP)
Jerry Valentine, Chair (University of Missouri)

Nominator Information

Nominator's Name _____

Nominator's E-mail Address _____

Nominated School Information_____

Name of Nominated School _____

School District: _____City _____State ____

Principal's Name _____

**Please provide evidence that this school meets two or three of the *Turning Points* principles.
Use the pull-down menu to indicate which principle your description addresses.**

1. Creating a community for learning
2. Teaching a core of common knowledge
3. Ensuring success for all students
4. Empowering teachers and administrators
5. Developing expert teachers of young adolescents
6. Improving academic performance through better health and fitness
7. Reengaging families in the education of young adolescents
8. Connecting schools with communities

Please select which *Turning Points* principle this description addresses ☐(pull-down menu)
Please describe how this school specifically meets this *Turning Points* principle:

Please select which Turning Points principle this description addresses ☐(pull-down menu)
Please describe how this school specifically meets this *Turning Points* principle:

Please select which Turning Points principle this description addresses ☐(pull-down menu)
Please describe how this school specifically meets this *Turning Points* principle:

SUBMIT   RESET

Appendix B:

Nominated Schools Invitation

Name _____ Date _____

Address _____

City, State, ZIP _____

Dear (Name):

At the beginning of each of the past two decades the National Association of Secondary School Principals (NASSP) sponsored a National Study of Middle Level Principals and Schools. The 1980 and 1990 studies provided significant information about developments in middle level education and the principalship, and the year 2000 finds us once again conducting this landmark study.

We have just recently concluded the data collection for the first phase of the study—an Internet-based survey in which every middle level principal in the United States had the opportunity to participate. The information we glean from this survey will help establish what the "state of the art" in middle level leadership and school practices is in the year 2000.

We are now beginning the second phase of the study, which is where your participation comes in. This phase of the study will be focused on 100 successful middle level principals and schools from across the nation. You and your school have been nominated by a middle level leader, expert, or advocate to participate in this phase of the study because he or she considers you and your school to be exemplary according to the principles of *Turning Points* (attached).

The purpose of this letter is to solicit your participation in the study by asking you to complete a survey that will help us more fully understand your school's mission, context, change processes, efforts to meet student needs, leadership practices, and programs that put into practice the recommendations from *Turning Points*. In order to facilitate your participation in this process, we have set up a website for you to electronically submit your responses. The website contains all of the directions you will need to complete the form. Please use this information to access the website:

Website address: [web address specified]

Password: [password specified]

While we know you are certainly busy, we truly appreciate the time you can take to help us in this next phase of the study. Please respond by (date). If you have any questions, please contact me by e-mail at valentinej@missouri.edu. Thank you for your time and help in this study.

Jerry Valentine
Director, Middle Level Leadership Center
University of Missouri

Appendix C:

Nominated Schools Web Response Form

(Welcome and Directions)

Welcome to the
National Study of Leadership in Middle Level Schools

Dear Principal,

Thank you for logging on. This study of successful middle level schools and principals is sponsored by the National Association of Secondary School Principals and is being conducted by the Middle Level Leadership Center at the University of Missouri–Columbia.

Please enter the user ID and password you received in your letter inviting you to participate in this phase of the study and then click on the continue button.

Username: _____   Password: _____   **CONTINUE**

If you have any questions about the study, contact us at: nationalstudy@coe.missouri.edu.

Jerry Valentine
Middle Level Leadership Center, University of Missouri

The NASSP Research Team:
Donald Clark (University of Arizona)
Vicki Petzko (University of Tennessee–Chattanooga)
Donald Hackmann (Iowa State University)
John Nori (NASSP)
Jerry Valentine, Chair (University of Missouri)

SCREEN TWO

(Directions and Study Information)

Thank you for logging in. The purpose of this phase of the National Study of Leadership in Middle Level Schools is to establish a knowledge base about the leadership characteristics and program practices in middle schools deemed to be "highly successful" in meeting the needs of early adolescent students. The following provides a brief explanation of the three-year study sponsored by NASSP and implemented by the Middle Level Leadership Center.

Study Explanation

Phase I. Since 1980 the National Association of Secondary School Principals has sponsored a "decade" study of middle level leadership and programs. In the 1980 and 1990 studies, and again in this 2000 study, an initial survey of principals across the nation was completed to develop a national profile of typical leadership, programs, and practices in the middle level schools of our country. That portion of the three-year study has been completed and information from that phase is being prepared for release as a paperback book by NASSP this fall. Preliminary results of that first phase of the overall project will be released for the first time at NASSP's National Convention in Phoenix this March

Phase II. The second phase of the study is a look at highly successful schools and the leadership and programs in those schools. Six steps are necessary for this second phase of the study:

1. Leaders in each state recently nominated schools to create a pool of highly successful schools. Your school has been nominated for that pool of schools from across the country.

2. The nominated school principals are being asked to complete two basic forms of information. One is a description of how their school addresses the *Turning Points* recommendations. The second is a set of several demographic questions about the principal and school. Those questions follow this explanation of the study.

3. From the pool of more than 250 schools, approximately 100 will be selected based upon their responses and their school demographics.

4. The principals of those 100 selected schools will be asked if they would like to participate in the next portion of the study. That portion includes a detailed survey this spring of school programs and practices and a set of teacher and student surveys to gain perspective about the school's culture, leadership, programs, and practices from the viewpoint of the teachers and students.

5. Five schools from the pool of 100 will be selected for two-day site visits this coming fall, with interviews and observations during those two days focused upon understanding the nature of the leadership and the processes of change and professional development implemented in the schools.

6. Information from the set of 100 schools and from the five site-visit schools will be prepared as a paperback book and distributed to all middle level principals who are members of NASSP.

This online survey represents the second step—collecting data from the 250 nominated principals about their schools. Information from this step will enable the research team to identify 100 "highly successful" middle level schools—successful because of the manner with which the school has implemented the basic tenants of *Turning Points 2000*, Carnegie Council's new report for middle level schools.

In this stage of the study, you will only be asked to complete the information in this online survey. However, you should be aware of the tasks we will be asking of the 100 schools at the next stage of the study. The following list describes the tasks remaining if you choose to complete this survey and are selected as one of the 100 highly successful schools. All of these tasks involve the completion of anonymous and confidential surveys.

Principal's Task

- Should your school be selected to participate in the study as one of the 100 "highly successful" schools, the principal will complete a second online survey later this spring.

Faculty's Task

- Should your school be selected to participate in the study as one of the 100 "highly successful" schools, each teacher will complete an online survey of about 115 multiple-choice items this spring.

Parent's Task

- Should your school be selected to participate in the study as one of the 100 "highly successful" schools, the parent leader of your school's formal parent organization (e.g., PTA, PTSA, PTO) will complete an online survey of about 15 items this spring.

Students' Task

- Should your school be selected to participate in the study as one of the 100 "highly successful" schools, approximately 10% of the students in your school's highest grade level will be asked to complete a 62-item multiple-choice, paper-and-pencil survey. Students will be required to obtain signed parental consent before participating in the survey. The study's research team will provide such consent forms for your use. The nature of this survey will require that it be administered under the supervision of a teacher during a single class period this spring.

By clicking on the "I Accept" button below, you agree to complete the survey that will immediately follow. This survey will take you about 30 minutes to complete. Additionally, by clicking on the "I Accept" button, you are indicating your understanding that your school might be asked to participate in the next stage of this study as described above.

Selection to the group of 100 schools will be an opportunity for your school to obtain significant free data about school practices, culture, climate, and leadership. Selection to that group of schools will also provide you with the opportunity to reinforce with your faculty and the school community the quality of your school's programs as measured by an outside group of middle school experts. In the previous decade studies, principals from the highly successful school groups were able to use that recognition in very positive ways.

By being at this stage in the study, you and your school have already been recognized by knowledgeable middle level persons in your state as high quality. The NASSP study is interested in learning about your school and others like it so that we can help all schools understand the processes and practices that best serve middle level students. In that process we will collect data and provide you and your faculty with those data in a format that will help you continue to be a quality school.

We hope we have provided an adequate explanation so you will see both the value of participation for your school and the value your participation can have to others who can learn from the dissemination of our findings of the study. If you have any questions about the information, don't hesitate to e-mail me at ValentineJ@missouri.edu or call at (573) 882-0944.

Jerry Valentine, *NASSP Research Team Chair*
Director, Middle Level Leadership Center
University of Missouri

I Accept ☐   I Decline ☐

Submit

(Part I Questions)

Part I: Principal/School Contact Information and Processes for Change, School Context, and Student Outcomes

Principal's Survey (Part 1 of 3)

Directions:

There are three parts to this survey.

- Part 1 has four open-ended questions about your school.
- Part 2 has seven open-ended questions about *Turning Points 2000.*
- Part 3 has 27 multiple-choice questions about your experience as a principal.

If you are not able to complete all sections in one sitting, you may return and finish the survey at a later time. It will retain all information that has been submitted. If you close your browser before you have completed the section and <u>submitted</u> the section, the information you have entered will be lost.

Human Subjects Research Explanation

- Please understand that the completion of this survey is voluntary, and you may choose to terminate your participation at any time.
- The information from this survey will be compiled with data from principals across the country and will be confidential and anonymous.
- The <u>User ID</u> and <u>Password</u> codes you used to access this survey are the only link the researchers have to your identity. Those links will be eliminated once the information has been collected and analyzed. The responses you provide to the survey questions will be the only information maintained. That information will remain confidential.
- Completing the survey and clicking the "submit" buttons throughout this survey indicates that you understand the nature of the survey study and agree to participate.

School/Principal Contact Information:

School:_____

School District: _____

Principal: _____

Years as principal at this school:_____

School Mailing Address: _____

City, State, ZIP:_____

E-mail:_____

Phone: _____Fax: _____

Grade configuration of school:_____Student enrollment: _____Full-time faculty: _____

Which of the following best describes your school's setting: ☐ Urban ☐ Suburban ☐ Rural

Open-ended questions on change processes, school context, and student outcomes:

1. Describe the process(es) by which change has come about in your school over the last five years.

2. What are your school's values, beliefs, mission, vision, and goals?

3. Describe the unique challenges or contexts that face your school.

4. What student outcomes demonstrate that your school is meeting the wide range of early adolescent needs?

SCREEN FOUR

(Part II Questions)

Part II: *Turning Points* Recommendations

Directions:

There are three parts to this survey.

- Part 1 has four open-ended questions about your school.
- **Part 2 has seven open-ended questions about *Turning Points 2000*.**
- Part 3 has 27 multiple-choice questions about your experience as a principal.

If you are not able to complete all sections in one sitting, you may return and finish the survey at a later time. It will retain all information that has been submitted. If you close your browser before you have completed the section and <u>submitted</u> the section, the information you have entered will be lost.

Human Subjects Research Explanation

- Please understand that the completion of this survey is voluntary, and you may choose to terminate your participation at any time.
- The information from this survey will be compiled with data from principals across the country and will be confidential and anonymous.
- The User ID and Password codes you used to access this survey are the only link the researchers have to your identity. Those links will be eliminated once the information has been collected and analyzed. The responses you provide to the survey questions will be the only information maintained. That information will remain confidential.
- Completing the survey and clicking the "submit" buttons throughout this survey indicates that you understand the nature of the survey study and agree to participate.

Turning Points Recommendations

Open-Ended Questions

Listed below are the seven recommendations from Turning Points 2000: Education Adolescents in the 21st Century. In the space provided beneath each recommendation, please describe specifically what your school is doing to meet those recommendations. Please take care to note programs and initiatives that your school has developed within the past five years, especially if they were developed primarily through collaborative efforts at the school site. [Recommendations deleted for space.]

(Part III Questions)

Part III: School and Leader Demographics

There are three parts to this survey.

- Part 1 has four open-ended questions about your school.
- Part 2 has seven open-ended questions about *Turning Points 2000*.
- **Part 3 has 27 multiple-choice questions about your experience as a principal.**

If you are not able to complete all sections in one sitting, you may return and finish the survey at a later time. It will retain all information that has been submitted. If you close your browser before you have completed the section and <u>submitted</u> the section, the information you have entered will be lost.

Human Subjects Research Explanation

- Please understand that the completion of this survey is voluntary, and you may choose to terminate your participation at any time.
- The information from this survey will be compiled with data from principals across the country and will be confidential and anonymous.
- The <u>User ID</u> and <u>Password</u> codes you used to access this survey are the only link the researchers have to your identity. Those links will be eliminated once the information has been collected and analyzed. The responses you provide to the survey questions will be the only information maintained. That information will remain confidential.
- Completing the survey and clicking the "submit" buttons throughout this survey indicates that you understand the nature of the survey study and agree to participate.

[To save space the 27 demographic items have been deleted from this document.]

(Optional Questions)

Thank You With Optional School and Leadership Issues (additional information)

Thank you for taking the time to complete all sections of this study. We have asked you about your school's (a) processes for change; (b) values, beliefs, mission, vision, and goals; (c) unique challenges and contexts; and, (d) desired student outcomes. We have also asked you to describe how your school addresses the seven recommendations from *Turning Points 2000*, the latest national report on middle level education. And, we have asked a variety of multiple-choice questions about your background as a school leader. We very much appreciate your willingness to respond to those varied questions about you and your school.

As you are aware, a primary purpose of this survey is to collect information necessary to identify and study 100 of the most highly effective middle level schools in the nation. If you would like to, please use the space below to provide any additional information that would help us better understand your school and/or your leadership as its principal. This response is optional.

Feedback on the Survey (optional)

If you wish to provide us with any feedback about the survey or the process used to collect data, please share that insight with us in the following space. This response is optional.

Thank you for your time. Please "submit" when you are finished.

Submit

(Thank You—Final Page)

Thank you for taking the time to complete all sections of this study. There are more than 14,100 middle level schools in the United States. Given that number and that only approximately 250 were nominated for this study, we encourage you to take advantage of the fact that your school was nominated and we encourage you to share that with your staff.

The NASSP research team will be reviewing the responses from all nominated schools. Many issues related to programs, practices, and demographics will be reviewed in the process of identifying the schools invited to participate in the group of 100 "highly successful schools." In March the NASSP research team will be contacting the principals of those 100 schools.

We wish you the best of luck as you continue your efforts to effectively meet the needs of your young adolescents.

Thank You.

Appendix D:

Letter of Invitation to 100 Highly Successful Schools

Name _____ Date _____

Address _____

City, State, ZIP _____

Dear (Name):

As you are aware, the National Association of Secondary School Principals is conducting the National Study of Leadership in Middle Level Schools. Because you and your school were nominated as "highly successful," you were invited to complete on online survey describing your school's mission, context, change processes, efforts to meet student needs, leadership practices, and programs that put into practice the recommendations from *Turning Points*. You also provided basic demographic information about yourself and your school.

Based upon the responses you provided, we are pleased to inform you that you and your school have been selected to participate in the national study of 100 highly successful middle schools. The purpose of this letter is to provide brief directions for you and your school's participation in this phase of the study. We will ship to you a package containing the materials listed below when you confirm that you and your school will indeed participate in this phase of the study.

As the school's principal, you will complete an online survey.

Your school's teachers and administrative staff will complete an online survey.

- The president or leader of your school's formal parent organization (e.g., PTA, PTSA, PSO) will complete an online survey.

- A portion of your school's students will complete a paper-and-pencil survey. While we know you are certainly busy, we truly appreciate the time you can take to help us in this important phase of the study.

- All of the tasks listed above will need to be completed by the end of March.

We have set up a website at (web address) to allow you to respond to this letter. Please log on to the site at your earliest convenience and provide the information requested there.

Jerry Valentine
Director, Middle Level Leadership Center
University of Missouri

Appendix E:
Teacher Surveys

E-001

NSLMLS Phase II Teacher Survey Items Form A

Teachers responded to these statements using the following Likert scale:

1 = Strongly Disagree, 2 = Disagree, 3 = Neutral, 4 = Agree, 5 = Strongly Agree

1.	Teachers utilize professional networks to obtain information and resources for classroom instruction.	1	2	3	4	5
2.	Leaders value teachers' ideas.	1	2	3	4	5
3.	Teachers have opportunities for dialogue and planning across grades and subjects.	1	2	3	4	5
4.	Teachers trust each other.	1	2	3	4	5
5.	Teachers support the mission of the school.	1	2	3	4	5
6.	Teachers and parents have common expectations for student performance.	1	2	3	4	5
7.	Leaders in this school trust the professional judgments of teachers.	1	2	3	4	5
8.	Teachers spend considerable time planning together.	1	2	3	4	5
9.	Teachers regularly seek ideas from seminars, colleagues, and conferences.	1	2	3	4	5
10.	Teachers are willing to help out whenever there is a problem.	1	2	3	4	5
11.	Leaders take time to praise teachers that perform well.	1	2	3	4	5
12.	The school mission provides a clear sense of direction for teachers.	1	2	3	4	5
13.	Parents trust teachers' professional judgments.	1	2	3	4	5
14.	Teachers are involved in the decision-making process.	1	2	3	4	5
15.	Teachers take time to observe each other teaching.	1	2	3	4	5
16.	Professional development is valued by the faculty.	1	2	3	4	5
17.	Teachers' ideas are valued by other teachers.	1	2	3	4	5
18.	Leaders in our school facilitate teachers working together.	1	2	3	4	5
19.	Teachers understand the mission of the school.	1	2	3	4	5
20.	Teachers are kept informed on current issues in the school.	1	2	3	4	5
21.	Teachers and parents communicate frequently about student performance.	1	2	3	4	5
22.	My involvement in policy or decision making is taken seriously.	1	2	3	4	5
23.	Teachers are generally aware of what other teachers are teaching.	1	2	3	4	5
24.	Teachers maintain a current knowledge base about the learning process.	1	2	3	4	5
25.	Teachers work cooperatively in groups.	1	2	3	4	5
26.	Teachers are rewarded for experimenting with new ideas and techniques.	1	2	3	4	5

27. The school mission statement reflects the values of the community.	1	2	3	4	5
28. Leaders support risk-taking and innovation in teaching.	1	2	3	4	5
29. Teachers work together to develop and evaluate programs and projects.	1	2	3	4	5
30. The faculty values school improvement.	1	2	3	4	5
31. Teaching performance reflects the mission of the school.	1	2	3	4	5
32. Administrators protect instruction and planning time.	1	2	3	4	5
33. Teaching-practice disagreements are voiced openly and discussed.	1	2	3	4	5
34. Teachers are encouraged to share ideas.	1	2	3	4	5
35. Students generally accept responsibility for their schooling; for example, they engage mentally in class and complete homework assignments.	1	2	3	4	5
36. The principal has both the capacity and judgment to overcome most obstacles.	1	2	3	4	5
37. The principal commands respect from everyone on the faculty.	1	2	3	4	5
38. The principal excites faculty members with visions of what we may be able to accomplish if we work together.	1	2	3	4	5
39. The principal makes faculty members feel and act like leaders.	1	2	3	4	5
40. The principal gives the faculty a sense of overall purpose for its leadership role.	1	2	3	4	5
41. The principal leads by "doing" rather than simply by "telling."	1	2	3	4	5
42. The principal symbolizes success and accomplishment within our profession.	1	2	3	4	5
43. The principal provides good models for faculty members to follow.	1	2	3	4	5
44. The principal provides for our participation in the process of developing school goals.	1	2	3	4	5
45. The principal encourages faculty members to work toward the same goals.	1	2	3	4	5
46. The principal uses problem solving with the faculty to generate school goals.	1	2	3	4	5
47. The principal works toward whole faculty consensus in establishing priorities for school goals.	1	2	3	4	5
48. The principal regularly encourages faculty members to evaluate our progress toward achievement of school goals.	1	2	3	4	5
49. The principal provides for extended training to develop my knowledge and skills relevant to being a member of the school faculty.	1	2	3	4	5
50. The principal provides the necessary resources to support my implementation of the school program.	1	2	3	4	5
51. The principal treats me as an individual with unique needs and expertise.	1	2	3	4	5
52. The principal takes my opinion into consideration when initiating actions that affect my work.	1	2	3	4	5

53. The principal behaves in a manner thoughtful of my personal needs.	1	2	3	4	5
54. The principal challenges me to reexamine some basic assumptions I have about my work at the school.	1	2	3	4	5
55. The principal stimulates me to think about what I am doing for the school's students.	1	2	3	4	5
56. The principal provides information that helps me think of ways to implement the school program.	1	2	3	4	5
57. The principal insists on only the best performance from the school faculty.	1	2	3	4	5
58. The principal shows us that there are high expectations for the faculty as professionals.	1	2	3	4	5
59. The principal will not settle for second best in the performance of our work as a faculty.	1	2	3	4	5
60. My principal leads formal discussions concerning instruction and student achievement.	1	2	3	4	5
61. Teachers in my school turn to the principal with instructional concerns or problems.	1	2	3	4	5
62. My principal provides frequent feedback regarding my classroom performance.	1	2	3	4	5
63. My principal assists faculty in interpreting test results.	1	2	3	4	5
64. My principal is an important instructional resource in our school.	1	2	3	4	5
65. My principal promotes staff development activities for faculty.	1	2	3	4	5
66. My principal communicates clearly to me regarding instructional matters.	1	2	3	4	5
67. My principal is accessible to discuss matters dealing with instruction.	1	2	3	4	5
68. My principal encourages the use of different instructional strategies.	1	2	3	4	5
69. My principal mobilizes support to help achieve academic goals.	1	2	3	4	5
70. Discussions with my principal result in improved instructional practice.	1	2	3	4	5
71. My principal makes frequent classroom observations.	1	2	3	4	5
72. My principal is knowledgeable about instructional resources.	1	2	3	4	5
73. My principal's evaluation of my performance helps me improve my teaching.	1	2	3	4	5
74. My principal is a strong instructional leader.	1	2	3	4	5
75. My principal is an active participant in staff development.	1	2	3	4	5
76. My principal is a "visible presence" in our building to both staff and students.	1	2	3	4	5
77. My principal uses clearly communicated criteria for judging my performance.	1	2	3	4	5
78. My principal provides a clear vision of what our school is all about.	1	2	3	4	5

NSLMLS Phase II Teacher Survey Items Form B

Teachers responded to these statements using the following Likert scale:

1 = Strongly Disagree, 2 = Disagree, 3 = Neutral, 4 = Agree, 5 = Strongly Agree

1.	The principal compliments teachers.	1	2	3	4	5
2.	Teachers have parties for each other.	1	2	3	4	5
3.	Teachers are burdened with busy work.	1	2	3	4	5
4.	Routine duties interfere with the job of teaching.	1	2	3	4	5
5.	Teachers "go the extra mile" with their students.	1	2	3	4	5
6.	Teachers are committed to helping their students.	1	2	3	4	5
7.	Teachers help students on their own time.	1	2	3	4	5
8.	Teachers interrupt other teachers who are talking in staff meetings.	1	2	3	4	5
9.	The principal rules with an iron fist.	1	2	3	4	5
10.	The principal encourages teacher autonomy.	1	2	3	4	5
11.	The principal goes out of his or her way to help teachers.	1	2	3	4	5
12.	The principal is available after school to help teachers when assistance is needed.	1	2	3	4	5
13.	Teachers invite other faculty members to visit them at home.	1	2	3	4	5
14.	Teachers socialize with each other on a regular basis.	1	2	3	4	5
15.	The principal uses constructive criticism.	1	2	3	4	5
16.	Teachers who have personal problems receive support from other staff members.	1	2	3	4	5
17.	Teachers stay after school to tutor students who need help.	1	2	3	4	5
18.	Teachers accept additional duties if students will benefit.	1	2	3	4	5
19.	The principal looks out for the personal welfare of the faculty.	1	2	3	4	5
20.	The principal supervises teachers closely.	1	2	3	4	5
21.	Teachers leave school immediately after school is over.	1	2	3	4	5
22.	Most of the teachers here accept the faults of their colleagues.	1	2	3	4	5
23.	Teachers exert group pressure on nonconforming faculty members.	1	2	3	4	5
24.	The principal listens to and accepts teachers' suggestions.	1	2	3	4	5
25.	Teachers have fun socializing together during school time.	1	2	3	4	5
26.	Teachers ramble when they talk at faculty meetings.	1	2	3	4	5
27.	Teachers are rude to other staff members.	1	2	3	4	5
28.	Teachers make "wise cracks" to each other during meetings.	1	2	3	4	5
29.	Teachers mock teachers who are different.	1	2	3	4	5
30.	Teachers don't listen to other teachers.	1	2	3	4	5
31.	Teachers like to hear gossip about other staff members.	1	2	3	4	5
32.	The principal treats teachers as equals.	1	2	3	4	5
33.	The principal corrects teachers' mistakes.	1	2	3	4	5
34.	Teachers provide strong social support for colleagues.	1	2	3	4	5

35. Teachers respect the professional competence of their colleagues.	1	2	3	4	5
36. The principal goes out of his or her way to show appreciation to teachers.	1	2	3	4	5
37. The principal keeps a close check on sign-in times.	1	2	3	4	5
38. The principal monitors everything teachers do.	1	2	3	4	5
39. Administrative paperwork is burdensome at this school.	1	2	3	4	5
40. Teachers help and support each other.	1	2	3	4	5
41. The principal closely checks teacher activities.	1	2	3	4	5
42. Assigned nonteaching duties are excessive.	1	2	3	4	5
43. The interactions between team/unit members are cooperative.	1	2	3	4	5
44. The principal accepts and implements ideas suggested by faculty members.	1	2	3	4	5
45. Members of teams/units consider other members to be their friends.	1	2	3	4	5
46. Extra help is available to students who need help.	1	2	3	4	5
47. Teachers volunteer to sponsor after-school activities.	1	2	3	4	5
48. Teachers spend time after school with students who have individual problems.	1	2	3	4	5
49. The principal sets an example by working hard himself or herself.	1	2	3	4	5
50. Teachers are polite to one another.	1	2	3	4	5
51. Students make provision to acquire extra help from teachers.	1	2	3	4	5
52. Extra materials are available if requested.	1	2	3	4	5
53. Students neglect to complete homework.	1	2	3	4	5
54. The school is vulnerable to outside pressures.	1	2	3	4	5
55. Teachers are provided with adequate materials for their classrooms.	1	2	3	4	5
56. Community demands are accepted even when they are not consistent with the educational program.	1	2	3	4	5
57. Teachers receive necessary classroom supplies.	1	2	3	4	5
58. Students respect others who get good grades.	1	2	3	4	5
59. Good grades are important to the students of this school.	1	2	3	4	5
60. Teachers feel pressure from the community.	1	2	3	4	5
61. Supplementary materials are available for classroom use.	1	2	3	4	5
62. Students seek extra work so they can get good grades.	1	2	3	4	5
63. Select citizen groups are influential with the board.	1	2	3	4	5
64. The school is open to the whims of the public.	1	2	3	4	5
65. A few vocal parents can change school policy.	1	2	3	4	5
66. The learning environment is orderly and serious.	1	2	3	4	5
67. Teachers are protected from unreasonable community and parental demands.	1	2	3	4	5
68. Teachers have access to needed instructional materials.	1	2	3	4	5
69. Teachers in this school believe that their students have the ability to achieve academically.	1	2	3	4	5
70. Our school gets its fair share of resources from the district.	1	2	3	4	5

NSLMLS Phase II Teacher Survey Items Form C

1. Which of the following most accurately describes your teaching assignment?
   - O **Core content area** (language arts, social studies, reading, math, or science)
   - O **Noncore exploratory or elective content areas** (e.g., art, music, speech, drama, family living, industrial education, health, physical education, foreign language)
   - O **Special education teacher** (whether you work in a fully included or partially included program or in a separate area with pull-out students or any combination, your primary teaching assignment is to work with special needs students)
   - O **Other or not sure which of the above to select.** (If you teach students on a daily basis as a regular classroom teacher and the above list does not fit your assignment or you are not sure which of the above to select, please describe your role on the next line.)

2. Which of the following most accurately describes your teaching assignment?
   - O I am a member of an interdisciplinary teaching team of four or more teachers.
   - O I am a member of an interdisciplinary team of two or three teachers.
   - O I am not a member of an interdisciplinary team.

For questions 3 through 18, the responses represent percentages of time in 10% increments. For example, in question 3, if you believe that you almost always select content that directly fits the district's curricular goals/objectives, you might select 90% as the most appropriate answer. If you believe you do that approximately half of the time, you would select 50% as the most appropriate answer.

Planning Strategies

3. When I design my lessons, I <u>consciously</u> select content that meets the district's curriculum, competencies, and/or performance standards.

4. When I design my lessons, I <u>consciously</u> select instructional materials based upon my knowledge of my students' developmental needs and learning styles.

5. When I design my lessons, I <u>consciously</u> select methods and strategies that accommodate individual needs and interests of specific students.

6. When I design my lessons, I <u>consciously</u> prepare lessons with high expectations designed to challenge and stimulate all students.

7. When I design my lessons, I <u>consciously</u> consider how to build upon my students' existing knowledge and experiences.

8. When I design my lessons, I <u>consciously</u> consider how to create active learning experiences for my students.

9. During each lesson, I monitor students' understanding of the content and make adjustments accordingly.

10. During each lesson, I move among the students, engaging individually and collectively with them during the learning experience.

Planning Strategies

11. During each lesson, I consciously implement a teaching strategy that stimulates higher-order thinking skills.

12. During each lesson, I create social interaction among students that enhances learning by requiring students to work as a team with both individual and group responsibilities.

13. During each lesson, I vary the size and composition of learning groups.

14. During each lesson, I discuss with my students the importance of courtesy and respect and I consciously model for my students the types of personal behaviors that promote responsibility and social development among early adolescents.

15. During each lesson, I consciously implement two or more learning activities.

16. During each lesson, I consciously implement a learning activity that requires students to read or write in my content area.

17. During each lesson, I consciously implement two or more learning activities.

18. During each lesson, I consciously implement a learning activity that requires students to read or write in my content area.

For the following assessment practices, please assign a percent of time that describes how frequently you use each assessment practice. In other words, as you look at the list, what percent of the assessments you give to students are multiple-choice tests, what percent are essay tests, etc.? When you complete the list, your total for items 19 through 28 should be 100%. Please limit your responses to the practices listed.

19. Multiple-choice tests

20. Essay tests

21. Short-answer tests

22. Fill-in-the-blank tests

23. Matching tests

24. Demonstrations to peers

25. Demonstrations to adults

26. Portfolios

27. Mastery checklists

28. Student projects

(Please review your answers to the above assessment practices. Does the total add up to 100%? If not, please adjust your responses as appropriate.)

After you have completed a lesson or unit of study and assessed each student's success or lack of success for the lesson or unit, you realize that a student in the class has not mastered the desired learning objectives of the lesson or unit. Please answer the next four questions based upon how you typically respond to that type of scenario. To help you formulate a response, think of all the units you teach and all the times one of the students does not demonstrate mastery of the content or competencies. Your responses to questions 29 through 32 should total 100%.

29. How frequently do you assign the grade the student has earned and move all students on to the next lesson or unit of study.

30. How frequently do you assign the grade the student has earned and create additional learning experiences for the student so he/she can master the objective. The initial grade remains unchanged, but the student has the opportunity to learn the material.

31. How frequently do you assign the grade the student has earned and create additional learning experiences for the student so he/she can master the objective. If the student masters the objective, you reassign or change the grade to one that reflects the student's newly developed competence.

32. If you frequently use a strategy other than the three described immediately above, please briefly describe the strategy and record _____ the percent of time you use that strategy.

Please remember to check your responses to items 29–32. They should total 100%.

Parent Relationships

Working effectively with parents is one of the most challenging tasks for most teachers. Please respond to the following items about parent relationships, based upon the practices you use to engage parents.

33. I typically interact personally (talk in person, talk on the phone, communicate via e-mail, etc.) with 10 or more of my student's parents:

___ Weekly   ___ Monthly   ___ Each semester   ___ Each school year

For questions 34 to 36, do not include in your responses any contacts with parents that occurred as part of regularly scheduled parent–teacher conference days at school. Think of the last 10 contacts you had with parents, such as phone conversations, home visits, and school visits, not associated with regularly scheduled reporting conferences. Your responses to items 34, 35, and 36 should total 10.

34. Of the last 10 contacts, how many of them did you initiate? _____

35. Of the 10 contacts, how many of them did the parent initiate? _____

36. Of the last 10 contacts, how many of them were a chance meeting that was not initiated by either you or the parent? _____

For items 37, 38, 39, and 40, think about those same last 10 contacts you had with parents. As previously, your responses to questions 37, 38, 39, and 40 should total 10.

37. Of the last 10 contacts, how many of them were by phone? _____

38. Of the last 10 contacts, how many were in the student's home? _____

39. Of the last 10 contacts, how many were at school? _____

40. Of the last 10 contacts, how many were at another site? _____

   Please describe site:_____

For items 41, 42, 43, and 44, think about the last five contacts you initiated with parents. Your responses to items 41, 42, 43, and 44 should total 5.

41. Of the last five contacts you initiated with parents, how many of them were to discuss a concern about student behavior? _____

42. Of the last five contacts you initiated with parents, how many of them were to discuss a concern about academic performance? _____

43. Of the last five contacts you initiated with parents, how many of them were to discuss positive growth in student behavior or academic performance? _____

44. Of the last five contacts you initiated with parents, how many of them were to discuss an issue other than student behavior or academic performance? _____

   Please describe the issue briefly_____

For items 45, 46, 47, and 48, think about the last five contacts parents initiated with you. Your responses to items 45, 46, 47, and 48 should total 5.

45. Of the last five contacts parents initiated with you, how many of them were to discuss a concern about student behavior? _____

46. Of the last five contacts parents initiated with you, how many of them were to discuss a concern about academic performance? _____

47. Of the last five contacts parents initiated with you, how many of them were to discuss positive growth in student behavior or academic performance? _____

48. Of the last five contacts parents initiated with you, how many of them were to discuss an issue other than student behavior or academic performance? _____

Please describe the issue briefly_____

Curriculum Development

Curricular goals/objectives and desired learner outcomes are typically identified by committees at the school and district level. However, teachers generally have some degree of flexibility in determining how they will teach to those goals/objectives/outcomes.

49. In your class, do you involve your students in the process of deciding what your students will study to accomplish the curricular goals?

O YES   O NO

If yes, briefly describe how you involve your students in determining what they will study.

_____

50. Do you involve your students in the process of deciding how your students will study the content to accomplish the goals?

O YES   O NO

If yes, briefly describe how you involve your students in determining how they will study the content.

_____

For the next three questions, consider the specific content your students study during a school year. (This is about the specific content to accomplish the goals, not about the broad goals.)

51. Of all the specific content your students study, what percent of that content is dictated by district curriculum? _____

52. Of all the specific content your students study, what percent of that content do you (or you and your colleagues) select? _____

53. Of all the specific content your students study, what percent of that content is selected by your students? _____

For the next three questions, think about the learning activities (not the content) you use to teach the content.

54. Of all the learning activities you use with your students, approximately what percent of those activities are dictated by district curriculum? _____

55. Of all the learning activities you use with your students, approximately what percent of those activities are selected by you? _____

56. Of all the learning activities you use with your students, approximately what percent of those activities are selected by you and other teachers in your school? _____

(NOTE: Your responses to the percentages for items 54, 55, and 56 should add to 100%.)

For the next two questions, again, think about the types of learning activities you use with your students and specifically the learning activities that you as the teacher have the opportunity to select.

	Percent of Frequency										
	0	10	20	30	40	50	60	70	80	90	100
57. Of all the learning activities that you have the opportunity to select, what percent are selected after discussion and/or input from your students?	O	O	O	O	O	O	O	O	O	O	O
58. Of all the learning activities that you have the opportunity to select, what percent are selected by your students?	O	O	O	O	O	O	O	O	O	O	O

Teachers responded to these statements using the following Likert scale:

1 = Strongly Disagree, 2 = Disagree, 3 = Neutral, 4 = Agree, 5 = Strongly Agree

59. District-adopted textbooks guide my planning of instruction.	1	2	3	4	5
60. Most students in my school will perform at about the national average in academic achievement.	1	2	3	4	5
61. I teach basically the same content that is taught in other classes at the same grade or same course in my school.	1	2	3	4	5
62. Many of my students will probably leave school before high school graduation.	1	2	3	4	5
63. Criterion-referenced tests are used to assess basic skills throughout the school.	1	2	3	4	5
64. Most students in my school are capable of mastering grade-level academic objectives.	1	2	3	4	5
65. Student assessment information, such as criterion-referenced tests, skill checklists, etc., is used regularly to give specific student feedback and plan appropriate instruction.	1	2	3	4	5
66. Teachers in my school generally believe most students are able to master the basic reading/math skills.	1	2	3	4	5
67. My school has effective programs for students who are in need of remediation.	1	2	3	4	5
68. I expect that most students in my school will perform above the national average in academic achievement.	1	2	3	4	5
69. The principal uses test results to recommend changes in the instructional program.	1	2	3	4	5

70. Nearly all of my students will be at or above grade level by the end of this year.　　1　2　3　4　5

71. My school has effective procedures for identifying students with special learning needs.　　1　2　3　4　5

72. Teachers in other schools would rate my school's level of academic achievement as good.　　1　2　3　4　5

73. Multiple assessment methods are used to assess student progress in basic skills (e.g., criterion-referenced tests, work samples, mastery checklists).　　1　2　3　4　5

74. Most of my students will show at least one year's growth in academic achievement this year.　　1　2　3　4　5

75. Teachers in my school frequently assess the progress of students in basic skills.　　1　2　3　4　5

76. The academic ability of students in my school compares favorably with students in other schools.　　1　2　3　4　5

77. The principal in my school is aware of student progress in relation to instructional objectives.　　1　2　3　4　5

78. I expect most students in my school will perform below the national average in academic achievement.　　1　2　3　4　5

79. What I teach in my class contributes to the content of the grade or course that follows it.　　1　2　3　4　5

80. My school is responsive to students with special learning needs.　　1　2　3　4　5

81. Most of the students in my school will ultimately graduate from high school.　　1　2　3　4　5

82. Staff review and analyze test results to plan instructional program changes.　　1　2　3　4　5

83. Students with special learning needs in my class are not receiving the instructional program they need.　　1　2　3　4　5

84. District curriculum documents guide my planning of instruction.　　1　2　3　4　5

85. What I teach in my class builds upon the content of the grade or course that precedes it.　　1　2　3　4　5

Appendix F:

Student Survey
Student Survey Items

Please indicate which of the following you have participated in this school year.

O 1. A school club such as math or science club.

O 2. A school sports program where you play teams from other schools.

O 3. An intramural sports program where you play other teams from your own school.

O 4. A spirit group such as cheerleading or pep club.

O 5. A school-sponsored music program such as orchestra, band, chorus, or choir in which your group performed for members of the community or others at events outside your school.

O 6. A speech, drama, or debate club that competes against teams from other schools or gives performances to parents or groups outside your school.

O 7. A school publishing group such as the school newspaper or yearbook.

O 8. A student council group.

O 9. An academic honors group such as National Honor Society.

Please indicate how much you agree or disagree with each of the following.

1 = Strongly Disagree, 2 = Disagree, 3 = Neutral, 4 = Agree, 5 = Strongly Agree

O 10. I am as good a student as I would like to be.

O 11. I am doing as well on schoolwork as I would like to.

O 12. I am good enough at math.

O 13. I am as good at reading and writing as I want to be.

O 14. I get grades that are good enough for me.

O 15. I feel OK about how good I am as a student.

O 16. I do as well on tests in school as I want to.

O 17. I get too many bad grades on my report cards.

O 18 I am happy with the way I can do most things.

O 19 I sometimes think I am a failure (a loser).

O 20. I think it is a waste of time studying for a class when the class is hard.

O 21. I often skip some parts of my schoolwork when the work seems too hard.

O 22. I think if I tried harder I could do a better job on my schoolwork.

O 23. I just try to get by on my schoolwork instead of doing the best I can.

O 24. I give up when my schoolwork is hard to do.

Please indicate the degree to which each of the following is a problem in your school.

1 = A Serious Problem, 2 = Somewhat of a Problem, 3 = A Minor Problem, 4 = Not a Problem at All

O 25. How much is student tardiness a problem in your school?

O 26. How much is student absenteeism a problem in your school?

O 27. How much is cutting class a problem in your school?

O 28. How much is physical conflict among students a problem in your school?

O 29. How much is robbery or theft a problem in your school?

O 30. How much is vandalism of school property a problem in your school?

O 31. How much is student use of alcohol a problem in your school?

O 32. How much is student use of illegal drugs a problem in your school?

O 33. How much is student possession of weapons a problem in your school?

O 34. How much is physical abuse of teachers a problem in your school?

O 35. How much is verbal abuse of teachers a problem in your school?

The following questions are about adults at your school (such as teachers, club sponsors, coaches, counselors, and administrators). Please select the answer that best describes how you feel.

Yes, Sometimes, No

O 36. Adults at my school back me up when I need them to.

O 37. I can count on adults at my school for emotional support (help with my feelings).

O 38. Adults at my school and I find it easy to talk to each other.

O 39. Adults at my school notice and give me help when I need them to.

O 40. Adults at my school are good at helping me solve problems.

Since the beginning of this school year, has either of your parents or guardians:

Yes, No, I Don't Know

O 41. Since the beginning of this school year, has either of your parents or guardians attended a school meeting?

O 42. Since the beginning of this school year, has either of your parents or guardians spoken to your teacher or counselor by phone?

O 43. Since the beginning of this school year, has either of your parents or guardians had a meeting with your teacher or counselor at school?

O 44. Since the beginning of this school year, has either of your parents or guardians visited your classes?

O 45. Since the beginning of this school year, has either of your parents or guardians attended a school event (such as a play, concert, or sports program) where you participated?

Please answer the following using the options provided.

O 46. Do you get free or reduced-price lunch at school?

O 47. What is your gender?

O 48. What grade are you in?

O 49. What is your race/ethnicity?

O 50. Which of the following people live in the same household as you?

Please read the following questions about school and select the best answer for you.

Yes, No

O 51. Do you have a place to study in your home where you can do homework, concentrate, and not be disturbed or interrupted?

O 52. Do you have a computer in your home that you can use to complete your schoolwork, such as typing reports?

O 53. Do you have a computer in your home that you can use to get onto the Internet to obtain information for your schoolwork?

O 54. Do you have an atlas, encyclopedia, or other general reference books in your home that you can use to complete your schoolwork?

O 55. Do you have a room of your own?

Not at All, Once or Twice, Three or Four Times, Five or More Times

O 56. During a typical school week, how often do you discuss school activities or events of particular interest to you with your parents or guardians?

O 57. During a typical school week, how often do you discuss things you have studied in class with your parents or guardians?

O 58. During a typical school week, how much time do you spend on homework for math?

O 59. During a typical school week, how much time do you spend on homework for science?

O 60. During a typical school week, how much time do you spend on homework for social studies?

O 61. During a typical school week, how much time do you spend on homework for English?

O 62. During a typical school week, how much time do you spend on homework for all other subjects?

Appendix G:

Parent Survey

Thank you for agreeing to participate in Phase II of the National Study of Leadership in Middle Level Schools. Your school's principal provided us with your name because you are a significant parent-leader at your school. As a parent-leader in one of our nation's most successful middle level schools, the information you share will be combined with the responses from parent-leaders in the other 99 schools to form a knowledge base about the leadership programs in "highly successful" middle level schools. Thank you for taking the time to complete this important survey.

This survey should take you about 30 minutes to complete. Before continuing with the survey, please read the statements below:

- The completion of this survey is voluntary, and you may choose to terminate your participation at any time.
- The information from this survey will be compiled with data from other parent-leaders from across the country and will be confidential and anonymous.
- The demographic information you provide in the survey is the only link the researchers have to your identity. These links will be eliminated once the information has been collected and analyzed. The responses you provide to the survey questions will be the only information maintained. That information will remain confidential.
- Completing and returning the survey indicates that you understand the nature of the survey study and agree to participate.

Please provide accurate demographic information (e.g., school name) so we can pair your responses with the correct school.

If you have any questions, please ask your principal or contact Professor Jerry Valentine at the University of Missouri by phone at (573) 882-0944 or e-mail at ValentineJ@missouri.edu.

Proceed with the survey making sure to answer all questions.

PARENT'S SURVEY (Part 1 of 2)

School: _____

School District: _____

City, State, ZIP _____

Email: _____ Phone: _____ Fax: _____

Survey Questions:

(Please type or print your responses to the following questions, attach them to the entire parent survey, and fax to Jerry Valentine, Middle Level Leadership Center, 573-884-5714.)

- Describe the process(es) by which change has come about in your school over the last five years.
- What are your school's values, beliefs, mission, vision, and goals?
- Describe the unique challenges or contexts that face your school.
- What student outcomes demonstrate that your school is meeting the wide range of early adolescent needs?
- How does your school's principal demonstrate and provide leadership for your school?

Please proceed to Part 2.

PARENT'S SURVEY (Part 2 of 2)

In November of 2000, an important national report was released to the public. The report, entitled *Turning Points 2000: Educating Adolescents in the 21st Century*, provided seven major recommendations for middle level schools. The purpose of this second set of parent questions is to obtain insight from parent-leaders' perspectives about the way in which your school has been addressing these recommendations. Please respond to these questions based upon your existing knowledge about the school. In other words, please do not visit with your principal or other school officials and ask for assistance in responding to these questions. We are looking for the perspective of the parent-leader on these issues.

Listed below are the seven recommendations from *Turning Points 2000: Educating Adolescents in the 21st Century*. **In your responses you provide to us, please describe specifically what your school is doing (based upon your knowledge) to meet <u>each</u> of those recommendations**. Please take care to note programs and initiatives that your school has developed within the past five years, especially if they were developed primarily through collaborative efforts at the school site. [Recommendations have been deleted for space.]

> **This concludes the Parent Survey for Phase II
> of the National Study of Leadership in Middle Level Schools.
> Please fax these four pages and your responses to
> Jerry Valentine, Middle Level Leadership Center,
> (573) 884-5714.**

Once again, thank you for your participation.

Appendix H:

Letter of Invitation to Site-Visit Schools

Date_____

Name _____

School _____

Address _____

City, State, ZIP _____

May I offer my congratulations to you and your faculty for having been selected as one of the six site-visit schools participating in NASSP's National Study of Leadership in Middle Level Schools. I have two basic purposes in this initial letter. First, I would like to provide you with some background information about the study and with some specifics about the second phase of the study and what transpired that led to the selection of the site-visit schools. I believe this information will be helpful to you both in your interactions within your school and district and for any comments you might need to make to the media. Second, I would like to discuss the site visit, providing you with insight about the events that will occur during the site visit.

NASSP has conducted a national study of middle level education for each of the past two decades. The first comprehensive study was conducted in 1980–83. It was the first comprehensive national study of middle level leaders and schools, and was, in fact, the origin of the term "middle level." All studies prior to that time were essentially about Junior High Schools or Middle Schools. The term middle level implies educational programs designed to serve the needs of young adolescents, and in the NASSP studies, we have defined Middle Level as those schools that serve students typically in combinations of grades five through nine. The Association again conducted a "decade" study in the early 1990s, which led to this third decade study that we began planning in 1999 and will conclude with the second book in 2003. Each of the three decade studies has had two major phases. The first phase was a comprehensive look at the "state-of-the-art" of middle level

leaders and schools and was designed around an extensive survey process of middle level schools across the United States. The second phase of each decade study was an attempt to understand how exemplary leaders and schools implement effective middle level education practices. In 1981, 50 "effective" school leaders were selected from a set of some 300 nominations. One person visited each school for a day to collect on-site data, primarily from a structured interview with the principal that focused on leadership. In 1992, the focus of the process was expanded from school leadership to school change processes and instructional programs. More than 50 schools were nominated and asked to participate in the survey data collection portion of the study. Fifty-four were invited to participate and 39 agreed to complete the set of survey instruments that provided school climate and leadership data. From the 39 schools, 25 schools completed the entire nomination process. Of the 25, eight were selected for the site visits.

In the current 2001 study, we received 275 nominations from school leaders in each of the 50 states. Most of the principals from those nominated schools completed the first round of nomination forms. From those data, the research team selected 100 schools to participate in the study. Two of those schools declined to participate, and two alternates were added to the pool. Once the 100 schools were identified, the data collection process from principals, teachers, students, and parents began. At this time, it appears that we anticipate having complete data sets from 98 schools. The research team analyzed all of the available data from the responding schools. This included data about school culture; school climate; leadership; school programs; instructional practices; change processes; implementation of *Turning Points 2000* recommendations; and school, student, community, and leader demographics. Data for these variables were collected from principals, teachers, students, and parents. Each school that provided data was considered eligible for the site visit. The only exceptions were the few schools where a new person assumed the principalship during the identification/data collection process.

Understanding the sophisticated process that led to the selection in your school as a site-visit school should reinforce the fact that every piece of information we had about your school implied that you and your staff have created a very special place for the young adolescents of your community. Based upon the data we have, your school is at the high end of the spectrum of schools in the pool of 100 schools, which in itself is a select group of schools. Please understand, however, that we are not implying that your school is one of the six "best" middle level schools in the country. To do so would be inappropriate. Our goal was not to identify the best schools, but to identify schools that were highly successful based upon the variables listed in the previous paragraph, particularly the recommendations associated with *Turning Points 2000*. But not being characterized as "the best" should in no way detract from the significant nature of this recognition. You undoubtedly have a superb school and we are looking forward to our visit and the opportunity to interact and observe within your school setting. We know that the media, parents, and others may, on occasion, overlook the subtleties of difference between what we are saying about your school being highly successful per the characteristics described. While they may characterize your school as the best, we ask that you refrain from reinforcing that misconception by inadvertently supporting that perception. To think that we could, based upon the information we have, definitively identify the six best schools in the country would be a false assumption. Far too many variables come into play to make such a statement. I have been a fan of the language used by the National Forum when they identified four "schools to watch." That implies that those schools

have something special about them and will, over time, continue to be special places for students. In a similar manner, we are saying your school is a highly successful place for young adolescents and you provide something very special for your students. We believe that, in itself, is a superlative compliment. You have much to offer others, both in what you do and how you arrived at what you do.

That brings us to the tasks for the site visit. First, you know that we will be in your school for two full school days. You know that there will be three researchers in your school. Each of us has been a teacher and administrator at the middle level and each of us has, for the most part, devoted our careers to studying and understanding middle level leadership and education. Here are some specific points of information to provide you with the big picture of the visit. The details of the visit will be provided in the attached schedule of events.

1. The leader of the site team will contact you by phone a few weeks prior to the visit to discuss final arrangements.

2. Prior to the site visit, we will send you a <u>list of artifacts</u> that we would like to ask you to compile and have available to us in a workroom when we arrive. The list will indicate which of those artifacts we will need to see only on-site and which ones we will need a copy of to keep for our records and study. We will send the list to you soon, but to give you an example, we are talking about things such as class schedules, teacher rosters, curriculum guides, etc. I would think that most of these are items you would have at your fingertips.

3. As you might have inferred from the above, we would like to have a private workroom to use during our visit. If possible, we would like a <u>small conference-type room</u> with a large table or two because we will have materials to spread out and manage. We would also like to have a dry-erase board, chalkboard, or easel for our work. We will be leaving laptop computers and small items of media equipment in the room when we are out in the building, so we would like to have a room that can be secured.

4. The leader will, if travel arrangements permit, <u>visit your school the afternoon prior</u> to the team visit

simply to meet with you briefly and become somewhat familiar first-hand with the school's layout and program. The team leader will determine the need or feasibility for this in his/her contact with you prior to the visit.

5. During the two full days of the site visit, members of the team will be meeting with and interviewing teachers, administrators, students, parents, and central office staff. We will need access to <u>two locations in addition to our team workroom to conduct those interviews</u>. Adequate accommodations might be a small workroom, a counselor's office, or a principal's office. We will need a location that is private. Please discuss the possibilities with the leader of your site-visit team.

As you review the attached schedule of events, please particularly note the following:

1. Times listed on the schedule are general time frames and will need to be adjusted based upon school start times, lunch times, etc. In other words, while it may indicate that the Principal's tour of the school is from 8:00–8:30, it may really end up occurring between 7:45 and 8:40, depending on school start time and length of time to take the tour. The leader of the research team and the principal will work together to adjust times as appropriate for the given school.

2. We would like to begin our visit with a brief faculty meeting the morning of the site visit to build some rapport between the research team and the faculty, orient the faculty about our research team's role and responsibilities, and reassure the faculty that we would like them to go about their days as they normally would. When we indicate "brief," that is what we intend. We believe we need but 15–20 minutes for our comments. You might wish to have the faculty meeting after school the day prior to the visit if that is a school day and if the team leader can make it to your school by that afternoon. However, in most cases, the whole team will not arrive in time for the meeting and for introductions. So, our preferred plan is to begin the first morning with the brief faculty meeting.

3. From 12:30 to 3:30 (remember that times are adjustable based upon school clock) of day one,

from 8:30 to 11:30 of day two, and from 1:00 to 3:00 of day two, research team members will be interviewing teachers who are available based upon their teaching schedule. In other words, we want to interview selected teachers who are on their planning period during those two time frames. To identify the teachers we wish to interview, I will need to ask you to send me a list of teachers who are on their planning times during the two days of our visit. With that list of names, please indicate <u>(a) the time the teacher can be available, (b) the content area the teacher teaches, (c) the teacher's gender, and (d) the number of years the teacher has been at your school</u>. (Note: if your schedules are different on those two days, we will need a separate set of times, etc., for each day). We will then select the teachers for the interviews based upon criteria designed to provide us with a balance of views from teachers by teaching area, gender, and experience in the school. You may e-mail that list of names, times, content areas, and years or you may fax it to me at (573) 884-5714. Please make a note to do so <u>approximately two weeks prior to the site visit</u> so I have time to make the selections and then share that schedule with both you and with the members of the site-visit team.

4. During the afternoon of day one and the morning of day two, one or more members of the research team will be moving throughout the building making <u>brief classroom observations</u>. Please share that fact with the teaching staff. The team leader will reiterate this during the brief faculty meeting at the beginning of the site visit. As we make those observations, we will simply be noting the nature of the instructional practices. We are not looking for "good" or "bad" practices. We will simply be making brief observations and will compile our notes on those observations in the form of feedback to the faculty. We may have those data compiled in time to share them during the exit faculty meeting. If not, we will e-mail them to you within a few days of our visit. This is not an evaluation of instructional practices, but rather a brief profiling of practice, i.e., a two-day snapshot in

time that may be valuable to you and your staff as a stimulus for future conversations about instructional practices.

5. You will notice that after school on day one we are asking you to select a group of <u>six diverse students to make a collective presentation</u> to our research team and the group of parents we would like to interview later that afternoon. Note that the presentation is to be no more than 15 minutes in length and should represent "how we (the students) view our school." Our research team suggests that you assign this responsibility to a counselor, dean, or other faculty member who can work with the six students to help them develop a way to express their views about life in their school. We envision a collective presentation from the students in an active-oriented expression; in other words, we prefer the students to be actively engaged in the presentation, not simply write a three-page paper and read the paper to us describing their feelings. Select students who represent the ethnic, cultural, and gender diversity of your school and who would find this an exciting opportunity. We will be bringing portable digital video equipment to the presentation and will videotape the presentation. I will send to you a permission sheet for the students and the students' parent/guardian to sign prior to the presentation. Please set this up in a room that will allow the students the opportunity to creatively express themselves and allow the three members of the research team, a few faculty, and the few parents described in the next item to view the presentation. Please do not open this to a large group session. We want the students to be comfortable and we want a small, intimate setting to fully appreciate what the students have to present. Following the student presentation, the team leader will use the room/location to visit/interview the students while the other two members of the team will move to other locations to interview the parents. That discussion will take approximately 30 minutes.

6. We would like for you to select <u>five or six parents</u> for the parent interview. We would encourage you to ask the parents/guardians of the six students who

are making the presentations as those parents will generally be a diverse group (assuming the students are a diverse group representative of your school's population). Two members of the research team will interview the parents in two small groups. The interviews will take approximately 30–40 minutes. Feel free to add another parent or two to the pool if you believe they would contribute to the conversation. Please ask all parents whom we interview to be present for the student presentation. We will need two locations large enough for the two small group parent interviews.

7. We would like to ask you to arrange for the <u>superintendent and/or an assistant superintendent</u> to have lunch with the team leader at the school site during day two. We realize that you cannot control their calendar, but if possible please make that request soon in order to increase the likelihood that the best people are available. If the superintendent is not available, we would like to visit with an assistant superintendent knowledgeable of your school. We will be particularly interested in the district's long-range vision and plan and any other insight or historical perspective the central office staff bring to our understanding of your school's success. For convenience, we can eat in the research team's workroom. While the team leader will be eating with the central office staff, team member B will be observing your role and responsibilities during the lunch time and team member C will be visiting informally with teachers as they eat lunch.

8. During the afternoon of day two the team leader will be interviewing selected counselors and librarians/media specialists while team members B and C interview teachers as per the directions established in paragraph 3, above.

9. At the end of day two, we would like to have a brief <u>exit discussion</u> with your faculty. We will keep this meeting brief (20–25 minutes). We will provide some general thoughts per our observations and interviews and answer any questions the staff might have about the study or the nature of the reports and writings developed from the study. It will be an opportunity for our team to say thank you and to offer, again, congratulations and compliments for providing such a quality school for the youth of your community and for us to study and

learn from so that other schools across the United States might benefit from your successes.

10. After the faculty meeting, you will note that the schedule describes a meeting of the school's "leadership team." The definition we use in this study for a leadership team is: "A group of teachers and administrators designated by the principal or elected by the faculty to assist in the leadership operation of the school. These staff members may have been formally designated, or they may be a more informal group obviously instrumental in the ongoing operation of the school." We would like to visit with you and your leadership team and have a general conversation about the school and the direction of the school over the coming years. It will be a more general and less structured discussion than many of the interviews throughout the two days. You will have heard us share some of our impressions during the faculty meeting and we will want to know what else we should know about your school to complete our knowledge about your school.

11. On the morning of day three, our research team will need a location to spread out materials, write on the board or easel, and get in a half-day of work before we depart. We will need access to our workroom for that morning. We would also like to have access to you as needed in case we find gaps in our information and need to ask additional or clarifying questions. It will be our opportunity to take stock of our information and add to that if needed.

I realize this is a rather lengthy epistle. I hope you will take the opportunity to mark those items that need to be addressed so when the leader of your site-visit team calls you a couple of weeks before the site visit to finalize the arrangements, you have addressed each of the items. Please don't hesitate to e-mail or call me if you have any questions. We want these visits to go as smoothly as you do so we can learn as much as possible about what makes your school a special place for young adolescents.

As stated previously, I am enclosing a copy of the schedule of events during the site visit. Prior to the site visit, I will be sending the following additional items:

(1) Consent forms for students and parents participating in the student presentation/interviews.

(2) List of artifacts for collection and/or review during the site visit.

(3) A press release from NASSP should be forthcoming in just a few days that you can use with your local media. The release has been drafted and is in the process of being finalized.

(4) A copy of the names, addresses and phone numbers of the entire research team. From that list you can identify your team leader should you need to contact him/her.

We look forward to our visit. Have a very joyous holiday season.

Sincerely,
Jerry Valentine
Professor and K-12 Leadership Program Coordinator,
Department of Educational Leadership
Director, Middle Level Leadership Center
Research Team Chair, NASSP National Study of
Leadership in Middle Level Schools

Appendix I:

Previsit Survey

National Study of Leadership in Middle Level Schools
Phase II: National Study of Highly Successful Middle Level Schools
Site-Visit Preinterview Survey

Section I: Educational Context

The following set of questions will help the site-visit team develop an understanding of the general conditions within which your school operates.

1. Please provide a general context that will help us understand the community this school serves. For example, community make-up by job roles, ethnicity, educational expectations, and population density.

2. Please describe this school's history as a middle level school. For example, when did it become a middle level school? What precipitated the grade changes if grade configuration was changed in the past 30 years?

3. Please characterize your faculty's perspective and capacity for addressing the educational needs of young adolescents.

4. What strengths do your faculty members bring to middle level education?

5. What do you view as the key areas for faculty growth?

6. Please provide a general context that will help us understand your student body. For example, how does it match with the community demographics previously described?

7. Please provide a general context that will help us understand this school's physical plant. For example, how does it fit your instructional program needs? Does it meet your technology needs? Does it provide a safe, clean environment?

Section II: Standards for Student Learning

The following set of questions will help the site-visit team develop an understanding of the relationships between standards and student learning in your school.

8. Does your school have a set of established standards that articulate desired learning outcomes? If so, are those established by the state, district, staff, or combinations thereof? Please explain. (Please include the standards with the materials you provide for the team during the site visit.)

9. To what degree do you believe that these are appropriate standards for your middle level students?

10. What evidence do you have that teachers, parents, and others support these standards?

11. Describe the process by which your faculty has engaged in discussions and/or study of the standards to shape curriculum and instruction for your particular students.

12. What process is used to collect evidence that students are meeting these standards?

13. How do you analyze and disseminate this evidence?

14. In what ways do you use this information to shape your school's instructional programs?

Appendix J: Site-visit Schedule

School Site Visit Schedule
National Study of Leadership in Middle Level Schools

Phase II: A Study of Leaders and Programs in Successful Middle Level Schools

DAY 1—A.M.

Time	Event	School	Team	Event goal	Instruments	Materials
Pre School	15- to 20-minute faculty meeting	All staff	Team Leader	Faculty orientation • Team member introductions • Overview visit • Establish expectation of "business as usual" • Build rapport	N. A.	Overview Handout to faculty • Goals of Visit • HSR Explanations • Schedule
8:00–8:30	Tour of school facility and programs	Principal	All	Orientation for research team to: • School facility • Faculty and staff roles • School Schedule • School Programs	N. A.	From principal: 3 master schedules 3 maps of bldg
8:30–10:30	Principal interview	Principal	All	Develop an understanding of principal's: • Philosophy, beliefs, and perspectives of leadership • Knowledge of school's vision and systemic change processes • Professional development practices • School's culture and learning organization	Principal Interview Form	Signed Interview Consent Form; If available, Principal provides at this time copies of school's: • Beliefs & Values • Mission • Vision • Goals • Plans
10:30–11:30	Assistant principal(s) interviews	Assistant principals	All	Same as for principal	Assistant Principal Interview Form	Signed Interview Consent Form
11:30–12:30	Lunch	None	All	General observations of school setting and casual conversations with staff and students (A—fac.; B & C—students)		

Note. Research team members are designated as members (A), (B), or (C) for clarity of which team member responsibilities.

DAY 1—P.M.

Time	Event	School	Team	Event goal	Instruments	Materials
12:30–3:30	Teacher interviews—two locations	Six to eight randomly selected teachers from planning time (min. 6)	A & B each interview one teacher for approximately 45 minutes per teacher; repeat three or four times	Develop an understanding of teachers' • Images of school's vision, goals, and change processes • Images of school's culture and learning organization • Images of school's leadership • Professional development practices	Teacher Interview Form	Signed Interview Consent Form
12:30–end of school	Observe instructional-practices	All teaching faculty (min. 50 obs)	C	Develop database of instructional practices	Classroom Observation Form	Signed Consent Form from principal to observe instruction
After school	Student presentation	Five to six students from highest grade who represent school's demographics (max. 6)	All	Brief presentation (max. 15 minutes) of "How we view our school." Suggest someone such as the counselor pull students together to create the presentation. The presentation will be videotaped by the research team.		Signed Consent Form by parents for students' presentation and videotaping
After school	Student interviews	Same students from presentation (max. 6)	Team Leader	Develop a richer understanding of the students' perceptions of the school. Students who will be interviewed as a group following the presentation.	Student Interview Form	Signed Interview Consent Form by parents for students
After school	Parent/ Guardian interviews	Selected by principal representing diversity of school	B & C	Develop an understanding of parents' images of the school. (Preferably use parents/ guardians of students who made the presentation.	Parent Interview Form	Signed Parent Consent Form
After school	Collect artifacts	Principal or designee	All	Develop an understanding of the school through identified artifacts.		See list of artifacts not already collected.
5:30–8:00	Working dinner at hotel	N.A.	All	Debrief day 1 and prepare for day 2 • Discuss impressions • Assess consistency of data • Identify specific issues that need more clarification		

Time	Event	School	Team	Event goal	Instruments	Materials
8:00–11:30	Teacher interviews— two locations	Six to eight randomly selected teachers from planning time (min. 6)	A & B each interview one teacher for approximately 45 minutes per teacher; repeat three or four times	Develop an understanding of teachers' • Images of school's vision, goals, and change processes • Images of school's culture and learning organization • Images of school's leadership • Typical instructional practices • Knowledge of middle level education and pedagogy	Teacher Interview Form	Signed Interview Consent Form
8:00–11:30	Observe Instructional practices	All teaching faculty (min. 50 obs)	C	Develop database of instructional practices	Classroom Observation Form	Signed Consent Form from principal to observe instruction
11:30–1:00	Lunch at building	Supt. and/or Ass't. Supt.	A w/ superintendent and/or assistant superintendent, B shadow principal, C w/faculty	Develop an understanding of the central office staff members' • Images of school's vision, goals, and change processes • Images of school's culture and learning organization • Images of school's leadership • Knowledge of middle level education and pedagogy		District Mission/ Vision District Strategic Plan

DAY 2—P.M.

Time	Event	School	Team	Event goal	Instruments	Materials
1:00–end of school	Teacher interviews—two locations	Six to eight randomly selected teachers from planning time (min. 6)	B & C each interview one teacher for approximately 45 minutes per teacher; repeat three or four times	Develop an understanding of teachers' • Images of school's vision, goals, and change processes • Images of school's culture • Images of school's leadership • Typical instructional practices • Knowledge of ML education	Teacher Interview Form	Signed Interview Consent Form
1:00–2:00	Counselor interview	School counselors (two randomly selected) (min. 1)	TL interviews one or two for at least 30 minutes each. Team will select whom on day 1.	Develop understanding of counselors' • Images of school's vision, goals, and change processes • Images of school's culture and learning organization • Images of school's leadership • Description of job role • Knowledge of ML education	Teacher Interview Form	Signed Interview Consent Form
2:00–3:00	Librarian and media specialist interview	Librarian and/or media specialists (two randomly selected) (min. 1)	TL interviews one or two for at least 30 minutes each. Team will select whom on day 1.	Develop understanding of librarian/media specialist's • Images of school's vision, goals, and change processes • Images of school's culture • Images of school's leadership • Description of job role • Knowledge of ML education	Teacher Interview Form	Signed Interview Consent Form
After school	20-minute faculty meeting	All staff	Team leader and team members	Perspective and thank you • Give overview of positive impressions • Explain tomorrow's schedule • Offer encouragement/thanks		
After faculty meeting	Leadership team interview	Leadership team members	All	Leadership team perceptions: (group) • "Here's what we've seen." • "What else do we need to know about your school?" (30 min.)	Leadership Team Comments Form	Signed Interview Consent Form
5:30–7:00	Dinner	None	All	Debrief day 2; prepare for day 3 • Discuss impressions • Assess consistency of data • Identify specific issues that need more clarification		

Time	Event	School	Team	Event goal	Instruments	Materials
AM	Team synthesis of interview data	Principal provides workroom with tables and writing board	All	Develop for writers a comprehensive matrix of information organized by principal, assistant principal, teachers, counselors, librarians/media specialists/students/parents/central office for issues such as: • Images of school's vision, goals, and change processes • Images of school's culture and learning organization • Images of school's leadership • Description of job role • Knowledge of ML education • Instructional practices • Curriculum standards • Assessment practices		Matrix of synthesized information and impressions for the selected issues. Matrix worksheets will be developed and used as needed; information can be put on laptop files and projected as needed for group discussion. Team leaders can select whether they want to work on laptops, worksheets, or chalkboards/easels. Team leader will develop a "master" three-ring binder of information that can be copied and provided to writing team as needed.
	Team follow-up	As appropriate	All	Team collects any last-minute data/insight from administration, teachers, staff, etc.		
	Team wrap-up	None	All	Team adds any last-minute information. Team organizes and files all artifacts, data, worksheets, materials according to folders provided by MLLC staff.		File folders, worksheets, and three-ring binders.
PM	Depart as appropriate	As appropriate	All	Team expresses appreciation to principal and available staff. Team leader confirms timeline for publication of study and provides a list of contacts (MLLC staff and site-visit team member names, addresses, and e-mails provided by MLLC)		Research Team Information Sheet

Appendix K: Site-Visit Principal, Teacher, Student, and Parent Interview Forms

National Study of Leadership in Middle Level Schools
Phase II: A Study of Leaders and Programs in Successful Middle Level Schools

Principal Interview Form

Researcher Notes:

Researcher-only notes are in italics. These should not be read to the interviewee. Statements underlined are information, not questions, that should be read as a preface to a question or set of questions.

We are making this site visit because your school has been identified as a very good middle level school. Following are some general questions about your school. Please tell us what you think about your school to the degree to which you are comfortable. If you decide you don't want to participate in this brief discussion, you can quit at any time. We are audio-taping simply because it enables us to take fewer notes and focus more on our conversation with you, thus making the interview shorter while providing the most accurate information. Your response will be kept confidential and will become anonymous as soon as we have transcribed the information.

Section I: Systemic Change Processes

We want this opening question answered before we provide the explanations about terminology and change processes and move to the subsequent questions. Remember not to bias this opening question

Your school has been recognized as being a highly successful school for your students. We are particularly interested in any change processes or strategies that helped your school develop and maintain this level of success. Please describe any change processes or strategies that are used in your school.

The following questions are about processes often associated with change in a highly successful school. You may or may not have described or discussed some of these processes in the previous question. Please help us understand some specifics about the change process as interpreted through five fundamental issues. The six issues we would like insight about are: "values and beliefs," "mission," "vision," "goals," "implementation strategies," and "the use of data." So that we have consistency in understanding these issues in each school, we are providing you with a sheet that defines each term as we are studying them in our successful schools. We realize that in your school you may or may not use these exact terms, so we are providing the terms so we can have a common language for this discussion. *(Distribute sheet of terms and discuss them briefly.)*

Values and Beliefs

The first questions are about the "values and beliefs" of your school. Please reference the definition we are using as you respond.

Is there a set of values and beliefs statements for this school?

The following questions are used if there is a set of values and beliefs.

Are the statements in written form? *(Remember to get a copy if you don't have one.)*

Please describe those values/beliefs.

How was this set developed? *(Interviewer—this is a critical question—probe for an extensive explanation.)*

What do you do as the principal to support and/or encourage the implementation of these values/beliefs?

What, if any, changes would you make to the set of value/beliefs?

The following questions are used if there is not a set of values and beliefs.

If you do not have a set of value and beliefs, have you discussed developing such a set? If so, please describe what you have discussed.

If you do not have a set of value and beliefs, what is the foundation upon which you and the faculty and others members of the school community base your decisions about the educational programs in this school.

School Mission

The following questions are about the "mission" of your school. Again, note the definition we are using. Please note that if this school uses different terminology to define the mission, help us understand your terminology so we can gain accurate information about the development and presence of a "mission" even if your school uses a different term.

Researchers: We must be particularly cautious here because some schools make no distinction between mission and vision, some blend mission and goals, and yet others blend vision and goals. We are trying to determine if the school has a clear picture of where they are now and what they want to become and we need to work through their particular terminology and adapt it to our terminology. The concept of mission that we are looking for in this set of questions is "Has this school consciously and formally defined its mission, it's purpose for being, and do they use that as a guiding light in their work?"

Is there a mission statement for this school (in other words, is there a succinct, written statement of purpose for this school)?

The following questions are used if there is a mission statement.

Is the statement in written form? *(Researcher: Remember to get a copy if you don't have one.)*

Please describe the mission as you would interpret it.

How was this statement developed? *(Interviewer: This is a critical question. Probe for an extensive explanation.)*

What do you do as the principal to support and/or encourage the implementation of the mission?

What, if any, changes would you make to the mission statement?

The following questions are used if there is not a mission statement.

If you do not have a mission statement, have you discussed developing such a statement? Please describe what has been discussed.

In the absence of a mission statement, how do you and your staff communicate to your constituents your school's primary purpose?

School Vision

The following questions are about the "vision" of your school. Again, note the definition we are using. If this school uses different terminology to define the vision, help us understand your terminology so we can gain accurate information about the development and presence of a "vision" even if your school uses a different term.

Researchers: We must be particularly cautious here because some schools make no distinction between mission and vision, some blend mission and goals, and yet others blend vision and goals. We are trying to determine if the school has a clear picture of where they are now and what they want to become and we need to work through their particular terminology and adapt it to our terminology. The concept of vision that we are looking for in this set of questions is "Have the members of this school community consciously and formally defined a "vision" of what they want this school to look like in the near future, particularly the next two to three years, and does this vision guide the decisions they make?"

Is there a vision statement for this school?

The following items are used if there is a school vision statement.

Is the statement in written form? *(Remember to get a copy if you don't have one)*

Please describe the vision as you would interpret it.

How was this statement developed? *(Interviewer: This is a critical question. Probe for an extensive explanation.)*

What do you do as the principal to support and/or encourage the implementation of the vision?

What evidence do you have that the staff support the school's vision?

What evidence do you have that parents support the school's vision?

What do you view as the viable "life" of this vision? In other words, how frequently do you think your vision statement should be reviewed?

Think about this school in five years. What, if any, changes would you make to the vision statement at that time?

The following items are used if there is not a school vision statement.

If you <u>do not</u> have a vision statement, have you discussed developing such a statement?

Please describe what has been discussed.

In the absence of a vision statement, how do you and your staff know the outcomes toward which you are working?

School Goals

<u>**The following questions are about the "goals" of your school. Again, note the definition we are using. If this school uses different terminology to define the goals, help us understand your terminology so we can gain accurate information about the development and presence of a set of "goals" even if your school uses a different term.**</u>

Researchers: We must be particularly cautious here because some schools make no distinction between mission and vision, some blend mission and goals, and yet others blend vision and goals. We are trying to determine if the school has a clear picture of where they are now and what they want to become and we need to work through their particular terminology and adapt it to our terminology. The concept of goals that we are looking for in this set of questions is "Has this school consciously and formally defined the primary goals that will guide the work of the school over the next year or two?"

Is there a set of goal statements for this school?

The following items are used if there is a set of goal statements.

Are the goal statements in written form? *(Remember to get a copy if you don't have one.)*

Please describe the goals as you would interpret them.

How were these goals developed? *(Interviewer: This is a critical question. Probe for an extensive explanation.)*

What do you do as the principal to support and/or encourage the accomplishment of the goals?

What do you view as the viable "life" of the goals? In other words, how long will the current set of goals effectively serve your school?

Think about the set of goals. What, if any, changes would you make to the goal statements at that time?

The following items are used if there is not a school goals statement.

If you do not have a set of goals, have you discussed developing such a set?

Please describe what has been discussed.

In the absence of a set of goals, how do you and your staff know the outcomes toward which you are working and how do you know when you have accomplished those outcomes?

Implementation Strategies

The following questions are about the "implementation strategies" of your school. Again, note the definition we are using. If this school uses different terminology to define the implementation strategies, help us understand your terminology so we can gain accurate information about the development and presence of a set of "implementation strategies" even if your school uses a different term.

Researchers: With this set of questions we are trying to determine if the school has a written set of strategies or an action plan for each goal. Do these strategies provide a blueprint of the tasks, timeline, and responsible parties so each goal can be accomplished? The school may have a completely different set of terminology that we must adapt to and document.

Is there a set of implementation strategies for this school?

The following items are used if there is a set of implementation strategies.

Are the implementation strategies in written form? *(Remember to get a copy if you don't have one.)*

Please describe the implementation strategies as you would interpret them.

How were the implementation strategies developed? *(Interviewer: This is a critical question. Probe for an extensive explanation.)*

What do you do as the principal to support and/or encourage the accomplishment of the implementation strategies?

What do you view as the viable "life" of the strategies? In other words, how long will the current set of strategies effectively serve your school?

The following items are used if there is not a set of implementation strategies.

If you do not have a written set of implementation strategies, have you discussed developing such a set? Please describe what has been discussed.

In the absence of a set of implementation strategies, how do you and your staff know what tasks are necessary to accomplish the school's goals and how do you know when you have accomplished those goals?

These questions are asked of everyone, regardless of whether they have a set of values and beliefs, mission, vision, goals, and implementation strategies.

Please describe a significant change that has occurred in your school in the past two or three years. Please describe the process used to make the change.

In the past two or three years, have you and your staff used your knowledge of best educational practice to make changes in the curricular programs and instructional practices (other than described in prior questions)? If so, please describe.

In the past two or three years, have you and your staff used data to make changes in the curricular programs and instructional practices (other than described in prior two questions)? If so, please describe.

Use of Data/Evidence in the Process of Change

The following questions are about the "use of data/evidence in the process of change" in your school. Again, note the definition we are using. If this school uses different terminology to define the use of data, help us understand your terminology so we can gain accurate information about the "use of data/evidence in the process of change" even if your school uses a different term.

Researchers: With this set of questions we are trying to determine how the school uses data/evidence in the process of change. Remember that this probe on data is about all types of desired outcomes for the school, not only about standards and desired learner outcomes. Does the use of data provide baseline and longitudinal information relevant to the school's continuous change? Do the data provide evidence of the accomplishment of school goals? Are data used to inform the process rather than drive the process? Is the vision driven by data or best practice; or, are the goals informed by data? The school may have a completely different set of terminology that we must adapt to and document.

In what ways do you use data and other forms of evidence to inform the process of change in your school?

What types of data and other forms of evidence do you use (artifacts)?

What are the sources of the data and other forms of evidence?

Why do you use each type of data and other forms of evidence?

How are these data and other forms of evidence analyzed?

How are these data and other forms of evidence disseminated?

How are these data and other forms of evidence used to change or improve your school's programs?

The following items are used if data are not used in the school to inform change:.

If you <u>do not</u> have a process for using data, have you discussed using such a process? Please describe what has been discussed.

In the absence of the use of data to inform school improvement, how do you and your staff know whether or not you are making progress toward the accomplishment of your goals and school vision?

Section II: Leadership Roles

Principals fulfill a broad range of leadership roles. Please help us develop insight into the various skills you bring to these roles.

Student-centered, collaborative culture

Please describe what you do as the principal to help your school develop and maintain a student-centered culture.

Please describe what you do as the principal to help your school develop and maintain a collaborative culture.

Please describe the roles you have defined for your Assistant Principals and other members of your administrative team (if you have assistants). How have you organized their roles to accomplish the goals of the school? Why have you organized your administration team in that manner?

We are interested in how you as the principal provide specific leadership for change at your school.

How do you collaboratively develop, articulate, and maintain the vision for your school?

How do you actively model the school's vision in your daily work as the principal?

What are the structures and processes you use to actively involve your faculty in your school's improvement?

How do you provide individualized support for teachers in the midst of the school change process?

How do you stimulate your faculty to think critically and reflectively about the nature of their work and the way they go about it?

How do you develop, communicate, and implement high expectations for faculty performance?

Leadership Teams

What is the basis for membership on the leadership team? (How are the members identified? Who makes the decision about who is on the team?)

If you have a leadership team, how would you describe the role/function/responsibility of the team?

If you have a leadership team, are they compensated for their work on the team? If so, how?

Are there any standing or ad hoc committees or councils in the school? If so, please describe the make-up and role of each.

How is the school organized to promote staff involvement in the decision-making process?

Section III: Knowledge of Best Practice

As a principal, maintaining your knowledge of best educational practices is obviously important. The following items are designed to help us understand how you stay current about best practice and provide leadership for your school or faculty to maintain knowledge of best practice.

Researchers: These questions deal specifically with the principal's personal professional development.

What do you do to advance your knowledge of best leadership practices, particularly current knowledge about change processes, collaborative cultures, and learning organizations?

What do you do to advance your knowledge of best instructional practice?

What do you do to advance your knowledge of best middle level practice?

What are some of the specific sources of information you use to maintain current knowledge? *(Interviewers: We are looking for specificity such as NMSA Internet site, Ed. Leadership, Middle School Journal, NASSP monographs…)*

Please provide specific examples that demonstrate how you have used current knowledge to improve your performance as a school leader?

What strategies do you use personally to modify or improve your performance? *(Researchers: Strategies could include reflection, participation in professional association and staff development, mentoring, etc.)*

Researchers: These questions deal specifically with the principal's leadership of or for professional development for the school.

What do you as a Principal do to advance knowledge of best practice for the whole faculty? In other words, how do you maintain currency of knowledge at a schoolwide level? *(Interviewers: This is a critical question about instructional leadership. Please probe.)*

Creating and maintaining a highly successful school requires resources. What strategies have you used in the past two or three years to garner the necessary resources to make this school an especially effective learning environment?

Researchers: Be sure to elicit specific examples of actual practices used for staff professional development (Please ask for artifacts, if possible).

K-2

National Study of Leadership in Middle Level Schools
Phase II: A Study of Leaders and Programs in Successful Middle Level Schools

Teacher Interview Form

Researcher Notes:

Researcher-only notes are in italics. These should not be read to the interviewee. Statements underlined are information, not questions, that should be read as a preface to a question or set of questions.

We are making this site visit because your school has been identified as a very good middle level school. Following are some general questions about your school. Please tell us what you think about your school to the degree to which you are comfortable. If you decide you don't want to participate in this brief discussion, you can quit at any time. We are audio-taping simply because it enables us to take fewer notes and focus more on our conversation with you, thus making the interview shorter while providing the most accurate information. Your responses will be kept confidential and will become anonymous as soon as we have transcribed the infor-

mation. As you are aware, we are visiting with some 20 to 30 randomly selected faculty members. After we collect our information we will be synthesizing all responses to gain insight about how faculty as a whole view the school. No specific statements will be able to be associated with any specific individual.

1. Please talk with us about your specific role as a teacher:
   a. What do you teach?

   b. How long have you been in your current role in this school?

   c. What position did you have prior to your current role?

2. Let's begin with a general perspective about the faculty. If the faculty were collectively asked to select five short phrases that describe what they believe and value, what would they say? *(Interviewer: Remember to quickly list the five so you can help the teacher if they cannot recall the five items as they try to answer question 2.)*
   a.
   b.
   c.
   d.
   e.

3. Which of those five statements would you personally endorse as the most important?

4. What has been the most important success for this school during the past 12 months? *(Interviewer: Remember that if the response is about recognition in this study, please ask for another response. The example should be concrete, specific, and something the school has done—celebrated. For example, do not accept recognition as a Blue Ribbon School or School to Watch. We are looking for accomplishments, not recognitions.)*

5. What distinguishes this school from other schools with which you are familiar?

6. When students come back to this school after graduating from high school, what do the students say about this school? *(Researchers: Phrase hypothetically if this question is inappropriate due to tenure of teacher.)*

7. Characterize the types of discussions you have about students' social and academic successes with: *(Interviewer: Try to obtain specific examples.)*
   a. Teachers/Counselors
   b. Administrators
   c. Parents
   d. Others

8. How do you advance your knowledge about best educational practices in instruction, curriculum, and middle level education? Please describe. *(Interviewer: Please remember to probe for an example to illustrate the response.)*

9. How does the faculty as a whole advance its knowledge about best educational practices in instruction, curriculum, and middle level education? Please describe. *(Interviewer: Please remember to prove for an example to illustrate the response.)*

10. When you stop to dream a little about how this school could become a better school, what do you dream about? *(Interviewer: Don't let the teacher off the hook on this if they say they don't dream. Probe for how they believe the school could become a better place for their students.)*

11. Is there a problem or issue that is persistent at this school that you think ought to be addressed? What is it?

12. When change is needed at this school, how does it occur? *(Interviewer: Probe for how it begins, who is involved. Is there a systemic or systematic process that the teacher can articulate?)*

13. Do you believe your school has a collaborative culture? Please explain. *(Interviewer: Probe for a specific example or two that supports the response.)*

14. How does the faculty exercise leadership for the school?

15. The term "mission" is often used to describe the basic purpose of a school. The term "vision" is often used to describe what the school should be like in three to five years. Please talk for a few moments about your perception of mission and vision. What do you see as the mission of the school? What do you see as the vision of the school?

16. How will you and your colleagues know when you have accomplished the vision of the school?

K-3

National Study of Leadership in Middle Level Schools
Phase II: A Study of Leaders and Programs in Successful Middle Level Schools

Student Interview Form

Researcher Notes:

Researcher-only notes are in italics. These should not be read to the interviewee. Statements underlined are information, not questions, which should be read as a preface to a question or set of questions.

We are making this site visit because your school has been identified as a very good middle level school. Following are some general questions about your school. Please tell us what you think about your school to the degree to which you are comfortable. If you decide you don't want to participate in this brief discussion, you can quit at any time. We are audio-taping simply because it enables us to take fewer notes and focus more on our conversation with you, thus making the interview shorter while providing the most accurate information. Your response will be kept confidential and will become anonymous as soon as we have transcribed the information.

We are very interested in how you, as students, view this school: what you like about it, what you wish you could change about it.

Let's begin there. What do you really like about school?

What are some of the things you would change in your school?

Researchers: These are the two stem questions you must remember to probe and nurture discussion.

National Study of Leadership in Middle Level Schools
Phase II: A Study of Leaders and Programs in Successful Middle Level Schools
Parent Interview Form

Researcher Notes:

Researcher-only notes are in italics. These should not be read to the interviewee. Statements underlined are information, not questions, which should be read as a preface to a question or set of questions.

<u>We are making this site visit because your school has been identified as a very good middle level school. Following are some general questions about your school. Please tell us what you think about your school to the degree to which you are comfortable. If you decide you don't want to participate in this brief discussion, you can quit at any time. We are audio-taping simply because it enables us to take fewer notes and focus more on our conversation with you, thus making the interview shorter while providing the most accurate information. Your response will be kept confidential and will become anonymous as soon as we have transcribed the information.</u>

<u>We are very interested in how you, as a parent, view this school: what you like about it, what you wish you could change about it.</u>

Let's begin there. What do you really like about school?

What are some of the things you would change in your school?

Researchers: These are the two stem questions you must remember to probe and nurture discussion.

About the Authors

Jerry Valentine is a professor of educational leadership in the Department of Educational Leadership and Policy Analysis at the University of Missouri—Columbia. He is the director of the Middle Level Leadership Center, program area coordinator for K-12 educational leadership, and coordinator for the Advanced Principal Preparation Program. He chaired the NASSP middle level studies in 1980 and 1990. He has served as a junior high principal and a high school assistant principal in Colorado and a teacher in Louisiana. He was editor of the monograph series of NASSP's National Alliance of Middle Level Schools, and has served as a member of the National Middle School Association's research committee.

Donald C. Clark is a professor emeritus of educational leadership, former head of the Educational Leadership Program at the University of Arizona, Tucson, and a former middle level teacher and administrator. He was codirector of the NASSP National Study of Eighth Grade and was a member of the research teams for the 1980 and 1990 NASSP middle level studies. He was also a member of the NASSP Council on Middle Level Education, served on the Research Committee of the National Middle School Association, and he currently serves as research consultant for the Western Regional Middle Level Consortium.

Donald G. Hackmann is associate professor of educational administration in the Department of Educational Organization and Leadership at the University of Illinois at Urbana–Champaign. He is also the program area coordinator for educational administration. He has served as a teacher, an assistant high school principal, and a middle level principal in Missouri, and a high school principal in Illinois.

Vicki Petzko is a University of Chattanooga Foundation associate professor of school leadership in the Graduate Studies Division of the College of Health, Education, and Applied Professional Studies at the University of Tennessee–Chattanooga. She is coordinator of the master's program in school leadership and the post-master's certificate in school leadership. She has experience as a middle level principal and high school assistant principal in Minnesota, where she was a divisional principal of the year in 1997.

About NASSP

The National Association of Secondary School Principals—the preeminent organization and the national voice for middle level and high school principals, assistant principals, and aspiring school leaders—provides its members with the professional resources to serve as visionary leaders. NASSP promotes the intellectual growth, academic achievement, character development, leadership development, and physical well-being of youth through its programs and student leadership services. NASSP sponsors the National Honor Society, the National Junior Honor Society, and the National Association of Student Councils.